HIDDEN FINANCE, ROGUE NETWORKS AND SECRET SORCERY

The Fascist International, 9/11, and Penetrated Operations

Adventures Unlimited Press

Other Books by Joseph P. Farrell:

The Third Way
Nazi International
Thrice Great Hermetica and the Janus Age
Covert Wars and the Clash of Civilizations
Saucers, Swastikas and Psyops
Covert Wars and Breakaway Civilizations
LBJ and the Conspiracy to Kill Kennedy
Roswell and the Reich
Reich of the Black Sun
The S.S. Brotherhood of the Bell
Babylon's Banksters
The Philosopher's Stone
The Vipers of Venice
Secrets of the Unified Field
The Cosmic War
The Giza Death Star
The Giza Death Star Deployed
The Giza Death Star Destroyed
Transhumanism (with Scott deHart)
The Grid of the Gods (with Scott deHart)

HIDDEN FINANCE, ROGUE NETWORKS AND SECRET SORCERY

The Fascist International, 9/11, and Penetrated Operations

Hidden Finance, Rogue Networks, and Secret Sorcery

by Joseph P. Farrell

ISBN: 978-1-939149-63-3

Published by:
Adventures Unlimited Press
One Adventure Place
Kempton, Illinois 60946 USA

auphq@frontiernet.net

www.adventuresunlimitedpress.com

Cover by Terry Lamb

10 9 8 7 6 5 4 3

*First of all, for my cousin, D.M.F., who asked the right
questions and made me think;*

*And to all my extended family and friends:
Scott D. deHart, and sons
Wesley, Calvin, Alex, and Bennett:
Thank You is inadequate;*

*To Catherine Austin Fitts and Daniel DiGriz, who keep me on
my toes;*

*To the "Dutch Inklings" Jeroen and Robert for so much hard
work in bringing things to light;*

*To "Al" in Norway, and the "Dark Journalist"
for penetrating questions;*

To R.C.H. in New Mexico, who showed me quite a few things;

*To all my website members and subscribers for your support
and prayers;*

*To "Maria" in Spain, for boundless support beyond my ability
to repay;*

And to the late George Ann Hughes, for so many good times;

To Matt S. for sharing your good heart and conversation;

*And Above All to T.S.F., who told me to write:
You are, and will always be, sorely and deeply missed.*

You are each and all a true

Table of Contents

Table of Contents

Table of Contents

PART TWO:
THE MYSTERIES OF THE MOTIVATION AND THE MECHANISM

Table of Contents

PREFACE AND PRÉCIS

"... (The) price for rejecting this conspiracy theory is to accept a
coincidence theory."
David Ray Griffin[1]

NYONE WRITING ON THE 9/11 TRAGEDY is doomed to invoke the ire of some faction within the 9/11 truth community. Everyone has some theory to advance on who did it and why, and in the case of the destruction of the World Trade Center complex, hypotheses about the mechanism of its destruction abound, with each party defending its favored hypothesis as to what constituted "the murder weapon" and hurling accusations—oftentimes of a very acrimonious and *ad hominem* nature—against advocates and adherents other hypotheses, to the extent detached discussion of the merits and demerits of each is all but impossible. The atmosphere of calm discussion and consideration has been all but poisoned by these debates. To be sure, the official explanation of the collapse of the twin towers—the so-called "pancake" theory that the structures were weakened by burning airplane fuel—is nonsense. The 9/11 truth movement quickly focused on some aspect of a controlled demolition theory as the murder weapon. The trouble is, this theory has at least four major variants, ranging from standard controlled demolitions using standard explosive techniques, to increasingly exotic explanations, from "nano-thermite" to "mini-nukes" and finally, to some sort of directed and/or exotic energy weapons system. Within the wider context of these re-interpretations, other theories are advanced: there were no airplanes at all, the airplanes were remotely piloted, the airplanes carried missiles, and so on. Nevertheless, the acrimoniousness of debate is somewhat comprehensible, for establishing the exact "mechanism" of the murder weapon is a profound clue as to who was ultimately responsible for the mass murders that took place on that day; the question of "who did it?" is inextricably linked to the questions of "what happened?" and "how was it done?" An equally pertinent question might be: can the various hypotheses of the mechanisms of the World Trade Center Twin Towers collapse be harmonized? If so, why bother to use several mechanisms? Were the same *parties* involved in the use of these mechanisms? Or do

---

[1] David Ray Griffin, *The New Pearl Harbor: Disturbing Questions about the Bush Administration and 9/11* (Northhampton, Massachusetts: Olive Branch Press, 2004), p. 141, emphasis in the original.

different mechanisms signal the involvement of different groups, perhaps in conflict with each other?

September 11, 2001 was a day few of us will ever forget. For me personally, most of my life has moved between the twin events that defined a whole history and transmuted American and world culture in an almost diabolically alchemical way. The other event was, of course, the assassination of President John F. Kennedy when I was a young boy. Then, as in 2001, I was at home, watching the events unfold on television as they happened. In 1963, I was six years old, and home sick from school. My mother sat on the couch, sewing and smoking a cigarette and watching one of her favorite soap operas, CBS's *As the World Turns,* while I sat on the floor eating some chicken soup. The program was interrupted with the announcement that the President may have been shot in Dallas. She said quietly, "Oh my God!"

In 2001, I had just finished my graveyard shift at the casino where I was an overnight floor manager and pit boss, and had come home and gone to bed. At that time, I had a friend staying with me who woke up, emerging groggy-eyed from the guest bedroom, just as I was going to sleep, and he had turned on the television to watch the morning news. As I began to doze off, suddenly, from the living room, I heard shouts of "Oh my God! Oh my God!" as if the echo of tragedy were rippling across time and space. In between those two events that have so defined American culture and domestic and foreign policy, I observed many others: the Watergate break-in and subsequent escalating crisis, the Ruby Ridge affair, the murder of the Branch Davidians at Waco, the Oklahoma City Bombing (which—again −I watched on local news in Tulsa as the events unfolded), the PanAm Flight 800-Lockerbie disaster, the 1993 World Trade Center Bombing, and a host of banking scandals from the collapse of the Bank of Credit and Commerce International, the Vatican bank scandal of the 1980s, the savings and loan scandal, the collapse of the Nugan Hand Bank, and so on. All of these things may seem entirely unrelated to the architecture of the 9/11 tragedy, and yet, as most research to date has uncovered, there are profound and detailed connections between them.

Consider just the parallels between the assassination of President Kennedy, and the 9/11 tragedy:

1) In both cases, the events signaled or were used to remake American foreign and domestic policy in a profound fashion, and this included the normalization of the use of war in that policy;

2) In both cases, there were clear examples of "security stripping" around the President, and in the case of 9/11, this extended to "security stripping" the entire country itself;

3) In both cases, the official version of events were analyzed by independent investigators unsatisfied with the official explanations; the results of their investigations, when viewed synoptically, uncovered a vast architecture of conspiracy consisting of various factional interests, each of which had the means, motive, and opportunity to orchestrate the events;

4) In both cases, many of these investigations uncovered indications that clearly implied some sort of connection to post-war Fascist and Nazi organizations, and as will be discovered in the main text, in both cases the 9/11 investigations largely ignored these clues in their hypothetical constructions of the architecture of the conspiracy: radical Islamic terrorists, rogue "neo-conservative" or "neocon" elements within the national security structure, the Bush family's connection to Saudi Arabia via the Carlyle Group, or even "moles" could be blamed for the event, but *never* Fascists;

5) In both cases, aspects of the events indicated that a coup d'etat had been successfully accomplished;

6) In both cases, the events were accompanied by suspicious financial activity indicating that someone had prior knowledge of the events, and profited from it, an indicator of deep planning and inside knowledge; and finally, and not the least significantly (though it is another of those "ignored sets of clues" by the vast majority of researchers),

7) In both cases, the events themselves were surrounded with aspects of an esoteric and occult symbolic context that gave indication that they were planned as deep rituals of ceremonial and alchemical magic, and as vast social engineering works.

The disturbing implication about this comparison—and there are many more such points of continuity between the two events—is that the M.O. or *modus operandi* of the perpetrators is essentially the same, and this an indicator that perhaps the perpetrators, or at least the organizational structures and networks behind both, are the same. This carries with it yet another equally if not more disturbing implication: the latter event was the logical end of the former.

In any case, n 2001, unable to go to sleep as my friend was exclaiming "Oh my God!," I put on my bathrobe and came out into the living room and asked him what was happening, and he pointed to the television screen and simply said "Look!" There I saw the North Tower of the World Trade Center in New York City burning. The news commentators were saying that apparently an airplane had flown into the tower. Then, as we watched, United Airlines Flight 175 struck the South Tower. The words "Oh my God!" were heard again, from both of us. At that moment, we and everyone else in America knew that the country was under attack. The question was—and remains—by whom?

We both watched, stunned into silence, glued to the television, when the south tower came down, and when it did, I made a little mental note to count. It appeared to have fallen at nearly free-fall speed. When the north tower collapsed at the same speed, I knew something was dreadfully wrong. In the coming hours (and days) the speculations from the talking heads on television immediately began; "witnesses" were interviewed who—to my mind at least—seemed to be rehearsing well-learned lines about the fires from the airplanes somehow causing the towers' collapse. The mechanism of the collapse appeared to me to be highly unusual; it both looked like, and did not look like, a standard controlled demolition. As it turned out, and as we shall see, I was not alone that day having doubts and questions about the emerging narrative.

As if to underscore my horrified intuitions, my friend and I watched as the news began to be reported that the Pentagon had been struck as well. In the coming days and weeks, as the story unfolded, the other question that began to disturb me "Where was the debris from the airplane that supposedly crashed into it?" I was not alone in asking this question either.

About four weeks after 9/11, another friend called me to ask me if the towers had collapsed due to the "same type of weird physics" (or words to that effect) that I had written about in my first book. I told him that this was in fact my opinion, but that I did not want to talk about it any further.

In other words, on 9/11 itself, the 9/11 Truth movement was born, as critics of the official conspiracy theory combed over every chronological, technical, and testimonial detail in the ensuing years, offering alternative explanations of how the towers had come down, of what had actually hit the Pentagon, of what had happened on Flight 93. Alternative theories and scenarios of who was responsible and what their motivations may have been, were proposed.

In the course of these investigations by several researchers in the years since 9/11, two basic theories have emerged, and have dominated the 9/11 truth research community ever since: the "Let It Happen On

Purpose" (or LIHOP) hypothesis, and the "Made It Happen On Purpose" (MIHOP) hypothesis.

A. LIHOP(Let It Happen On Purpose) and MIHOP (Made It Happen On Purpose)
1. The Basic Premises of LIHOP and MIHOP

The first, and at that time most popular, emergent theory was that there were essentially *two different intertwined levels* to the events of 9/11. At one level −the public level and the government's own officially sponsored "conspiracy theory"−there were the alleged terrorists flying the planes themselves. But at a deeper level were the agencies of the US Federal Government, which, the critics argued, had known of the operation in advance, and which had "Let It Happen On Purpose" in order create a crisis of public opinion that would allow them to project American military power into the Middle East in order to secure the region's energy resources.

The second theory, that of a distinct but growing minority, was that the first level of the operation, the terrorists, were simply "patsies" and that the *entire* operation was planned and executed at the second deeper level by "rogue elements" or a "rogue network" operating within and under the cover of the American military and intelligence establishments. This group pointed out that the whole 9/11 operation was conducted at exactly the same time there were a number of American military drills taking place, some of them involving—you guessed it—hijacked airliners being used for attacks on American targets. This group pointed out that the probability of terrorists planning and conducting their operations coincidentally with these drills was vanishingly small, and hence, the operation had to have been planned at some level with some degree of participation and complicity by the American national security structure itself. It was here that the whole idea of a "rogue network" idea was born.

But again, the goal was the same; it was all precisely for the purpose of creating an incident to shock the climate of domestic and world opinion to allow the projection of American military power into the Middle East, to seize and dominate the world's oil supplies. The late Michael Ruppert, for example, viewed 9/11 in the context of what he called "the most significant event in human history: the end of the age of oil."[2] Many if not most researchers share this view of the ultimate geopolitical motivations behind the attacks.

On this rather conventional analysis of the motivations behind the attacks, 9/11 was a classic—if bloody—textbook case of a "false flag operation". Advocates both of the LIHOP theory and of the MIHOP theory often point to the neo-conservative group behind *The Project for a New American Century* as being a potential contender for the "rogue elements" within the American intelligence-military-industrial-finance complex that had pulled off the event. This group had stated that a "new Pearl Harbor" would be needed to galvanize American public opinion for a vast and prolonged military effort in the Middle East. Oil was the motivation, terrorism was the cover story, and 9/11 was the activating event, the "new Pearl Harbor" that provided the pretext for war. Even President Bush himself at one point obliged this interpretation and its advocates by calling the event "a new Pearl Harbor."

2. Critiques of the Oil Motivation: A Multi-Layered Operation with Multiple Objectives

While certainly true at one level, 9/11 is about much more than oil and terrorism. For author Laurent Guyénot, 9/11 was really but the pretext for the American "militarization of the planet,"[3] an agenda that upon a little reflection might be about much more than just controlling the petroleum resources of the planet. As Guyénot observes, President George W. Bush in a speech delivered on September 20th, 2001, stated that this new type of war was a war against an invisible enemy, and that it would not end "until every terrorist group of global reach has been found, stopped, and defeated."[4] Global wars against invisible enemies convey the real significance of the 9/11 attacks, for viewed in this light, it was an event that could be used—and was—to justify perpetual war, and the domestic policies and surveillance state required to conduct it. The day after the attacks, Presidential rhetoric quickly transformed the event from a terrorist attack into a cosmological and even metaphysical conflict, as the President announced "a monumental struggle of Good

---

[2] Michael C. Ruppert, *Crossing the Rubicon: The Decline of the American Empire at the End of the Age of Oil* (Gabriola Island, British Columbia: New Society Publishers, 2004), p. 19.

[3] Laurent Guyénot, *JFK-9/11: 50 Years of Deep State* (San Diego, California: Progressive Press, 2014), p. 103.

[4] Ibid., p. 104.

versus Evil."[5] Others, picking up on this cosmological meme, have noted that the event served really to legitimize the criminality and criminalization of "the upper echelons of the State."[6] For occult and Nazi-survival scholar Peter Levenda, 9/11 additionally functions as the sanctioning event for state sponsored paranoia:

> Paranoia becomes institutionalized. It is appropriated by the government as its own prerogative. The state determines the nature and quality of the paranoia; it creates intelligence agencies whose sole purpose is to give a form to paranoia, to enshrine paranoia as one of the necessary qualities of an observant and caring state. To prove that paranoia is an acceptable characteristic of the paternalistic regime.
>
> The citizens are not allowed to become paranoid unless it is at government direction and sanction. Individual cases of paranoia are frowned upon. The state tells us that if we are not paranoid the way it is paranoid—and about the same things—it's because we don't have all the facts: about terrorism, fundamentalism, communism, foreign countries, weapons of mass destruction, sleeper cells. The state has all the facts: classified documents, wire-tap transcripts, intelligence feeds, high-altitude reconnaissance images, none of which the citizen is permitted to see.
>
> It does not realize that the logical conclusion of all this paranoia is suspicion of the state apparatus itself.[7]

But 9/11 is much more than even this, because for Levenda and fellow occult researcher S.K. Bain, 9/11 is also an event with the clear and detailed components of a magical ritual sacrifice of massive scale;[8] it exemplifies detailed planning in depth for an act of ceremonial magic,[9] and thus can be studied as a textbook or grimoire for magical operations.[10]

---

[5] David Ray Griffin, *The New Pearl Harbor: Disturbing Questions about the Bush Administration and 9/11* (Northampton, Massachusetts: Olive Branch Press, 2004), p. xiv.

[6] David MacGregor, "September 11 as 'Machiavellian State Terror' in *The Hidden History of 9-11*, ed. Paul Zarembka, 183-214 (New York: Seven Stories Press: 2008), p. 188, citing Michel Chossudovsky, *America's war on terrorism* (Pincourt, Quebec: Global Research, 2005), no page number given.

[7] Peter Levenda, "Prologue: Knock, Knock," v-ix, in S.K. Bain, *The Most Dangerous Book in the World: 9/11 as Mass Ritual* (Walterville, Oregon: Trine Day Press, 2012), p. vi.

[8] Ibid., p. viii.

[9] S.K. Bain, *The Most Dangerous Book in the World: 9/11 as Mass Ritual*, p. 18.

[10] Ibid., p. 19.

Hovering in between these extremes of interpretation −from the mundane one of a false flag event to seize the oil of the Middle East and Central Asia, to the arcane one of ritual magic and sacrifice in a cosmological struggle of good and evil −are those theories that view 9/11's primary motivation as that of a *financial crime* of a high order; 9/11 was a financial crime to cover-up a vast fraud and fraudulent system, rather than a political act.[11]

Such analyses, taken at face value and in combination, imply that 9/11 was more than a terrorist or even a false-flag operation. It was, and was planned as, a multi-layered operation whose architecture was designed to accomplish several objectives in one efficient event, and this in turn implies that its planners were much more than Islamic fundamentalists, but people with detailed inside financial, political, and even occult knowledge. The financial, and occult, clues are profound indicators of the various perpetrators involved in each layer of the operation, and what their motivations were.

3. Webster Griffin Tarpley's Critique of the LIHOP Hypothesis: A Coup, Thermonuclear Blackmail, and Possible Indications of a **Third** Player

One of the most well-known and respected researchers of the 9/11 conspiracy's architecture is Webster Griffin Tarpley, who has exposed indications of a possible *third* layer to the event, above and beyond that of the "rogue element" within the US national security apparatus required by the LIHOP and MIHOP hypotheses. While this case will require the detailed examination of the main text to be completely comprehensible, an overview is necessitated here, in order to make the theses and methodological approaches of this book more readily apparent.

Tarpley argues the MIHOP position in his celebrated and detailed book *9/11 Synthetic Terror: Made in the USA*, now in its fifth edition. The MIHOP hypothesis "represents the analytical point of view which sees the events of September 11, 2001 as a deliberate provocation manufactured by an outlaw network of high officials infesting the military and security apparatus of the United States and Great Britain, a network ultimately dominated by Wall Street and City of London

---

[11] E.P. Heidner, "Collateral Damage: U.S. Covert Operations and the Terrorist Attacks on September 11, 2001," (PDF manuscript, 2008), p. 1. This study is available at www.futurefastforward.com/feature-articles/3988-collateral-damage-us-covert-operations-and-the-terrorist-attacks-on-september-11-2001-by-ep-heidner-6810.html.

financiers."[12] With this in hand, Tarpley notes that the LIHOP hypothesis is subject to a number of problems which, in the end, render it an inadequate analytical and synthetic template by which to view the events and aftermath of that day:

> LIHOP assumes that Bin Laden, al Qaeda, Atta, and company actually have at least a semi-independent existence and possess the will and the physical-technical capability to strike the United States in the ways seen on 9/11. But LIHOP also posits that the al Qaeda attack could not have been successful without the active cooperation of elements of the Pentagon and Bush administration who deliberately sabotaged US air defenses so as to allow the suicide pilots to reach their targets at the World Trade Center and Pentagon...
>
> In 2002 and 2003, LIHOP represented progress beyond the unanswered questions way station. But here too, as more new material has come to light, LIHOP has also become untenable...
>
> LIHOP is increasingly at war with masses of evidence. A more outré version of LIHOP admits that Atta and his cohorts were working for the CIA, but only as gun-runners and drug-runners, not terrorists. At a certain point, this view alleges, the drug-runners decided to revolt against their arrogant CIA masters by blowing up the World Trade Center and the Pentagon! But even this recondite scheme cannot address the absence of air defense for one hour and forty-five minutes, nor the controlled demolition which overtook the two trade towers.[13]

There thus emerged what Tarpley calls the Bush-Cheney MIHOP position, i.e., that the President and Vice-President were active planners of the operation, a position Tarpley does not find credible, since it would mean leaving part of the operational details in the hands of a "moron" and a man who has a history of heart trouble and "who is living on borrowed time."[14] Bush and Cheney may have had some limited knowledge or even planning role, but were not involved at the deepest level of level two, and certainly not in that all-important third level

Given these objections to LIHOP, and various versions of the Bush-Cheney MIHOP hypothesis, Tarpley goes on to argue that the tragedy of

---

[12] Webster Griffin Tarpley, *9/11 Synthetic Terror: Made in the USA* (Joshua Tree, California: Progressive Press, 2011), p. 275.

[13] Ibid., pp. 276-277.

[14] Ibid., p. 277. Tarpley also notes that there is a MOSSAD MIHOP position, a position he finds questionable due to the lack of a credible motivation for Israeli involvement in the operation. See p. 277.

9/11 was an orchestrated coup d'etat, a false flag event of state-sponsored "synthetic terror" designed to unleash the "clash of civilizations" of Samuel Huntington's famous book by that name.[15]

> The goal was to shock the entire US political system—the White House, the executive departments, the Congress, the courts, the political parties, the mass media, publishing and journalism, and the public in general out of their inertia of normal everyday life into a kind of war psychosis and paranoid obsession with phantom threats agreeable to the outlook of the neocon faction, the modern heirs of Carl Schmitt, Hitler's lawyer. The United States had to be mobilized, on the basis of pure hysteria, for the clash of civilizations.[16]

The mention of a Nazi connection, albeit in the tenuous and purely ideological and methodological reference to one of Hitler's lawyers, is significant, for this book argues that the *third* layer of 9/11, above and beyond the *American* rogue element—the second layer—is in fact an international Fascist one.

Before continuing with this cursory review of Tarpley's research, a brief word is necessary about what I mean by this Fascist or Nazi International. Many researchers have pointed out the connections of various intelligence agencies—the CIA, KGB, GRU, and so on—to international criminal undergrounds and their drug running networks.[17] The utility of this intelligence-drug running nexus is twofold, for it allows such agencies a source of large income that is completely free of the oversight of their respective governments, income that can be used in turn to fund a variety of covert operations and black research projects. However, it also provides them not only with a means both of monitoring those criminal organizations and their connections, but also provides them with an independent internationally-extensive source of intelligence. I have contended that in the post-World War Two period, the Fascist and Nazi elites were connected with these underground criminal organizations, and further, liaised with the similarly-minded rogue elements within various

---

[15] Webster Griffin Tarpley, *9/11 Synthetic Terror: Made in the USA*, p. 278.

[16] Tarpley, op. cit.., p. 279.

[17] See, for example, Henrik Krueger's *The Great Heroin Coup*, Stephen Handelman's *Comrade Criminal: Russia's New Mafia*, and the many writings of Professor Peter Dale Scott. Scott's work is particularly invaluable for providing a host of details connecting the American "deep state", its security services, to the international underground criminal drug running operations.

nations' "deep states." In America's case, this meant an effective alliance with the "Sullivan and Cromwell" crowd, with the American financial and business interests that shared the basic Fascist ideology and outlook. I hasten to add that for both parties, this was a post-war marriage of convenience, and from that point of view, 9/11 may have been the announcement of divorce.

With this in mind, we return to our review of Tarpley's research, for he presents a number of details and analyses that suggest not only the MIHOP hypothesis, but the "divorce" hypothesis. For example, crucial to Tarpley's MIHOP hypothesis is the fact that a significant number of wargaming exercises and drills were occurring on 9/11, and that the 9/11 attacks themselves took place within this context, using the cover of the drills to provide confusion in the command and control structure of the country. This fact alone indicates that the detailed planning of 9/11 *had to have come at some point from within the American national security and military structure.* It is this level that we are calling "level two" or "the rogue network."

Global Guardian was one of these drills, involving all of America's strategic nuclear and thermonuclear arsenal: ICBMs, SLBMs, nuclear bombers, and the "Doomsday/Night Watch/Looking Glass flying command posts". This drill involved airbases that house hydrogen bombs, such as Barksdale in Louisiana, and Offut in Omaha, Nebraska, both bases where President Bush flew on 9/11 after leaving Florida on Air Force One.[18] The probable reasons for Bush's appearance at these two airbases on that day will be addressed in a moment. Tarpley notes, however, that the motivation for Bush's flight to Offut Air Force Base in Omaha, Nebraska is suggested by the presence at Offut, on 9/11, of General Brent Scowcroft and Warren Buffet, as a kind of potential "Committee of Public Safety".[19] In other words, a group had converged at the command headquarters of America's strategic nuclear forces as a potential element of a coup d'etat, necessitating that President Bush be *personally present to reassert control over America's nuclear forces.*

> Thus, on the morning of 9/11, before a single hijacking had been reported, the US had assumed a strategic nuclear posture comparable to that observed during the Cuban missile crisis: B-1 and B-52 bombers were in the air; ballistic missile submarines were at their launch points, presumably near Russia and possibly China, and land-based ICBMs were ready for launch. The air defenses of North America were also on high alert, both in terms of

---

[18] Tarpley, op. cit., p. 318.
[19] Ibid.

interceptor aircraft and space assets. Everything, in short, was ready for a nuclear first strike like the neocons have talked so much about in recent years. All of this was observed in real time from Moscow by General Leonid Ivashov and his colleagues of the Russian General Staff.

The combination of mobilization for nuclear war plus the spectacular self-inflicted terrorism of 9.11 was unquestionably designed to provide the backdrop for Bush's announcement, first to Russian President Putin and soon thereafter to the world, that the US would seize Afghanistan and also bases in former Soviet central Asia. Anyone wanting to resist such plans had the US nuclear striking force—presumably under the control of the neocon fascist madmen who had organized the attacks—staring him in the face. It is also highly significant that Bush's 9/11 flight itinerary included both Barksdale (Air Force Base) and Offut (Air Force Base), two US nuclear command centers which were part of Global Guardian. Global Guardian was a massive exercise in nuclear blackmail...[20]

But how does this constitute a coup d'etat? And why would Bush need to have reasserted control over the nuclear command structure by his personal presence at Barksdale and Offut?

Tarpley points out that among the components of the Global Guardian thermonuclear wargame exercises on 9/11 was the "Global Guardian Computer Network Attack" exercise. This exercise, he observes, was designed to simulate a cyber attack on STRATCOM's computer network command and control structure by use a variety of methods, from denial of service attacks to simulation of an attack from "a 'bad insider with access to a key command and control system," an exercise that suggests the unthinkable, for this "bad insider" could easily have flipped the drill to "live" status by being a plant or mole for "some 'other organization', namely the "rogue network" and thus "missiles might actually have been launched. Here was the invisible government's back door to worldwide thermonuclear escalation, if that had been necessary, on 9/11."[21]

It is precisely here that we begin to get closer to the possibility that the architecture of 9/11 was not a two-tiered operation, i.e., an

---

[20] Webster Griffin Tarpley, *9/11 Synthetic Terror: Made in the USA*, fifth edition, p. 319. It should be noted that Barksdale was the *backup* command center to Offut, which is headquarters to STRATCOM, the successor command to SAC(Strategic Air Command), the command and control center for America's strategic nuclear forces.
[21] Webster Griffin Tarpley, *9/11 Synthetic Terror: Made in the USA,* fifth edition, pp. 320-321, emphasis added. Tarpley cites Pentagon newsletters for the details of this aspect of the Global Guardian drill.

operation involving the "outer layer" of the "terrorists", the effective patsies of the event, and a "deeper layer" involving a rogue element within the US military-intelligence complex, but a *three-tiered* operation, with the deepest layer penetrating the operations of the second layer, and threatening it with blackmail via a compromised command and control structure.

Tarpley summarizes the possibilities of a coup d'etat on 9/11 with Global Guardian as its effective instrument of cover, as a surrender of the Bush White House to the coup planners, a surrender

> ...that owed much to the fear that the coup faction were extremists capable of unleashing nuclear war. Here is a portal through which the rogue network could have launched nuclear missiles without the help of Bush... The targets for such missiles could have been Arab or Islamic capitals, if Bush had refused to initiate the war of civilziations in conventional form by attacking Afghanistan. The target could also have been China or Russia. *We must never lose sight of the Bush-Putin telephone call on 9/11, which was the central diplomatic and strategic event of the day, even though most 9/11 books do not even mention it.* In that telephone call, Bush in effect delivered an ultimatum that the United States was determined to seize Afghanistan... plus bases in former Soviet central Asia.[22]

Tarpley argues that Putin acceded to these demands, knowing that the USA's effort in Afghanistan would be no more successful than the Soviet one, and because such a large effort in Central Asia and the Middle East would ultimately sap America's strength.[23]

There are other significant clues that at its deepest level, 9/11 was not about terrorism, but about a coup attempt *by level three against level two*, that is to say, by some faction turning against the rogue group of the American national security-military establishment. These clues are found in Bush's statements to the nation on 9/11, and in some statements by his staff shortly thereafter.

For example, according to some reports on September 12th and 13th, 2001, Bush's press secretary, Ari Fleischer, indicated that the Secret Service had received credible threats on 9/11 from the attackers—notably unspecified—that indicated the White House and Air Force One were also targets. The *New York Times* itself reported that the threats were viewed as credible because they had been accompanied by the use of transmission and identification codes unique to the presidency

---

[22] Tarpley, op. cit., p. 321.
[23] Ibid.

itself.[24] French researcher Thierry Meyssan disclosed the *depth and breadth* of the attackers' apparent knowledge of these secure and highly classified codes:

> And more astonishing still, *World Net Daily*, citing intelligence officers as its sources, said the attackers also had the codes of the Drug Enforcement Agency(DEA), the National Reconnaissance Office(NRO), Air Force Intelligence(AFI), Army Intelligence(AI), Naval Intelligence(NI), the Marine Corps Intelligence(MCI) and the intelligence services of the State Department and the Department of Energy. Each of these codes is known by only a very small group of officials. No one is authorized to possess several of them. Also, to accept that the attackers were in possession of them supposes either that there exists a method of cracking the codes, or that moles have infiltrated each of these intelligence bodies. Technically, *it appears to be possible to reconstitute the codes of the American agencies by means of the software, Promis, that served to create them.*[25]

We shall return to the crucial role of the PROMIS software in the main text. For the moment, it is quite crucial to note (and to remember) that some of the codes the attackers allegedly knew were those of the super-secret National Reconnaissance Office, the center coordinating all of America's spy satellites, and the center coordinating their reconnaissance data.

For Meyssan, however, the use of the codes to establish the attackers' credibility and *capability* meant that the American state, and more importantly, the highest and deepest levels of its national security and military establishment, was penetrated by traitors and moles,[26] in other words, again one finds the possibility that there was a *third* level at work, above and beyond the rogue network planning the event as a financial crime, and as a social engineering incident to inject American power into the Middle East. By calling the White House and revealing their existence, they could only have had a specific objective in mind, the blackmail of the US government, for with such an extensive access to codes, the possibility existed that they could "usurp the authority of the President of the United States" and conceivably order the use of nuclear and thermonuclear weapons, and flip the Global Guardian drill to live status. And thus, "the only means," argues Meyssan, "allowing George W.

---

[24] Thierry Meyssan, *9/11: The Big Lie* (London: Carnot Pub. Ltd., 2002), pp. 43f.
[25] Ibid., p. 44, emphasis added.
[26] Ibid.

Bush to retain control of the military was to physically hold the headquarters of the U.S. Strategic Command, at Offut, and to personally issue orders and counter-orders from there. That's why he went there in person."[27] It is in this analytical context that Meyssan and Tarpley analyze Bush's statements on 9/11, noting an interesting progression of concepts, and some intriguing omissions of others.

At 9:30 AM, after he had finished reading "My Pet Goat" to the schoolchildren of the Emma Booker elementary school in Sarasota, Florida, President Bush conferred briefly with his staff, then appeared to the press to read the following statement:

> Ladies and Gentlemen, this is a difficult moment for America. I, unfortunately, *will be going back to Washington after my remarks.* Secretary Rod Paige and the Lt. Governor will take the podium and discuss education. I do want to thank the folks here at Booker Elementary School for their hospitality.
>
> Today we've had a national tragedy. Two airplanes have crashed into the World Trade Center *in an apparent terrorist attack* on our country. I have spoken to the Vice President, to the Governor of New York, to the Director of the FBI, and have ordered that the full resources of the federal government go to help the victims and their families, and to conduct a full-scale investigation to hunt down and to find those folks who committed this act.
>
> *Terrorism against our nation will not stand.* And now if you would join me in a moment of silence. May God bless the victims, their families, and America. Thank you very much.[28]

Tarpley notes that the key and crucial remark is the reference to an "*apparent* terrorist attack."[29] But also to be noted is that Bush explicitly states he will be returning to Washington after concluding his remarks, suggesting that at some point between his departure from Booker Elementary School to his departure from Sarasota on Air Force One, the threat had become clearer and the decision was taken to divert to Barksdale and then Offut in order to assert personal presidential control over the military's strategic command structure. Indeed, Tarpley states that shortly after leaving the school, the Secret Service learned of a

---

[27] Thierry Meyssan, *9/11: The Big Lie*, p. 45.
[28] Webster Griffin Tarpley, *9/11 Synthetic Terror: Made in USA*, fifth edition, p, 345, emphasis added.
[29] Ibid.

threat to Air Force One.[30] It seems most probable that this threat was precisely that conveyed with the use of classified presidential codes.

Then, circa 9:42 AM, the ABC television network "broadcast live images of a fire that had broken out in the White House annex, the Old Executive Office Building," home to a number of key offices of the executive, including that of the Vice President. As Meyssan observes, "No information has ever leaked out concerning the origin of the blaze, or its exact scale." All that ABC showed was a "fixed shot of plumes of black smoke escaping from the building."[31] Approximately fifteen minutes later, according to Meyssan, Vice President Dick Cheney was taken by the Secret Service and escorted to the White House situation room below ground, while sharpshooters "armed with rocket launchers" were deployed around the now evacuated White House complex. These troops, notes Meyssan, were capable "of repelling an assault by airborne troops. In short, they were facing a threat of a very different nature to that later described by Vice President Cheney."[32] That is, at that moment, the threat was not terrorism; it was something else entirely.

At approximately the same time this was happening, Air Force One departed Sarasota, sometime between 9:55 and 9:57 AM at the same time that the South Tower of the World Trade Center was about to be demolished. According to Bush Communications Director Dan Bartlett, the presidential airplane climbed at such a steep angle for about 10 minutes that it seemed that the aircraft was "going almost straight up." Most significantly, however, Air Force One, in a classic example of "security stripping," *had no fighter escort as it left Sarasota, and would not acquire one until an hour after it had been in the air.*[33]

Air Force One eventually landed at Barksdale Air Force Base in Louisiana, where most of the press corps was jettisoned, and where, at 1:04 PM, President Bush made another statement, before proceeding on to Offutt Air Force Base in Omaha, Nebraska. The text of this statement is unique, not only for what it says, but what it does *not* say:

> I want to reassure the American people that the full resources of the federal government are working to assist local authorities to save lives and to help the victims of these attacks. Make no mistake: The United States will hunt down and punish those responsible for these cowardly acts.

---

[30] Webster Griffin Tarpley, *9/11 Synthetic Terror: Made in USA*, p. 345-346.
[31] Thierry Meyssan, *9/11: The Big Lie*, p.46.
[32] Ibid.
[33] Webster Griffin Tarpley, *9/11 Synthetic Terror: Made in USA*, p. 346.

I've been in regular contact with the Vice President, the Secretary of Defense, the national security team and my Cabinet. We have taken all appropriate security precautions to protect the American people. Our military at home and around the world is on high alert status, and *we have taken the necessary security precautions to continue the functions of your government.*

We have been in touch with the leaders of Congress and with world leaders to assure them that we will do whatever is necessary to protect America and Americans.

I ask the American people to join me in saying a thanks for all the folks who have been fighting hard to rescue our fellow citizens and to join me in saying a prayer for the victims and their families.

The resolve of our great nation is being tested. But make no mistake: we will show the world that we will pass this test. God bless.[34]

As Meyssan and Tarpley both observe, there is *not a single mention* of terrorism in this speech, but only of a "test," and Bush's words could therefore equally and just as easily refer to an internal revolt, coup, or military conflict, as to terrorism.[35] Similarly, a simple terrorist threat, no matter how big or dire, is unlikely to provoke the statement that indicates Continuity of Government operations were begun: "We have taken the necessary security precautions to continue the functions of your government."

Meyssan observes that there are two possible readings of this action:

In such a context, one can interpret in two different ways the activation of the Continuity of Government (CoG) procedure. The simplest explanation is to consider the need to protect the President and other political leaders from the actions of traitors capable of starting a fire in the Old Executive Building and stealing the secret codes of both the Presidency and the intelligence agencies.

One might also consider whether, on the contrary, the C0G plan was put into effect not to protect political leaders from traitors, but was initiated by the traitors themselves to isolate those leaders. The account given by Vice President Dick Cheney is truly strange.

---

[34] President George W. Bush, Text of Statement at Barksdale Air Force Base, 1:04 PM, September 11, 2001, emphasis added, in Thierry Meyssan, *9/11 The Big Lie*, pp. 46-47.

[35] See Webster Griffin Tarpley, *9/11 Synthetic Terror: Made in USA*, fifth edition, p. 345, and Thierry Meyssan, *9/11: the Big Lie*, p. 47.

He claims that men from the Secret Service seized him in his office and bundled him into the White House bunker without receiving his consent. He appeared to suggest that the same was true for the principal members of the government and Congress. And what else is an operation where the secret services take elected officials and put them in bunkers *"for their own security"*, if not a *coup d'etat*, or at least a palace coup?[36]

In other words, the government in Washington had been seized by the coup, placing its key members under "protection," leaving the President to attempt to reassert control over the strategic command structure of the military by his personal presence at its headquarters, forestalling a potential nuclear conflict, by surrendering to the demands of the attackers.[37]

These considerations, however, still do not add up to a deeper *third* layer or faction, coopting and penetrating the "rogue element" or network within the American national security apparatus. Let us now make an assumption, to be argued in the main text more thoroughly, that Bush and Cheney and other elements of the federal government knew, to some degree, of the 9/11 operation, and perhaps even assisted in its planning. Once one adds this assumption, one sees the third level revealed, for Bush and the federal government are then *reacting to an operation they know has gone wrong, and that has been penetrated or coopted by someone else.* The explanatory power of this assumption, as will be seen, rationalizes certain behavior of the federal government and its domestic and foreign policies quite well, and additionally provides a different perspective from which to view certain statements not only of President Bush, but of the British Prime Minister at that time, Tony Blair.

On January 29, 2002, President Bush delivered his famous "axis of evil" State of the Union address before the Congress. In that speech, as is now known, he accused North Korea, Iraq, and Iran and "states like these and their terrorist allies" of attempting to acquire missiles and weapons of mass destruction, including weaponized anthrax, nerve gas, and nuclear weapons. These states, however, could not acquire the technological infrastructure for the production of such weapons on their own without acquiring them from some great power. I suggest, in this context, that the allusion to an "axis of evil" was a deliberate hint on the part of Bush as to whom the *real* hidden players may have been.

---

[36] Thierry Meyssan, *9/11: The Big Lie*, pp. 47-48, emphasis in the original.
[37] Webster Griffin Tarpley, *9/11 Synthetic Terror: Made in USA*, fifth edition, p. 339. Tarpley notes that "Better than 'Bush knew'...is 'Bush surrendered.'"

More importantly, according to 9/11 researcher Daniel Hopsicker, British Prime Minister Tony Blair may have let something highly significant out of the bag:

> It was left to British Prime Minister Tony Blair to present the prosecution's case against Bin Laden, and he sketched out the Cliff Notes version of the evidence. Tony Blair said, "Al Qaeda is a terrorist organization *with ties to a global network*."
>
> That made sense. The idea that Mohamed Atta and his henchmen needed help from an international organization while they were in the U.S. was easy to understand.
>
> Logistical support is difficult to arrange from caves.
>
> But what *kind* of global network? Blair didn't say. Blair's "global network" remained elusive, un-named, shadowy, and undefined.
>
> Several weeks later the FBI denied that this *global network* existed, and proposed instead a "Lone Cadre Theory" which became the operative assumption in their investigation.[38]

But what, exactly, *is* that network? That "axis of evil"?

Before answering that question, a personal aspect of my interest in its answer must now be recounted.

B. A Personal Perspective: An Email to a Cousin

In the years during which the 9/11 truth movement combed over the evidence, testimony, and analyses of various researchers, I read and gathered their writings, dreading to find any confirmation that my intuitions about who had perpetrated the event were true. My intuitions, formed on that terrible day itself, were firstly that no such event could take place without, at *some* level, the knowledge and complicity of some group in the military-national security apparatus of the federal government, and secondly, that whatever that second rogue level consisted of, their own spokesmen were behaving in a manner that suggested *genuine*, and *not insincere* panic, and that in turn suggested a third level, and a penetrated operation. I came to that conclusion in turn also because, when watching the destruction of the Twin Towers, I thought that I may be looking at the application of exotic modalities of destruction, including exotic energy weapons.[39]

---

[38] Daniel Hopsicker, *Welcome to Terrorland: Mohamed Atta and the 9-11 Cover-Up in Florida* (Venice, Florida: Mad Cow Press: 2007), pp. xiii-xiv, emphasis added.

[39] Note I say "exotic energy weapons" and *not* "directed energy weapons." This will become an important consideration in the main text.

This is hardly a popular view in the 9/11 truth community. Indeed, it is the one hypothesis concerning the "murder weapon" that the overwhelming majority of researchers—with the exceptions of Webster Tarpley, Dr. Judy Wood, and a few others—who are trying to understand the architecture of the conspiracy reject out of hand. The hypothesis of exotic energy weapons in my view is not exclusive of the presence of other modalities of the destruction of the Twin Towers. Nevertheless, of all the hypotheses (hotly) debated in the 9/11 truth community, it is the one which has the most problematical elements, not the least of which are the enormous energy requirements that such a mechanism would involve. In the main text, I shall propose some hypothetical models for consideration.

The problem of the exact mechanism of the controlled demolition of the Twin Towers (and standard explosives, nano-thermite, mini-nukes, and exotic energy weapons systems are all variations on the mechanism of controlled demolitions) is the *crux interpretum* of the 9/11 event, for in all four cases, they render a simple "terrorism" interpretation impossible, for in the first three hypotheses of controlled demolition, the buildings would have had to have been elaborately and deliberately prepared by careful placement of the explosives, be they standard, thermite, nuclear, or otherwise, and in the final instance, that of an energy weapons system, it is *almost* inconceivable that a mere terrorist organization such as al Qaeda or anything similar to it would have access to such technologies.

It was during this period of research, in late 2008 and after the now infamous "bail out" hearings, that I received an email from one of my paternal cousins, we'll simply call him "Douglas", whom I had not heard from since we were both nine years old (he had been born in the same year as I, just a few months later). He had been reading some of my books when, in a conversation with his father, my uncle, he realized he was reading his cousin's books, and hence he had decided to contact me to find out my views on who I thought was responsible for 9/11, as he had been doing his own digging, and had come to question the narrative of the officially-approved conspiracy theory, but also to doubt aspects of the LIHOP and MIHOP versions of events that were then popular. I responded in a lengthy email, outlining what I had read in other critics' accounts. Later I shared this email with Mr. Richard C. Hoagland, where a portion of it appeared on his website, enterprisemission.com.[40] In that email, I summarized my difficulties with the various versions of

---

[40] http://www.enterprisemission.com/Norway-Message3.htm

standard controlled demolition of the twin towers, and why I thought some form of exotic technology might also be involved, and on that basis, went on to outline in crude fashion what I intuited to be the basic architecture of the conspiracy:

> ... so we are left with ...some version of my Nazi International extra-territorial state, with, in my mind, an all but proven track record of the postwar investigation of precisely the technologies to bring down the Towers. Radical and wild and woolly as I think this scenario sounds, it does in my mind rationalize the rather odd signs of "panic" that "our" elite has shown since 9/11, for consider the almost frenzied rush into Afghanistan and Iraq (whose true and ultimate purpose, I think, involved much more than oil, and I hint about that ultimate purpose in my books repeatedly). Realizing that they were faced with an extra-territorial state with possession of extraordinarily sophisticated "scalar-torsion" technology that had been successfully weaponized, they launched a 'war on terror' with radical Islam as the fall guy, when in fact, the real target is something completely different and much more frightening. The behavior of the financial elite during the bailout crisis is another signal, at least to me, that someone has the gun to their heads; they acted like people being blackmailed by some hidden "protection racket" by insisting on "no oversight" back in 2008. The only people in the historical record that wielded such financial and technological clout that I can think of were, in fact, the postwar Nazis.
>
> There is a final, even weirder, consideration, and that's Ian Fleming and his James Bond novels/films. Many people have always considered that he was "leaking information in the guise of fiction." Well, consider the movie "You Only Live Twice," where you have the following elements clearly displayed:

1) An international conspiracy that is extra-territorial, called SPECTRE (Society for the Promotion of Extortion, Criminality, Terrorism, Revenge...);
2) That society has a secret space program and is using it to interfere with Russian and American space launches (shades of the recent collision of an American and Russian satellite in orbit above the earth), and to bring the two nations to the brink of war;
3) That society has a heavy presence of Japanese criminal underground; and finally,
4) It is headed by an obviously German fellow named Ernst Stavro Blohfeld (played by Donald Pleasance, and thus, plump, middle aged, and almost Bormann-esque in appearance).

So if one grants the proposition that Fleming is "leaking information", then the conclusion is obvious as to what he's trying to say. And I believe this to be the case because in effect this is what my own research has been able to verify, in that, I have been able to argue points 1,2, and 4 are most likely true, and that would seem to indicate that point 3 is as well.

So my "op within an op within an op" scenario is basically that someone, with probable access to hidden space technologies, and with all but certain access to weaponized versions of "scalar-torsion technologies", brought the Twin Towers down. That "someone" is some sort of *rogue extra-territorial organization, with deep and historical connections to the radical Islamic underworld*, and that leaves me with, guess who, the Nazis. Thus, I believe the second level of that 9/11 conspiracy, our own home-grown elitists, were once again played the fools by the outer and innermost rings of it, in a sort of "squeeze from below squeeze from above" methodology, a methodology that elite has used itself numerous times.

By using that specific methodology against the very people that use it themselves, the message was sent: "we know your game, and lookee-lookee what we can do, what we have possession of. We can literally turn your centers and instrumentalities of power to dust before your very eyes. We are deeply penetrated into your own covert agencies and plans, and the game is now afoot."

Consider also the Masonic symbolism of what was struck in that way: the Twin Towers, the twin Masonic pillars of Jachin and Boaz, sitting in the heart of the Anglo-American elite's financial district. Richard's analysis of the esoteric symbolism "Who's the Enemy, Really?" at http://www.enterprisemission. com/tower2.htm] is as far as I'm concerned right on target, as is his analysis of why radical Islam would be involved. I think, too, he might be willing to entertain my particular "twist" on his scenario, in that one has not only radical Muslims, but worse, unreconstructed Nazis involved with it, after all, the historical connections between the two run very deep. The Muslims do not have access to such technologies, whereas the Nazis were investigating them with a vengeance since at least 1933!

So, that's it in a nutshell ....

While many if not most 9/11 researchers, whether defenders of the official scenario or its critics, would be inclined to dismiss my informal musings as the wildest, most bizarre ravings, and the least probable of all the alternative scenarios available, when reduced to its bare conceptual essence, the scenario I proposed to my cousin is not really all that different than that proposed by others. I merely am willing to connect the dots they have provided, with that greatest genocidal-technological ideology of the last century, and its long association with radical Islamic terrorism: Nazism. This postwar Nazi group as I have noted elsewhere had deep post-war ties with "rogue elements" of a basically fascist mindset within the American financial and intelligence deep state in the postwar period, that group represented by Allen and

John Foster Dulles, John McCloy, and others of the "Sullivan and Cromwell crowd".

This hypothesis is not easily dismissible when one ponders the actual details—uncovered by many in that 9/11 truth community itself—which suggest that this Nazi element *is* involved. *They* have uncovered these details, but like all such uncomfortable details, they have chosen to ignore these clues, and thus no effort has yet been made to integrate their significance and their implications into the architecture of the various conspiracy theories concerning 9/11 that have been proffered.

I contend that this failure does egregious harm to the interpretation of 9/11 itself, and that in part is what this book explores in the following pages. Webster Griffin Tarpley, as we have seen, has had no hesitation in describing Tony Blair's "global network" as a Fascist network, centered in London and New York. It is therefore no a great leap of the imagination to state that this network also has centers in Frankfurt, and that some of its historical and technological roots lie in Nazism. This third layer, as I shall attempt to argue in the main text, exposes itself in a variety of clues, not the least of which are those clues which suggest exotic modalities of the Twin Towers' destruction, be that "nano-thermite," "mini-nukes" or exotic "energy weapons." Viewed in this way, such an approach to 9/11 is an attempt to view the event from the perspective of Mr. Richard Dolan's idea of a "breakaway civilization" that secretly emerged over the decades since World War Two, a civilization that emerged because of its decades' long access to secret funds, a great deal of which came from the exploitation of Axis loot, and that emerged because of its use of that vast war chest to fund the secret development of various exotic technologies.

Such an approach is not meant to delegitimize the efforts of those 9/11 researchers who stick to "nuts and bolts" and who do *not* consciously attempt to integrate their speculations about the architecture of the conspiracy into such a wide historical and interpretive context. Indeed, their approach has uncovered most of the clues re-examined in this book. I merely argue that it is perhaps time to reconsider these clues within a much larger technological and historical context, for that context leads us to UFOs, to the black projects world, to the national security structure and Mr. Dolan's "breakaway civilization" hypothesis, and to that post-war extra-territorial Nazi organization, with its own deep ties to the criminal underworld, drug trafficking, and, of course, to Islamic radicalism and terrorism.

This third level is not therefore exclusively, at its deepest level, merely or exclusively Anglo-American Fascist nor composed simply of corrupt financial oligarchs in London or Wall Street as Mr. Tarpley observes. It *is* that, but it is also much more; it is also at that deepest level, Nazi, and German, and international, all at once. Like all Mafias, it has its factions, and like all Mafias, its alliances are always and only of convenience. It can and does go to war with itself. So in this sense, this book is a development and continuation of my examinations in previous books, begun in *Reich of the Black Sun*, continued in *SS Brotherhood of the Bell, Secrets of the Unified Field, The Philosophers' Stone, The Nazi International, Roswell and the Reich, Saucers Swastikas and Psyops, Covert Wars and Breakaway Civilizations, Covert Wars and the Clash of Civilizations*, and finally, my most recent book *The Third Way*.

In that last book, I pointed out that one of the goals of the post-war Nazi International was precisely to destabilize Anglo-American petroleum interests in the Middle East,[41] and that the war on terror might be a convenient front for a war against this Nazi International, connected as it was and is to Islamic terrorist groups.[42] Consider only the utility of a "global war on terror" from a variety of points of view. A war on terror is essentially a war against an invisible extra-territorial enemy; it provides a rationalization and justification for overt and/or covert action anywhere in the world, and thus, for any ideology bent on world domination—from American unipolarism through the special claims of "religion" to Nazism—a war on terror works as well for extra-territorial organizations as it does for American imperialists.

Consequently, by no means do I mean to suggest that all the careful deliberations and analyses of other researchers are *wrong* with respect to this architecture and the perpetrators of this mass murder. I mean merely to suggest that the interpretive net must be cast much wider, and that the suggestive Fascist links they themselves have uncovered must be appropriated into any hypothetical 9/11 scenario.

That Fascist devil is in the details, and these details the 9/11 truth community itself has uncovered, and then ignored, perhaps because dealing with them is to deal with the historically and apocalyptically unthinkable.

I propose in this book not to ignore those details.

They are chilling.

For like it or not, there's a clear and palpable Nazi connection that constantly hovers on the edges and centers of the drama.

Was there such a third level to 9/11? I have always suspected there is, and this book is an attempt to elaborate that suspicion.

---

[41] Joseph P Farrell, *The Third Way* (Kempton, Illinois: AUP, 2015), pp. 26-27,
[42] Ibid., p. 112.

PART ONE:
PROBLEMS AND PROBLEMATICS

"It was left to British Prime Minister Tony Blair to present the prosecution's case against Bin Laden, and he sketched out the Cliff Notes version of the evidence. Tony Blair said, 'Al Qaeda is a terrorist organization with ties to a global network.'"
Daniel Hopsicker,
Welcome to Terrorland: Mohammed Atta and the 9-11 Cover-up in Florida, p. xiii

1

THE PROBLEMATIC OF THE PERPETRATORS:
OF PATSIES AND PILOTS AND PRESCOTT'S PROGENY

Patsies can... be used in many combinations. They can be merged together in false flag terror operations. These organizations will assume a distinct ideological or religious coloration and will advertise it, and that will become the key to the process of creating or reinforcing the enemy image desired by the terrorist controllers after the terrorist action has been successfully carried out.
Webster Griffin Tarpley[1]

THE DIABOLICALLY DULL, SOPHOMORIC, SOPORIFIC EYES of Mohamed Atta, heavy-laden with the life of a Faustian bargain with its accompanying debaucheries, and perhaps with personal knowledge of the events of 9/11 that he took with him to his doom, have been staring at us from the pages of a thousand newspapers and television screens since 9/11 itself. Of all the images of 9/11, it is Atta's face that is the visual, iconic symbol of that day, perhaps second only in stature as an icon of those events to the endlessly looped videos of planes slamming into the World Trade Center Twin Towers.

Mohamed Mohamed al-Amir Awad el-Sayed Atta (1968-2001)

---

[1] Webster Griffin Tarpley, *9/11 Synthetic Terror: Made in USA*, fifth edition, p. 92.

The Problematic of the Perpetrators

It is entirely appropriate that Atta's visage has attained such iconic status as a symbol of 9/11 along with the videos and photos of the airplanes slamming into the Twin Towers of the World Trade Center in New York City, for Atta's hijacked aircraft, American Airlines flight 11, was the first aircraft to crash into the North Tower of the Twin Towers, beginning the day's tragic events. More than any other individual, he symbolizes the events of the day, and like most salient features of 9/11, he is a profound clue to the architecture and levels of the conspiracy, and of the motivations and means of the various groups involved with it. The hijackers in general, and Atta in particular, are the gate of entry into this labyrinthine structure.

A. The Problem of the Hijackers
1. The Shifting List of Hijackers

9/11 researcher Jay Kolar observes that the Director of the FBI during and subsequently to the 9/11 attacks, Robert Mueller,[2] admitted the FBI's case against the nineteen hijackers eventually named by the agency, would never be adequate in a court of law.[3] Doubtless, the fact that no one knows exactly *how* the FBI established the original list of nineteen hijackers,[4] a list which contained grievous errors and which had to be subsequently modified, doubtless has something to do with this, as, no doubt, also does the fact the some of the individuals named on its final "official" list "have since turned out to be alive, documented as such by authorities and interviews with those named," while the FBI has "stubbornly refused to adjust its list to reflect these facts."[5] Perhaps the fact that the passenger manifests of the airlines in question were so quickly confiscated by the FBI, but when the airlines eventually released the names of passengers, none of their passenger lists contained the nineteen hijackers might have something to do with it, or maybe the fact that the television network CNN had the first FBI list of nineteen hijackers within a day after the attacks, and that this list contained Mohamed Atta's name plus that of four other alleged hijackers, which

---

[2] One of the details that some researchers have found suspicious about 9/11 is the fact that Mueller assumed the FBI directorship only one week prior to the attacks, on September 4, 2001. He held this post until September 4, 2013.

[3] Jay Kolar, "What We Now Know About the Alleged 9-11 Hijackers," in Pau Zarembka, ed., *The Hidden History of 9-11* (New York: Seven Stories Press, 2008), 3-44, p. 3.

[4] Ibid., p. 4.

[5] Ibid.

were later dropped "and replaced with four other Arab names"[6] might have something to do with Director Mueller's hesitance about the ability of the FBI's hijacker list to withstand the scrutiny of a court of law.

To be sure, and to be fair, in an investigation of such intensity and enormity, the FBI, like any other investigative agency, is bound to follow every lead, and such clues may lead to dead ends, and to revisions while the investigation is in progress.

However, as Jay Kolar also observes, this is not the principal problem with the FBI's "final list." The problem is that four years after the events of that day, at least *ten* of its named hijackers were still alive, and one other alleged hijacker, "Ziad Jarrah, had his identity doubled and therefore fabricated."[7] This raises the question of whether obfuscation of data was being deliberately introduced into the picture, and the question is not merely an academic one, for at one level, namely, that of the official narrative itself, the nineteen alleged hijackers are the murder weapon, and hence obfuscation on this matter recalls to some extent the similar obfuscation that occurred over the murder weapon of President Kennedy: was it a 7.65 Mauser rifle, as originally reported, or a 6.5 Mannlicher-Carcano, the murder weapon of the subsequent "official narrative".

Kolar points out that with respect to the early list, the four "corrected names" of CNN's list might have been made with a view of substituting people known to be dead and who were *not* in the USA, so that the FBI list could not be challenged by uncomfortable incidents like Adnan Bukhari, who was on the initial list, but who showed up at a local FBI office to show that he was quite alive.[8]

With the FBI's hijacker list, one is already in the presence of the LIHOP-MIHOP problem. As Kolar notes, why was it necessary to publish

---

[6] Jay Kolar, "What We Now Know About the Alleged 9-11 Hijackers," in Pau Zarembka, ed., *The Hidden History of 9-11* (New York: Seven Stories Press, 2008), 3-44, p. 3

[7] Ibid., pp. 11-12. Kolar lists these eleven names as being (1) Walled al-Shehri, (2) Wail al-Shehri, (3) Mohand al-Shehri, (4) Abdurahman al-Omari, (5) Abdul Aziz al-Omari, (6) Khalid al-Mihdhar, (7) Salem al-Hazmi, (8) Marwan al-shehri, (9) Saeed al-Ghamdi, (10) ahmed al-Nami, and (11) Zaid Jarrah. Kolar also gives the sources for the verification that these alleged hijackers were still alive, which in Marwan al-Shahri's case (number 8), is listed as being the *Saudi Gazette* of September 18, 2001 and *The KJhaleej Times*, of September 20, 2001. The question of whether Saudi sources are to be trusted with respect to 9/11, when there is clear indication of Saudi involvement at *some* level in the events (as we shall see later in this chapter), is not adequately addressed by Kolar in my opinion with respect to this issue.

[8] Ibid., pp. 12-13.

a list so quickly after the events, and then to correct that list, and then maintain the correctness of that list in the face of evidence that at least some of its named individuals did not even belong on it, since they were still alive? The answer, he says,

> ...is fivefold: (1) to implicate an outside, foreign, Arab source and, more specifically, to set up al-Qaeda as overall patsy. Conveniently for the US war machine, al-Qaeda lacks a specific national identity, a fact which makes it necessary for the US military to hunt them down in multiple countries: Afghanistan, Iraq... (2) to give the perpetrators a decidedly fanatic, fundamentalist Islamic "face," captured so well in Atta's "death-mask" photograph, and thereby convince us that this enemy had the necessary religious extremism to martyr themselves as the hijacker/"suicide bombers" the official story needed as cover story; (3) to act as a red-herring used *to divert attention away from government insider moles, the only perpetrators **capable** of carrying out an attack using multiple wargames as a crucial part of its strategy*; (4) to divert attention away from the use of computer technology and Global Hawk by which piloting of the planes could have been overtaken from a remote location, for example the military command bunker that the Vice President occupied...

(With that last comment, note that we are already in the Bush-Cheney version of the MIHOP hypothesis, a hypothesis that this author, like Tarpley, finds dubious for all the reasons mentioned in the preface. Continuing:)

> ...and (5) with the construction of hijackers flying planes in suicide missions as the agency that brought down the WTC twin towers, *to divert attention from the actual agency of the towers' destruction: pre-planned, controlled demolition explosives.*[9]

It is important to note that while it is likely that President Bush and Vice President Cheney knew to some degree of all the vast wargames taking place on that day, and that they may have been involved in some of the planning for them, as we shall discover later in this chapter, there are indications that at one level, they were *not* surprised at the *real* events taking place, and yet, that at another level, they *were* surprised. It is also important to note that the official narrative of suicide hijackers from the

---

[9] Jay Kolar, "What We Now Know About the Alleged 9-11 Hijackers," in Pau Zarembka, ed., *The Hidden History of 9-11* (New York: Seven Stories Press, 2008), 3-44, p. 14, all emphases added.

al-Qaeda network, and therefore the "official narrative" of the events of 9/11 *is quite simply **impossible** on its own, for the concurrence of wargames and drills during the day which effectively cloaked the operation means that the operation was planned with knowledge of those drills, and that knowledge could only have come from within the American national security and military establishments, and from people with the security clearance to have access to them.* Note finally that while Kolar is an adherent to the "standard explosives controlled demolition" hypothesis for the destruction of the Twin Towers, that the suicide hijackers could just as easily function as a diversion for all *other* hypotheses of the Twin Towers' destruction. And indeed, the "standard explosives controlled demolition" hypothesis and any supporting evidence for it could *also* function as a diversion from the other more exotic hypotheses of their destruction.

To put all this "country simple," the official narrative points ineluctably to its own falsification and interior contradictions, and as much as anything else about 9/11, points to the existence of a second and deeper level lurking in the events of that day. This level is the celebrated "rogue network" existing within the superstructure of the American national security-military establishment that the 9/11 truth movement has so consistently insisted exists as a kind of deep state or parallel bureaucracy.

2. The Dulles and Portland, Maine, Airport Security Videos

There are *other* difficulties with the general picture of the hijackers. Kolar points out that the alleged security camera video of the hijackers at Dulles International Airport outside Washington DC, purportedly showing some of the hijackers boarding their flight, is problematic in the extreme, lacking any of the standard features of closed circuit television security videos, such as the camera number which would clearly identify the location, the date of the recording, and the running digital clock. Additionally, the camera on this video is apparently being jostled and manipulated by humans, and there is further evidence of cuts and splices in the video, and hence, of heavy editing.[10] Additionally, the video does not even show Hani Hanjour, the alleged pilot of flight 77

---

[10] Jay Kolar, "What We Now Know About the Alleged 9-11 Hijackers," in Pau Zarembka, ed., *The Hidden History of 9-11* (New York: Seven Stories Press, 2008), 3-44, pp. 6-7.

which allegedly crashed into the Pentagon,[11] a problem which we shall confront later in this book.

The significance of these problems with the Dulles Airport video is that its dubious nature is the basis "upon which the entire weight of the official story" rests, and ultimately, collapses" for the simple reason that "No airport security video has appeared for the other flights." And the bottom line of *this* implication is in turn that "no evidence exists that any of the 'hijackers' ever boarded planes that crashed on 9-11."[12]

The reader might well ask, however, "but what about the security camera footage of Mohamed Atta and Abdul Azis al-Omari captured at the Portland, Maine airport?" This *is* indisputably authentic airport security camera footage. Unfortunately, however, this is *not* footage of Atta and al-Omari boarding American Airlines Flight 11 for its fateful encounter with the north tower of the World Trade Center, but of them boarding a *connecting* flight for flight 11.[13] Kolar theorizes that the reason so many people assume that this is a video of them boarding flight 11 is because in the stress of the day, it was easy to confuse and conflate two entirely different things, and he goes on to suggest that "This factor was most likely taken into account in the overall plan of the real perpetrators of 9-11, and it may be why Atta and al-Omari took the detour from Boston to Portland, Maine, only to fly the connecting flight back to Boston."[14]

In proffering this explanation for the Portland video and the connecting flight, Kolar is addressing another problem raised by many 9/11 researchers with respect to the official story. Why would Atta and al-Omari have *risked* the entire operation on a connecting flight? Connecting flights can be late, and hence, the possibility existed that they might not have made their appointment with Allah due to a late flight, or some other factor that might have "gone wrong." So again, why did Atta and Omari risk the whole thing, rent a Nissan car, drive from Boston to Portland, Maine, board a connecting flight *back* to Boston, and then board Flight 11?

Kolar's answer to these questions is worth citing extensively, for it brings us back to the *original* list, and to two people who were originally on it, Adnan and Ameer Bukhari, who were eventually *replaced* by Atta and al-Omari:

---

[11] Jay Kolar, "What We Now Know About the Alleged 9-11 Hijackers," in Pau Zarembka, ed., *The Hidden History of 9-11* (New York: Seven Stories Press, 2008), 3-44, p. 8.

[12] Ibid.

[13] Ibid., p. 5.

[14] Ibid.

The two Bukharis chapter of the official 9-11 myth is instructive for an additional reason. The press reported they rented a Nissan Altima at Boston's Logan Airport, drove it to Portland, Maine, the day before 9-11, and just abandoned it at the Portland Jetport on the morning of the attacks when they took the connecting flight back to Boston, there to board Flight 11 into history books. Strike the word "history," however, and write in "unexplained mystery," because, due to the problems the FBI had with one Bukhari having been dead for a year and the other turning up alive on its doorstep, the FBI had to perform a quick switcheroo. Now, it is uniformly reported that Atta and Abdul Aziz al-Omari rented the Nissan Altima at Boston Logan, drove to Portland, left the Nissan there, and took the connecting flight back to Boston. Add to this latter inexplicable mystery the fact that *another* car rented allegedly by Atta, a White Mitsubishi, was abandoned at Boston Logan. When their destination was Boston, why would Atta and al-Omari rent one car in Boston and leave it at the Boston airport, then rent another car in Boston and leave it at the Portland, Maine, airport, and take a flight back to Boston. The whole story makes no sense.[15]

Here let us pause and interject that the story makes no sense from any normal point of view, but *does* make sense when viewed from the standpoint of standard surveillance tactics, and the types of *counter-measures* that can be used to throw off surveillance if one has available a team of people to do this type of bait-and-switch operation. With this in mind, Kolar continues:

> What this story does suggest, however, is that just as the story about the two Bukharis renting the Nissan was found to be an impossibility—one of them being dead—and as such a fabrication by the FBI, so also was the substitute story of Atta and al-Omari a fabrication and a myth.[16]

The reasons it was a myth?

Kolar, like most other 9/11 researchers, finds the amount of evidence connecting Atta to the rented cars just "too good to be true," i.e., just too good not to have been planted evidence. In fact, Atta took *luggage* with him when he boarded the connecting flight to Boston in

---

[15] Jay Kolar, "What We Now Know About the Alleged 9-11 Hijackers," in Pau Zarembka, ed., *The Hidden History of 9-11* (New York: Seven Stories Press, 2008), 3-44, p. 16.

[16] Ibid., pp. 16-17.

Portland, Maine, luggage which included, among other things, instruction manuals on the use of Boeing flight simulators, a cassette tape of religious instruction of an obviously "Islamicist" variety, a written instruction to other hijackers concerning mental preparation for their impending appearance before Allah, his passport, his international driver's license, and last and not least, his last will and testament![17] Fortunately, and quite conveniently, Atta's luggage did *not* make the connecting flight back to Boston, which allowed the authorities to "discover" its treasure-trove of incriminating evidence. The problem here, however, is obvious: "If Atta knew he was going to hijack and crash Flight 11, and everything would be burnt to a crisp, why would he pack, among other things, his Will?"[18]

Finally, there is the well-known "passport problem" with respect to this hijackers and the official narrative. Most people are aware that a passport from one of the hijackers on Flight 11, Satam al-Suqami, was found on the streets of Manhattan by an anonymous pedestrian, who then supposedly handed it over to the FBI. Supposedly, the passport was conveniently ejected from the aircraft, while the aircraft itself disintegrated and burned after its impact with the north tower. Additionally, the passports of Majed Moqed and Ziad Jarah were supposedly found in the environs of the Pentagon and Shanksville, Pennsylvania, respectively.[19] These latter two passports are particularly problematic when one considers the "problematic of the planes and the Pentagon", which will occur subsequently.

For the moment, it is to be noted that the entire official narrative and the behavior of Atta and his companion al-Omari, and for that matter, of the FBI in its data obfuscation efforts, all point compellingly to

---

[17] Jay Kolar, "What We Now Know About the Alleged 9-11 Hijackers," in Pau Zarembka, ed., *The Hidden History of 9-11* (New York: Seven Stories Press, 2008), 3-44, p. 17.

[18] Ibid. This is, notes Kolar and renowned 9/11 researcher David Ray Griffin, one of those inconvenient facts the official 9/11 Commission refused to comment on. Thierry Meyssan puts the question differently: Why would one bring baggage in the first place if one was going to commit suicide? (Thierry Meyssan, *9/11: the Big lie* [London: Carnot Publishing, Ltd., 2002] p. 54.) One answer is that if one is involved in an intelligence operation, as Atta might have believed himself to be, *not* bringing luggage would be suspicious. Nonetheless, on any view, including his last will and testament in the luggage is the most suspicious element. Realistically, wills are normally kept with a lawyer, or in private papers in one's dwelling or safe deposit box, etc.

[19] Laurent Guyénot, *JFK-9/11: 50 years of Deep State* (San Diego: Progressive Press, 2014), p. 130.

the existence of a second, deeper level and player behind the events of 9/11.

Similarly, it should now be obvious that there are all sorts of problems with Mohamed Atta. And we have only barely *begun* to explore them.

B. Mohamed Atta: Study in Bizarre Connections
1. Bizarre Theology and Behaviors

It is now more or less well-known that Mohamed Atta, like many other of the alleged hijackers, was a student in a flight school, in this case in Venice, Florida, where the official narrative alleges he learned how to fly just well enough to crash airliners into buildings. Atta's behavior while at this flight school was, however, hardly normal from almost any viewpoint. For the so-called Islamic terrorist mastermind of the 9/11 events, Atta's behavior was hardly that of a devout Muslim. Additionally, his behavior was so outlandish that it might reasonably be asked if Atta was trying to draw attention to himself.

Not the least of these incongruities is the bizarre theology supposedly espoused by the "Islamic fundamentalist hijackers," for in standard Muslim theology, suicide is absolutely forbidden. If the hijackers were kamikazes, then they could not, according to Salman Rushdie, be Muslim fundamentalists.[20] Nonetheless, the strange theology of the hijackers was apparently confirmed when the FBI found handwritten Arabic "suicide notes", one in the debris of flight 93 in Pennsylvania, one in a rental car left abandoned by Nawaf al-Hazmi at Dulles Airport , and finally one in the luggage of Mohamed Atta which, as we have seen, conveniently did *not* make the connecting flight from Portland, Maine to Boston.[21] These suicide notes, however, all shared one tiny little problem, easily detectable by anyone with even a rudimentary knowledge of Islam, for they all begin with an invocation of God, as do most pious Muslim documents: "In the name of God..." But here, the invocation continues in a most un-Islamic way: "In the name of God, of myself and of my family."[22] From the viewpoint of standard Islamic theology, such an invocation is close to blasphemy, since no Muslim would likely leave out reference to the prophet Mohammed at *some* point. But even then, no Muslim would include *any* human, not

---

[20] Thierry Meyssan, *9/11: The Big Lie*, p. 51.

[21] Ibid., p. 52. Meyssan actually quotes brief sections of these "Islamic" suicide notes on this page.

[22] Ibid.,

even Mohamed, much less himself or anyone else, in an invocation made in God's name. Such would be considered blasphemy and idolatry.[23]

This dubious theology appears to be mirrored in Atta's own acts and lifestyle, for Atta was a regular visitor to Las Vegas' Olympic Garden, "the biggest topless cabaret in the world,"[24] a fact that suggests to French researcher Thierry Meyssan that perhaps Atta was simply trying to disguise his "fundamentalism."

Researcher Daniel Hopsicker, whose book *Welcome to Terrorland: Mohamed Atta and the 9-11 Cover-Up in Florida* has become such a standard in the 9/11 truth community, and with which we shall be much concerned in this chapter, noted that Atta's behavior in Florida was so outlandish and so bizarre, so *noticeable*, that it could only be classified as psychotic.[25] Indeed, one does not need to second guess Hopsicker's evaluation that Atta's behavior in Florida including, as we shall discover, drug parties and alcohol consumption—in some instances apparently on a grand scale—and shacking up with pink-haired women, "fits no definition of 'Islamic fundamentalist' we've come across. Pink hair doesn't seem Wahabbi."[26] Atta and his fellow terrorists at the Venice, Florida flight school appear as if they are deliberately trying to create a high profile, very visible legend, as they partied up and down the peninsula "and stuffed $20 bills down stripper's g-strings in skin joints all up and down the state."[27] His behavior towards women was no less bizarre and noticeable than his other behavior. At one point, he demanded that one of his girlfriends never look him in the eye when talking to him, but rather, look down.[28] While such attitudes might indeed be seen as typical of fundamentalist Islamic pieties, nonetheless for a mad terrorist soon to embark on mass murder as part of a complex intelligence operation, such behavior was bound to attract attention.

Drugs formed a consistent component of Atta's life in Florida. One of Atta's landlords informed authorities that Atta's apartment was frequently visited by "a lot of visitors" and that when this occurred they smoked a lot, and that it smelled like marijuana.[29] On one occasion, which we shall return to subsequently, Atta attended a meeting in Key

---

[23] Thierry Meyssan, *9/11: The Big Lie*, p. 52.

[24] Ibid., p. 53

[25] Daniel Hopsicker, *Welcome to Terrorland: Mohamed Atta and the 9-11 Cover-up in Florida* (Venice, Florida: The MadCow Press, 2007), p. 1.

[26] Ibid., p. 39.

[27] Ibid., p. 4.

[28] Ibid., p. 38.

[29] Daniel Hopsicker, *Welcome to Terrorland*, p. 42.

West, Florida, where he and the other participants snorted cocaine.[30] One particularly notable event was an apparent "pre-9/11 party" on September 8, 2001, held at a local seafood bar called Shuckums, where Atta and his "Islamic fundamentalist" companions drank rums-and-coke, Stolichnaya vodkas and fruit juices, where Atta himself flashed a thick wad of money, and where he and his companions shouted curses in Arabic that "roughly translates as 'F—k God.'" The party was reported by *Newsweek* and *Time*.[31]

One of Atta's girlfriends, who liked animals and kept a pet dog and several cats, recounts an episode when one of her cats had born a litter of kittens. Arriving at her apartment one day, she discovered that Atta had apparently butchered the little animals alive, severing their heads and limbs and scattering the body parts all over her apartment after she had broken off the relationship. He had told her "you will be sorry."[32] Such psychotic behavior, coupled with drug and alcohol abuse, raise the distinct possibilities that Atta may have been "mind controlled" in some fashion, for such abuse of innocent and helpless life is often the traumatizing "shock" designed to fracture a person's mental and moral conscience and render it susceptible to manipulation. Bear this possibility in mind, for it will surface later. To round out all this strange and anomalous behavior, Atta apparently *already* possessed various pilot's licenses from six nations by the time he found himself in Venice, Florida, attending the flight school at Huffman Aviation.[33] Why does one need to attend flight school if one already knows how to fly?

When one probes the flight school itself—Huffman Aviation—as Daniel Hopsicker did, the bizarre and strange connections multiply like rabbits.

The only problem is, in this case, the various rabbits' warrens these connections lead to do not involve Islamic fundamentalism save only in the most round-about way.

2. The Bizarre Flight School: Drug and Technology Smuggling

As one of Hopsicker's contacts pointed out to him, Florida has a long history of attracting a criminal underworld, and a long history of association with drug-running, criminal cartels, and paramilitary organizations,[34] dating all the way back to the anti-Casto Cuban exiles

---

30 Ibid., p. 45.
31 Ibid., p. 57.
32 Ibid, p. 12.
33 Ibid., p. 36.
34 Daniel Hopsicker, *Welcome to Terrorland.*, p. 3.

who trained there and elsewhere in the American southeast for the disastrous Bay of Pigs invasion dubbed Operation Zapata, an operation some researchers have quite convincingly connected to George Herbert Walker Bush.[35] Perhaps not coincidentally, Florida's governor at that time was the younger brother of President George W. Bush, Jeb Bush. Additionally, the Bush family had at that time deep connections to the Saudis and to the giant Saudi construction consortium, the Bin Laden Group, via its own family connections through the Carlyle Group. Hopsicker quips that "since 15 of the 19 terrorist hijackers were Saudi, the story of the terrorist conspiracy is, perforce, a story about *Saudis in Florida.*"[36]

But given all these connections, perhaps it is better to view it as a story about Saudis in the Bushes of Florida.

At the center of the Florida-Atta mystery, is Huffman Aviation, the so-called flight school that Atta and his merry band of "Islamic fundamentalists" attended. Huffman's "student body" composition alone raises questions, and indeed, sends the needle on the "suspicion meter" into the red zone, for the national and ethnic composition of its student body was primarily Arab...

...and Dutch...

...and German.[37]

Atta himself at one time had roommates, one of whom turned out to be Ziad al Jarrah, and two other friends named Pierre and Patrick, the latter being, in spite of his Celtic-Irish name, from Holland.[38] On top of all of this high strangeness, Atta's girlfriends also state that he spoke fluent French, Hebrew,[39] and German.

a. Hopsicker's Methodology

All of this compels certain questions. Is the Dutch connection to Huffman Aviation significant? Was Atta and his cadre of "Islamic fundamentalists" ordered to Venice, Florida and to attend Huffman Aviation? Why was Atta's and his companions' behavior so at odds with anything that could be reasonably associated to the behavior of pious Muslims?

---

[35] See the documentary *Dark Legacy: George Bush and the Murder of John F. Kennedy*, Terra Entertainment, Los Angeles, 2009.

[36] Hopsicker, op. cit, p. 2, emphasis in the original.

[37] Ibid., p. 36.

[38] Ibid., p. 41.

[39] Ibid., p. 84

These types of questions prompted Hopsicker to assume a different methodological approach from the "official narrative" of 9/11, and to assume that Atta was not "the wild-eyed religious zealot we've been told he is" and on that basis, to discover whether or not "that clears up any of the many 'anomalies' about the official explanation of who he was."[40] Indeed, Hopsicker quips on yet another odd parallel between the 9/11 event and the Kennedy assassination:

> Remember: "Your legend" is your cover story, the lie that holds together long enough to let you slip away." Mohamed Atta's "Islamic extremist" legend had begun falling apart in South Florida's bars and strip joints, just as Lee Harvey Oswald's "communist" legend did when news of his presence at anti-Castro paramilitary camps in Louisiana came out.[41]

What he discovered when the official narrative was suspended as an investigative template had little to do with Islamic terrorism, and a great deal to do with international criminal organizations and activities:

> Atta's U.S. associates were responsible for or involved in: a Lear jet seized in Orlando by Uzi-toting DEA agents with 43lbs., of heroin on board with it's(sic) pilot talking unconcernedly on his cell phone while agents leveled their guns; suspected skullduggery in the Mormon Temple in Orlando; a gold mine in the Caribbean; high technology smuggling out of southwest Florida; missionary flights to Havana carrying—not the word of God—but bag-fulls of gold Rolexes for sympathetic Cuban officials who already had Bibles; the interesting part-time job of the chief pilot of Venezuela's Air Force One; robot planes at the Venice Airport; and a "really tall blond woman whose parents were KGB."
>
> For somebody looking to go unrecognized, Atta knew a lot of people. Far from being the secretive ringleader of a "lone cadre" which slipped through Europe and America unnoticed, Atta moved in some pretty interesting circles.[42]

Additionally, one of Atta's instructors at Huffman Aviation stated that Atta had some sort of relationship to the Saudi royal family, and was a part of the Saudi elite.[43]

---

[40] Daniel Hopsicker, *Welcome to Terrorland.*, p. 103.
[41] Ibid., p. 138.
[42] Daniel Hopsicker, *Welcome to Terrorland.*, p. 104.
[43] Ibid., p. 105.

Huffman Aviation's owner, Dutchman Rudi Dekkers—with whom we shall be greatly concerned later on—contradicted this assertion, stating that he had no knowledge of this alleged Atta-Saudi elite connection, and that Atta dressed rather plainly, like an ordinary American, in sneakers and jeans, but this story was in turn contradicted by other witnesses from the flight school who recall seeing Atta in leather shoes and silk shirts.[44]

b. Huffman Aviation's Rudi Dekkers, and International Smuggling

Huffman Aviation's owner Rudi Dekkers is a large component of the Atta mystery, as is the flight school itself. Having purchased Huffman aviation a little over a year prior to the arrival and influx of Arab "flight students," the timing seemed a little more than suspicious to Hopsicker, who discovered a whole world of intrigue swirling around the Dutchman. This led him to posit that Huffman Aviation, and similar flight schools, might be a part of Prime Minister Tony Blair's "global network" that lay behind the terrorist organizations.[45] Dekkers, it turned out, had a connection to another Dutchman associated with flight schools, one Arne Kruithof, and they in turn were connected to a German named Pascal Schreier, who was a corporate officer for a company named Florida Sunrise Aviation, and who had recruited flight school students in Hamburg, Germany, and sent them on to Dekkers and Kruithof.[46] This is an important point because, of course, it is part of the acknowledged official narrative of 9/11 that Atta resided for some time in an apartment in Hamburg, Germany. This is another connection to bear in mind, for this German connection will eventually bear huge dividends.

For the moment, however, our focus remains on Rudi Dekkers, the Dutch owner of Huffman Aviation. To say that Dekkers' Huffman Aviation flight school was engaged in a variety of suspicious activities would be putting it mildly. For one thing, Huffman Aviation was in turn linked to a variety of aviation companies that claimed they held leases on Boeing 757 and 757 airliners from companies that did not even *own* any of these types of aircraft.[47] In fact, this activity (and many others) meant that Dekker's Huffman Aviation was hemorrhaging money, a fact that made matters even more suspicious, because he and his business partner, Florida businessman Wally Hilliard, already owned *another*

---

[44] Ibid., pp. 105-106.
[45] Ibid., p. 128.
[46] Ibid., p. 141.
[47] Daniel Hopsicker, *Welcome to Terrorland*, p. 134.

flight school in Florida that was losing money to the tune of $40,000 per month when they bought Huffman Aviation a little more than two and a half years prior to 9/11.[48] Upon further investigation, Hopsicker discovered that Dekkers "never made a dime teaching people to fly airplanes, and the 'legend' of Rudi Dekkers as 'flight school owner" is a sham."[49] For Hopsicker, Dekkers was "not just a run-of-the-mill con-man and quick-fading historical footnote. Dekkers was at the critical nexus of the terrorist conspiracy."[50]

So what *was* Dekkers doing with Huffman Aviation, and why was it when Mohamed Atta moved from Hamburg, Germany to Venice, Florida, that Rudi Dekkers was "assigning bunks on this side of the pond?"[51] If Huffman Aviation flight school was just a cover, what was it a cover *for?*

One informant told Hopsicker that Dekkers also owned a computer company at the Naples, Florida airport called International Computer Products.[52] Through this company, Dekkers was apparently running a smuggling operation and securing loans which he had no intention of repaying, an activity that brought him to the investigative attentions of a Florida state's attorney.[53] Through this company, Dekkers was apparently smuggling high technology computer chips out of the USA and into the Netherlands, a fact which brought him to the attention of the Dutch authorities, and to the attentions of the United States Drug Enforcement Agency (DEA)![54] Obviously, Dekkers must have been smuggling something else besides computer chips to come to the attentions of the DEA.

But note now what we have: a high tech computer chip smuggling ring, and drugs. Recall that in the Preface, we mentioned the fact that during the events of 9/11, the attackers apparently contacted the White House, and conveyed a threat that was validated by their apparent knowledge of highly classified American codes, which included those of the Drug Enforcement Agency.

This was not, however, the only thing Dekkers was allegedly smuggling. One of Hopsicker's contacts stated that Dekkers "was smuggling aircraft back into the U.S. over the Arctic."[55] The significance of this one point alone, if true, cannot be overestimated, for *all* aircraft

---

[48] Ibid., p. 148.
[49] Ibid.
[50] Ibid.
[51] Ibid.
[52] Ibid., p. 153.
[53] Ibid., p. 165.
[54] Ibid., p. 166.
[55] Daniel Hopsicker, *Welcome to Terrorland*, p. 153.

activity over the Arctic is carefully monitored not just by American radar, but by British and Russian radar for the simple reason of preventing surprise nuclear attacks. Thus, any smuggling of aircraft via this route implies the tacit knowledge of *someone* within the military command structures of those three countries. And this, in turn, implies...

...a global network, existing within and behind the military command structures of those countries, able to "turn a blind eye" when needed in order to accomplish the smuggling.[56]

This point is crucial for another reason, for as Hopsicker also notes, Dekkers had become the darling of the television networks after 9/11, giving interviews about his "first hand contact" with the alleged terrorists and their mastermind, Mohamed Atta. He was even invited to testify before Congress when he was at the same time "the target" not only of multi-agency American federal investigations, but the target of Florida state investigations, and investigations by the Dutch government!

> Didn't the U.S. *know* Dekkers was a crook before he went on television? There is only one answer, we think. Rudi Dekkers was one of their own, or he belonged to them, at least. He said what they wanted him to say... because he *had* to.
>
> He was a criminal. He had been caught by federal authorities back in the mid-90s. But he had never been charged. Why not?
>
> The answer is simple, and yet stunning: Rudi Dekkers had "rolled," and become a government "confidential informant."[57]

But there are other possible explanations besides this one. One possibility is that Dekkers was part of something *else*, some *other* network, and that he was protected by elements within the U.S. government whose loyalties were to the same network. And the other possibility is that the U.S. authorities were simply *blackmailed* into covering for Dekkers, and into promoting him as "most favored interviewee" in the wake of 9/11. Hopsicker himself implies these possibilities when he admits that Mohamed Atta did not just "stumble into his Venice, Florida flight school," and that with Dekkers, one might indeed be looking at the "'Southeast Regional Manager' for the global network said to have assisted the hijackers."[58]

---

[56] In this respect, recall the allegations of Major Jordan of a similar high-tech smuggling effort hidden within American Lend-lease aid to the Soviet Union during World War Two, reviewed in my previous book, *The Third Way*.

[57] Hopsicker, op. cit., p. 167.

[58] Daniel Hopsicker, *Welcome to Terrorland*, p. 158.

c. Drugs and Some Unbelievable Connections

The fact that Dekkers had come to the attentions of the DEA implies that at some point his smuggling operations were about more than just aircraft of high-tech technology and computer chip smuggling. It suggests a drug-running operation.

Here the connections between Mohamed Atta, Huffman Aviation, and prior historical scandals become complex and labyrinthine. They seem almost too deep-reaching to be credible, but nonetheless, they are real. Hopsciker notes that every day, as Atta and companions drove from their apartments to the flight school they would have passed by an old twin engine DC-3 aircraft, a workhorse legend of aviation technology that has been in service since the World War Two era.

This particular DC-3, however, is painted like Noah's Ark, and once belonged to Frank Moss, a 1980s era drug smuggler connected to the Iran-Contra scandal.[59] The connection of Huffman Aviation to the drug-smuggling of the 1980s group of former covert operatives "gone private and rogue" is, however, more than symbolic. The Iran-Contra era drug smuggler Dietrich Reinhardt was linked to notorious drug smuggler and pilot Barry Seal, connected to the smuggling operations at the Mena, Arkansas airport, so much a part of the early scandals surrounding the late G.H.W. Bush and early Clinton Administrations. One of Reinhardt's companies was based in Venice, Florida, and conducted business with, you guessed it, Rudi Dekkers' Huffman Aviation.[60] Barry Seal was, in fact, "a close associate of Iran-Contra figures like Frank Moss and Dietrich Reinhardt."[61]

This is by no means the least of the bizarre connections of Rudi Dekkers' and Huffman Aviation. Another was Mark Shubin, an associate of Dekkers' business partner, Wally Hilliard. Shubin's father was a KGB colonel who was caught spying for the United States, and was traded

---

[59] Ibid., p. 97.

[60] Ibid., p. 100.

[61] Ibid., p. 210. Another connection that looms, unbelievably, in connection to Iran-Contra and the 9/11-Huffman Aviation relationship is Jackson Stephens, Arkansas millionaire, contributor to the campaigns of G.H.W. Bush and Bill Clinton. Stephens owned a nursing company based in Venice, Florida, and was rumored to be connected to the Mena, Arkansas "enterprise." Hopsicker states that "Interestingly enough, the U.S. intelligence agency to which Jackson Stephens' name has been persistently linked, the National Security Agency, was accused by furious government intelligence officers with destroying data pertinent to the Sept. 11 probe, meaning that possible leads stemming from the Sept. 11 attack weren't being followed because of the NSA action, reported the *Boston Globe*." (q.v. pp. 200-201)

with shot-down U-2 spy aircraft pilot Francis Gary Powers. Shubin himself became a U-2 pilot for the CIA, and in turn was connected to Kenneth Good, a partner in the Silverado Savings and Loan during the Savings and Loan Scandal. Another of Silverado's partners was, of course, one of President G.H.W. Bush's sons.[62] And as if this twisted set of relationships could not possibly become more bizarre, Shubin was connected to various Ukrainian oligarchs, having been a private pilot for them after "retiring" from flying spy aircraft.[63]

As if all this were not enough, Rudi Dekkers and his Huffman Aviation partner Wally Hilliard also found yet another business partner for their operations, one Rock Boehlke, who was allegedly involved in the looting of some three hundred-and forty million dollars from Mafia-led union pension funds.[64] What was all this money for? One possibility, suggested by Hopsicker, is that yet *another* company associated with Dekkers, Florida Aviation, was a smuggling company. Boehlke in turn was associated with Jeff Grayson, who turned a tidy six million dollar profit investing in a Georgia company called Title Loans of America, a company owned by Jewish lawyer Alvin Malnik, whose son, Mark, converted to Islam, married a daughter of Sheik al-Fazzi, "whose other daughter is married to Prince Turki."[65] Prince Turki at the time ran Saudi intelligence.

The circle now closes, for Dekkers' recruitment efforts for pilots in Europe to come and "study" at his flight school could be sweetened by a track record of one hundred percent successful "job placement rates" by the school's "job placement office." And the school itself could well-afford to "hemorrhage" money, since short falls could be made up by the profits from the smuggling.[66]

"We have," says Hopsicker,

> been looking for evidence of a global network which authorities, early on, said must have been aiding the terrorists while they were in this country.
>
> Boehlke, because of his proximity to terrorist flight school owner Dekkers and his concurrent participation in what the Securities and Exchange Commission has called "the biggest fraud by an investment manage in U.S. history," seemed to offer some clues.

---

[62] Ibid., p. 221.

[63] Ibid., pp. 300-301.

[64] Ibid., p. 176.

[65] Daniel Hopsicker, *Welcome to Terrorland*, p. 188.

[66] Hopsciker hints at this analysis repeatedly. See p. 177.

Might the same "international network" responsible for stealing $340 million have been simultaneously training a terrorist air corps in Southwest Florida?

...

Perhaps Rudi Dekkers, Wally Hilliard, and Rick Boehlke worked for a single unnamed airline, devoted exclusively to a very large client, a client—after the pension fund scam—more than $300 million dollars richer.

Call it "Global Network Air."

Lurking just beneath the surface of American life, it seemed, was massive corruption on an unheard of scale, presided over by modern-day Untouchables, members of an organization—a *global network*—operating well outside the law.

And getting away with it.[67]

All of this returns us, once again, to the hijackers, to Mohamed Atta, and what, exactly, they were doing at flight schools.

d. Welcome To Flight School, Here's How You Fly Into Buildings: Stonewalling U.S. Intelligence Efforts

When Mohamed Atta was not visiting strip clubs, getting drunk, or snorting cocaine, he did manage to attend flight schools. The trouble is, the flight schools had little to do with Huffman Aviation, and apparently everything to do with U.S. *military* flight schools. For example, the *Los Angeles Times* reported on the Saturday after 9/11 that two of the hijackers were Saudi fighter pilots who had received U.S. military aviation training as part of an exchange program conducted at Lackland Air Base in Texas and Maxwell Air Base in Alabama.[68] As Hopsicker observes, this story was picked up the very next day and expanded by *Newsweek,* the *Washington Post,* and the *Miami Herald* which reported that "as many as seven of the terrorist hijackers in the Sept. 11th attacks received training at secure U.S. military installations."[69] Even more inconveniently, one Mohamed Atta had apparently attended the

---

[67] Ibid., p. 189.

[68] Daniel Hopsicker, *Welcome to Terrorland.*, p. 107. It is perhaps worth mentioning that both airbases are also connected to post-war Nazi activities, and Maxwell was the home to the documentation of Nazi exotic technology in the Air Force's Project Lusty files.

[69] Ibid.

International Officers' School at Maxwell Air Base, a fact that quickly called forth a response, as the media reminded everyone how common the name Mohamed was in Islamic culture, and that Atta itself was a very common surname.[70] More inconveniently, many Saudis were being trained at Maxwell; and had to be evacuated the day after the attack.[71]

The problem, however, is that if the Mohamed Atta of the Maxwell Air Base Officers' School and the Mohamed Atta of Huffman Aviation are one and the same, then the problem is that his flight school instructors are almost universal in their testimony that Atta and his terrorist companions were both poor students and poor pilots, whereas by all professional assessments of the pilots' performance on 9/11, the piloting skill exhibited on that day was of very high caliber. Indeed, one ex-military pilot told Hopsicker that even a commercial pilot would have had difficulty hitting the World Trade Center and the Pentagon with such precision—and in a subsequent chapter we shall discover how precisely targeted the areas struck in each instance really were— and that such skills were more indicative of an exposure to military piloting training. "Was Atta," Hopsicker asks, "a better pilot than they let on?"[72]

Whatever the answer to that question may be, Atta's possible presence at an American flight school connected to the training of Saudi pilots raises the specter of a heavy Saudi involvement at more than just the surface level of the events of 9/11. The question is, how did so many future Saudi terrorists gain entry to the country? Once again, the answer

---

[70] Ibid., p. 108.

[71] Ibid., p. 112. Nefeez Mosaddeq Ahmed notes that Saudi Arabia, like all other countries sending its pilots to military flight training and officers' school at Maxwell and other participating U.S. air bases, paid for the training of their officers. See Ahmed, *The War on Freedom: How and Why America was Attacked on September 11, 2001* (Joshua Tree, California: Tree of Life Publications, 2002), p. 97. Ahmed also states that Abdul Aziz al-Omari, Sayeed al-Ghamdi attended similar military flight training programs at Brooks Air Base in Texas, and the Defense Language Institute in Monterrey, California, respectively (see p. 98). Ahmed also provides an additional perspective on Hopsicker's attempt to contact the Pentagon to clarify whether the Mohamed Atta of Maxwell Air Base and the Mohamed Atta of Hufffman Aviation and 9/11 were one and the same. According to Ahmed *and* Hopsicker, the Air Force Major whom Hopsicker contacted, when asked if they were one and the same, or different individuals, replied that Hopsicker was not going to get that information.(See p. 99, and compare to Hopsciker's account in *Welcome to Terrorland*, p. 111)

[72] Daniel Hopsicker, *Welcome to Terrorland.*, p. 137. N.B.: I am leaving aside, for the moment, a discussion of the remote-control piloting theory in order to review Hopsicker's research as he himself presents it.

points to a rogue element, operating at a deeper level than the public story of al Qaeda terrorist cells:

> The freedom with which Al-Qaeda operatives entered and left the U.S. should be understood in the context of testimony from Michael Springmann former head of the Visa Bureau at the U.S. Consulate in Jeddah, Saudi Arabia, between 1987 and 1989. Springmann, has had 20 years of experience in the U.S. government, and is now a practicing lawyer in Washington DC. He stated on (the) BBC's 'Newsnight' that: "In Saudi Arabia I was repeatedly ordered by high level State Dept(sic) officials to issue visas to unqualified applicants. These were, essentially, people who had no ties either to Saudi Arabia or to their own country.
>
> In another interview with CBC's Radio One, he stated that according to confirmation he received from U.S. government officials, the "CIA was recruiting terrorists to fight against the then Soviets." Osama bin Laden, moreover, "was their asset, and was working with them." There were "as many as a hundred" recruits, people "with no ties to any place in particular... Afghanistan was the end user of their facilities. They were coming to the U.S. for training as terrorists. The countries that had supplied them did not want them back." Springmann testified that CIA officials had consistently violated State Department regulations to issue visas to these people.
>
> CBC: Does this demonstrate a relationship between the CIA and Osama Bin laden dating back as far as 1987?
>
> SPRINGMANN: That's right, and as you recall, they believe that this fellow Sheikh Abdurrahman who was tied to the first New York World Trade Center bombing had gotten his visa from a CIA case officer in the Sudan. And that the 15 or so people who came from Saudi Arabia to participate in the attacks on the WTC and the Pentagon had gotten visas through the American consulate general in Jeddah.
>
> CBC: So what does that suggest, that this pipeline was never rolled up, that it's still operational?
>
> SPRINGMANN: Exactly...
>
> CBC: If what you say may be true, many of the terrorists who allegedly flew those planes into those targets, got their U.S. visas through the CIA and your U.S. consulate in Jeddah. That suggests a relationship ongoing as recently as obviously September. But what was the CIA presumably recruiting these people for as recently as September 11th?
>
> SPRINGMANN: That I don't know. And that's one of the things that I tried to find out through a series of Freedom of Information

Act requests starting ten years ago. At the time the State Department and the CIA stonewalled my requests. They're still doing so.

CBC: If the CIA had a relationship with the people responsible for September 11th, are you suggesting therein that they are somehow complicit?

SPRINGMANN: Yes, either through omission or through failure to act...[73]

Additionally, at the very time that there were increasing warnings about terrorist acts both within the U.S. intelligence community and from abroad, a matter that we shall explore more completely in a subsequent chapter, the administration of President G.W. Bush actually *instituted* this fast-tracking of visas from Saudi Arabia.[74]

While the implications of this fact are obvious, for the moment we shall forego stating them to raise one final point, that of the forewarning of impending terrorist attacks by U.S. attorney David Philip Schippers. Schippers, in an interview two days after the 9/11 attacks given to Pittsburgh station WRRK, stated that he had received information from a variety of American intelligence sources including FBI agents, who had shared intelligence about impending terrorist attacks with him after having been stonewalled in their efforts to bring it to the attention of superiors. During the interview, Schippers revealed that he had attempted to warn U.S. Attorney General John Ashcroft about the impending attacks fully six weeks prior to their actual occurrence. Additionally, Schippers maintained that this information was specific as to the "names of the hijackers, the targets of their attacks, the proposed dates, and the sources of their funding, along with other information."[75] Confirming this story of high-level blocking and outright frustration of U.S. intelligence efforts, the U.K.'s *Guardian* newspaper reported that "U.S. intelligence agencies... are complaining that their hands were tied... They said the restrictions became worse after the Bush administration took over this year. The intelligence agencies had been told to 'back off' from investigations involving other members of the Bin Laden family, the Saudi royals, and possible Saudi links to the acquisition of nuclear weapons by Pakistan."[76]

---

[73] Nafeez Mosaddeq Ahmed, *The War on Freedom*, pp. 104-105.
[74] Ibid., p. 106.
[75] Nafeez Mosaddeq Ahmed, *The War on Freedom*, p. 107.
[76] Ibid., p. 111, citing Gregory palest and David Pallister, "FBI Claims Bin Laden Inquiry was frustrated," *The Guardian* November 2001.

The implications here are obvious, and decidedly foul, for they imply that at the second deeper level of the 9/11 events, there was indeed not only foreknowledge of the impending attacks by American intelligence, but active attempts to block any counter-measures, and this implies that the Bush administration was, at least minimally, involved in a LIHOP version of the 9/11 scenario. However, the fact that visas were being provided to questionable applicants via the consulate in Jeddah, Saudi Arabia, under pressure from the CIA and that the Bush administration actually promoted this, indicates that the MIHOP version of the scenario not only is a likely and plausible interpretation of these facts, it also means that *whatever rogue network as may be in place and involved in the 9/11 attacks, that network had knowledge extending to the highest reaches of the American federal government.*

As we shall see, this will become quite a crucial point when we turn to consider the question of the potential existence of a *third level* unknown to the other two—the terrorists and the "rogue network"— that had penetrated the other two levels. One may also view this point somewhat differently, by assuming the "rogue network" of level two incorporated various factions within it, and that on the day of 9/11, one faction turned *against* the rest of the network, and announced its presence in a stark fashion, as indicated by the use of the presidential codes, and the decision of President Bush to personally fly to Barksdale and then Offut to reassert personal presidential command and control over the nation's strategic nuclear forces.

What level two knew, level three knew.

3. Atta's Most Bizarre Connection

It is when one scrutinizes Mohamed Atta's connections in Florida more closely, and when one sifts through the history of how he came to Florida in the first place, that one discovers the most disturbing connections of them all, connections which invariably raise the question of just what, *exactly*, constitutes that putative "third level" or "rogue faction within the rogue" network. Indeed, when one confronts the question of how Atta managed to get from Hamburg, Germany, to Venice, Florida, one also confronts the question of how, and why, Atta, an Egyptian, ended up associated with Saudis, and how he came to be in Hamburg, Germany, in the first place.

Here again, it was Daniel Hopsicker who unearthed a crucially significant clue that has now become well-known in the 9/11 truth community, while its potential significance continues to be ignored by that same community. The Chairman of the Congressional Intelligence Committee investigating 9/11, Senator Bob Graham gave an interview on the American television network CBS's *Face the Nation* broadcast, and Hopsicker points out that during this broadcast Senator Graham stated that "there is a piece of information which is still classified which I consider to be the most important information that's come to the attention of the joint committee." While most 9/11 researchers think that this refers to the role of Saudi Arabia, due to the vast number of data points and relationships that connect the Saudis to 9/11, they miss what Graham went on to say: "I was surprised at the evidence *that there were foreign governments involved in facilitating the activities of at least some of the terrorists in the United States.*"[77] Senator Graham's Republican counterpart and co-chairman, Senator Richard Shelby, dropped another bombshell, stating that "There is explosive information that has not been publicly released. I think there are some bombshells out there."[78]

The clear implication of these remarks is that Saudi Arabia, whatever its role in 9/11, *was not alone*; *other* governments were involved, and the implication of Shelby's remarks is that if this became public knowledge, it would be "explosive", and that there were "other bombshells" regarding 9/11 that neither he nor Senator Graham could disclose. The question of who these governments are is signally

---

[77] Daniel Hopsicker, *Welcome to Terrorland*, p. xvi, emphasis added.
[78] Ibid.

important, for as Hopsicker puts it later in his book, it involves, the deep "puzzle of who declared war on the United States and why."[79]

The question thus becomes, what governments' involvement could be considered a "bombshell" and "explosive"? The usual suspects—Pakistan, for example—seem predictable enough, and not all that explosive. Israel's involvement would certainly seem to be explosive and a bombshell, but are there other candidates? If there *is* a "rogue network within the rogue network", what might it be and consist of?

Once again, Mohamed Atta is the key, for as already noted, Atta came to Rudi Dekkers' Huffman Aviation from Hamburg, Germany, and thus, "if Atta was in contact with Dekkers' recruiters while still in Hamburg, instead of just showing up in Venice, that could explain statements by officials early on that the key to unraveling the plot might not lie in the United States, but in Germany."[80] Indeed, we have already encountered one fact that indicates this might be the case, namely, the close association with Rudi Dekkers, Arne Kruithof, and the German Pascal Schreier.[81]

One of Atta's girlfriends in Florida recounts an event when he and some friends were parting at a club in Sarasota, Florida, with friends of his, including two people named Juergen and Wolfgang.[82] Atta had a coterie of German friends that appeared to have been more or less a consistent presence during his stay in Florida, for at the meeting in Key West mentioned earlier, the whole purpose of the meeting was so that Atta could meet two Germans who had flown all the way across the Atlantic for the sole purpose of meeting and conferring with him.[83] In fact, it could be stated without any exaggeration that many of Atta's closest associates in Florida, besides Dekkers and his fellow "Islamic fundamentalist extremists" were Germans or Austrians, with names like Peter, Juergen, and Stephan.[84] One of Atta's girlfriends told Hopsicker that Atta attended "meetings" with these Germans and Austrians.[85]

Nor was the German-Austrian connection limited simply to contacts with the mysterious Peter, Stephan, and Juergen. According to NBC news reporter Brian Ross, the FBI was greatly interested in the wire transfers of money to Atta not only from the Middle East, but from

---

[79] Daniel Hopsicker, *Welcome to Terrorland*, pp. 46.

[80] Ibid., p. 142.

[81] Ibid., p. 141.

[82] Ibid., p. 10, the club in question was Margarita Maggie's.

[83] Ibid., pp. 48-49.

[84] Ibid., p. 66.

[85] Ibid., p. 68.

Germany.[86] Atta also apparently had close Swiss and French associates in Florida as well.[87] On these occasions, Atta apparently spoke German to his German associates, especially to his friend Wolfgang, who turned out to be one Wolfgang Bohringer, a Swiss-German, and possessed of a rather dubious past, including the operation of an illegal flight school in Florida in the 1990s.[88] Bohringer also hated Jews, and was known to make jokes about blacks, Jews, ovens, and bread, [89] remarks that could as easily be associated with Nazism as with extremist Islam.

However, the most significant, and damning, association of Mohamed Atta is not with people, but with a *foundation:*

> For at least four of Atta's seven years living in Hamburg he was part of a "joint venture" between the U.S. and German Governments, an elite international "exchange" program run by a little-known private organization which has close ties to powerful American political figures like David Rockefeller and former Secretary of State Henry Kissinger.
>
> This fact has escaped notice as well.
>
> Before becoming a terrorist ringleader, Atta enjoyed the patronage of a government initiative known as the "Congress-Bundestag Program, overseen by the U.S. State Department and the German Ministry of Economic Cooperation and Development, the German equivalent of the U.S. Agency for International Development.[90]

This program footed the bill for Atta's junkets to Cairo, Aleppo, and Istanbul during 1994-1995.

It is when one digs deeper into the associations of this program that one finds an even murkier connection: the *Carl Duisberg Gesellschaft,* or Carl Duisberg Society, a private corporate foundation that listed Mohamed Atta as a "scholarship holder" and "tutor" from 1995-1997.[91] Jay Kolar, whose work has been referred to earlier in this chapter, wrote this about the Carl Duisberg Society:

> Atta's association with these nefarious members of the wealthy elite in South Florida was just the tip of the iceberg of his

---

86 Ibid., p. 79.
87 Ibid., p. 281.
88 Ibid., pp. 282-283.
89 Ibid., p. 314.
90 Ibid., p. 285.
91 Ibid., p. 285.

connections. The deeply submerged part of the berg is where we find those with the deepest pockets, powerful American political figures like David Rockefeller and Henry Kissinger who, according to Hopsicker, were closely tied to a little-known private organization that ran an elite international exchange program known variously as "Carl Duisberg Gesellschaft," or CDS, or Carl Duisberg Society International. The list of CDS elite power-broker supporters also includes Bill and Hillary Clinton. In 1987, both Kissinger and Clinton praised CDS International's service not only for keeping close business ties between Germany and the US, but also for supporting career development programs for its participants, namely, young German engineers.[92]

If the name Carl Duisberg sounds vaguely familiar and sinister, it should.

Carl Duisberg, 1861-1935

Carl Duisberg was a renowned German chemist and industrialist, becoming head of the large German chemicals combine, Bayer, in 1900. Duisberg also advocated that 60,000 Belgians from German occupied Belgium in World War One to be sent to Germany to make up for manpower shortages in German industry.

---

[92] Jay Kolar, "What We Now Know about the Alleged 9-11 Hijackers," in Paul Zarembka, ed., *The Hidden History of 9-11*, 3-44, p. 32.

The Problematic of the Perpetrators

But most importantly, it was Carl Duisberg who with fellow chemical industrialist Carl Bosch of BASF(*Bayrischen Analin und Soda Fabrik*), pushed for the consolidation of all of Germany's massive chemical and dyes industry into the gigantic international cartel, *Interessen Gemeinschaft Farbenfabrikenindustrie, A.G.*, known to the world by its more popular, and notorious, name, I.G. Farben.

And the society that bears his name? Notably it was founded in the year 1949, the same year as the formal beginning of the West German Federal Republic, ostensibly as a society funding development and education, especially for people from "developing countries." The question few people seem to be asking is, where would such a society get any money in post-war West Germany, still suffering under brutal poverty, and only beginning to clear away the piles of rubble that the country had been reduced to?

The answer to this question is highly speculative, but one answer that immediately suggests itself is the association to IG Farben itself, a company with very deep pockets, and the resources to hide its funds from prying postwar Allied prosecutors.

But there's another possibility, one I mentioned in my previous book, *The Nazi International.* In August 1944, Martin Bormann sponsored a meeting of German industrialists at the *Hotel Maison Rouge* in Strasbourg, France. At this meeting, German firms were informed that they were to prepare a variety of overseas holding companies and a variety of fronts, each of which would have a liaison officer from the Nazi party itself overseeing the disbursement of party funds to the firms to aid in the postwar rebuilding of Germany, and the extension of its international business contacts, all for the purpose of an eventual Nazi return to power.[93] Given its connection to IG Farben, and the latter's deep connection to the Nazi war machine, it requires no great leap of the imagination to see that perhaps the Carl Duisberg Society may have been, at least initially, one of those front organizations.

Whatever one makes of these speculations, one thing remains uncomfortably true: Mohamed Atta's involvement with the Carl Duisberg Society means, howsoever surreal it may sound, that there is a direct connection between him and I.G. Farben via a society named for one of its founders.

---

[93] Joseph P. Farrell, *The Nazi International: The Nazis' Postwar Plan to Control Finance, Conflict, Physics and Space* (Kempton, Illinois: Adventures Unlimited Press, 2008), pp. 69-76.

The issue of this connection is an important one, for it colors how one interprets events from this point on. For example, writing of this connection, Jay Kolar states:

> Why would CDS International's elite sponsors, apparently influential enough to keep their organization name out of the media, want to keep their generous support of such an international student secret in the first place? Were they psychic? Or did they know what role Atta might play in the future because they had a hand in grooming him for it?[94]

Notably, neither he, nor Hopsicker, nor any other 9/11 researcher that I am aware of, points out the obvious, namely, that Carl Duisberg was a founder of the infamous I.G. Farben cartel, the cartel that was almost synonymous with and identical to the Nazi war machine.

Once one points this out, however, it is clear why the American sponsors would wish to keep the society's connection to Atta out of the light of widespread exposure to the public by the mainstream media, for it would raise the issue of their own potential fascist worldviews, and the reasons they were involved in a society with such notorious associations. One might go even deeper and suggest that the presence of people like David Rockefeller in the Carl Duisberg Society might represent the "American contingent" of a Fascist International. Adding grist for this mill, it is to be recalled that there are indications of profound connections between postwar laundering of Nazi and Axis loot and the Rockefeller Chase Manhattan bank, and that these connections are in turn indicative of an even deeper hidden system of finance that was put into place and run by American intelligence after World War Two, with the complicity and compliance of the defeated Axis elites, to fund covert operations and long term secret technological research projects.[95] Exposing the Carl Duisberg Society connection, in other words, could conceivably open a Pandoras' box of vast connections to Faustian deals with the Fascist devil and their complicity in such bargains, and to hidden systems of finance and a vast network of

---

[94] Jay Kolar, "What We Now Know about the Alleged 9-11 Hijackers," in Paul Zarembka, ed., *The Hidden History of 9-11*, 3-44, p. 33.

[95] For these points, see my *Nazi International*, pp. 69-83, 176-177, and my *Covert Wars and Breakaway Civilizations: The Secret Space Program, Celestial Psyops, and Hidden Conflicts* (Kempton, Illinois: Adventures Unlimited Press, 2012), pp. 71-99, 133-212. For postwar Nazi plans to involve the US in prolonged Middle Eastern and East-West conflicts, see my *The Third Way: The Nazi International, European Union and Corporate Fascism* (Kempton, Illinois: Adventures Unlimited Press, 2015), pp. 1-34.

intelligence, drug running, and secret technological developments that they would rather keep from widespread public scrutiny.

And there is one final, possible and highly speculative reason the Carl Duisberg Society's powerful American "elite" sponsors may have wished to keep the association with Mohamed Atta from public view, for if there was indeed a "rogue network within their own rogue network", and if that "rogue network within their own rogue network" had broken its long alliance with them and somehow signaled it to them (to their doubtless great shock and surprise) during the sad events of 9/11, then this too would be a reason to keep it quiet, for after all, they had already created an operation designed to blame "Islamic terrorists" in order to inject American power into the Middle East. To expose the other possibility would expose the fact that the "war on terrorism" was really a cover story for a war on a very *different* enemy, one far more sophisticated, a war between two rival fascist ideologies and camps, each willing to "weaponize Islam" for use against the other.

As if to underscore these disturbing possibilities, Hopsicker mentions a story that ran on March 7, 2003 in the *Chicago Tribune*:

> Under the headline "9/11 haunts hijacker's sponsors: German couple talks of living with pilot Atta," the article described the 1992 meeting in Cairo between Atta and a German couple running an "international student exchange program."
>
> Atta was recruited in Cairo by this mysterious German couple, dubbed the "hijacker's sponsors." It was this meeting, said the *Tribune*, which led Atta to move to Hamburg.
>
> But although *Tribune* correspondent Stevenson Swanson cites this German couple for "having played such an important role in Atta's move to Germany," he never gives their *names*, nor that of the organization they worked for.[96]

Atta studied German in Cairo, then arrived in Germany in July 1992, where he lived rent-free in the couple's home in Hamburg "in a quiet, middle-class neighborhood."[97]

Here, again, interpretation in the 9/11 community fails to consider all the possibilities. Jay Kolar notes that "according to Hopsicker, secret US government hosts were grooming and financially supporting Atta and other key operative patsies."[98] Certainly the associations of

---

[96] Daniel Hopsicker, *Welcome to Terrorland*, p. 287, emphasis in the original.
[97] Ibid., p. 288.
[98] Jay Kolar, "What We Now Know about the Alleged 9-11 Hijackers," in Paul Zarembka, ed., *The Hidden History of 9-11*, 3-44, p. 33.

powerful members of the American political and financial elite with the Carl Duisberg Society make this a possibility. But the IG Farben connection of Duisberg himself raises the prospects of *other* more sinister, much more overtly Fascist, and much more deeply hidden sponsors, sponsors moreover, with their own long intelligence and covert-ops history with Islamic fundamentalist groups in Egypt.[99]

Adding to the mystique of Atta as a high target of intelligence activities is the fact a self-described former Navy seal was hired as a night time cab driver in Venice, Florida about a month before 9/11, and quit one day after 9/11. Since Atta would drink excessively on his nighttime outings to various local strip clubs, he always traveled by taxi. This raises the possibility that U.S. military intelligence, in the form of the Office of Naval Investigations, had Atta under surveillance.[100] Egyptian and German intelligence also had Atta under surveillance.[101]

The FBI also had Atta under surveillance, ostensibly for his apparent activity in "stockpiling bomb-making materials." And last, but not least, the Canadian press stated that Atta had already been implicated for a bombing in Israel,[102] raising the question of his ultimate motivations, and his ultimate handlers: was this an *Islamic* terrorist bombing, or a *Nazi* one, or both?

4. Another Bizarre Parallel between 9/11 and JFK: Mohamed Atta, the **Other** Mohamed Atta, and Lee Harvey Oswald

Atta's alleged involvement in a terrorist bombing in Israel brings one chin-to-chin with yet another uncomfortable fact about the whole 9/11 operation, namely, its strong resemblance in some of its facets to the murder of President John F. Kennedy. We have already encountered suggestions that there may have been more than one Mohamed Atta in the fact that there was apparently a Mohamed Atta training at American military flight schools at Maxwell Air Force Base in Alabama.

In point of fact, the Israeli incident was the bombing of a bus in 1986, by a man with the same name, but who was already 33 years old in 1986, making him in his fifties in 2001, and thus considerably older than the Mohamed Atta of Huffman Aviation-9/11 infamy.[103] There

---

[99] For the connections of postwar Nazis to intelligence operations in Egypt and to radical Islamic groups, see my *Nazi International*, pp. 191-196.

[100] Jay Kolar, "What We Now Know about the Alleged 9-11 Hijackers," in Paul Zarembka, ed., *The Hidden History of 9-11*, 3-44, p. 34.

[101] Nafeez Mosaddeq Ahmed, *The War on Freedom*, p. 95.

[102] Ibid., p. 96.

[103] Daniel Hopsicker, *Welcome to Terrorland*, p. 114.

were thus *two* Mohamed Attas, both associated with terrorism, and even though the Israeli bus-bomber of the same name was not the same man, the mere fact of his involvement, as Hopsicker points out, would have meant that the *name* "Mohamed Atta" would have been placed on a watch-list. This in turn raises the question of how the 9/11 Mohamed Atta gained such easy entrance to the United States.[104]

Worse yet, the local Florida media eventually learned that one of Mohamed Atta's girlfriends was actually in a relationship with a *Mohammed* Atta, i.e., with someone who spelled his first name differently than the 9/11 Mohamed Atta.[105] If you're counting, that makes now at least two, and possibly three, Moham(m)ed Attas.

Two, and possibly three Moham(m)ed Attas, just like two, and possibly three, Lee Harvey Oswalds.

The "M.O." is suspiciously familiar.

And if one has *really* been paying attention, (1) the name itself would have been on a watch list, but (2) nonetheless Atta #1 gained easy entry to the USA, where (3) he was placed under surveillance by the FBI and possibly by US military intelligence in the form of the Office of Naval Investigation (ONI).

With this in mind, it is now time to look at some of the other *dramatis personae*, President George W. Bush, and his younger brother Jeb, Governor of Florida during 9/11.

C. Prescott's Progeny: The Bushes, Saudis, and Bin Ladens
1. Jeb Swoops in to Remove the Evidence

Within eighteen hours of 9/11, according to local Venice, Florida police sergeant Marty Treanor, the FBI swooped down on the sleepy village and confiscated all of Huffman Aviation's files, and those of the local police department concerning Rudi Dekkers and Huffman, loaded it all on Ryder rental trucks, and "then drove them right onto a C-130 military cargo plane at the Sarasota airport, which took off for Washington with Jeb Bush aboard."[106] Jay Kolar's version of this episode is slightly different, with Governor Jeb Bush showing up in Venice personally at 2AM on September 12th, 2001 in order to supervise the FBI's confiscation of the police and Huffman Aviation records, "file

---

[104] Daniel Hopsicker, *Welcome to Terrorland*, p. 115.
[105] Ibid., p. 55-56.
[106] Ibid., p. 8.

cabinets and all, thence to be taken to the waiting C-130 at Sarasota's airport "to be flown to...the Bermuda triangle for all we know."[107]

Here again, the possibilities of interpretation change, depending upon whom one assumes the various players and levels are. On the view that 9/11 was simply a "two-tiered" operation involving the outer level of the hijackers, and an inner, deeper level of a rogue element within the American power structure, Governor Bush's activity is usually understood, or implied to be, the actions of attempting to cover up evidence that could implicate either that power structure, or even the Bush family itself, with some degree of the planning of the operation.

But on the view that it may have been a *three*-tiered operation, with a "rogue element within the rogue element" turning upon the operation's planners and revealing its presence by communicating classified codes of various agencies, then two other basic interpretive possibilities emerge for this action: either Governor Bush was *ordered* to remove evidence by that rogue element within the rogue element that could implicate it, or he may have done so on orders from other members of the second level of the operation, who may have been fearful that those files might have revealed the existence of the third level, and hence jeopardized the planned war on terrorism; a war on terrorism is easy to sell to the public, a war against "fascist internationals", with no clear national or other localized centers of power, is not.

2. President George Walker Bush's Strange Behavior on 9/11

One of the most subtly revealing facts that there may be not two, but *three* levels behind the events of 9/11 is the strange behavior of President Bush himself on that day, as he was conducting his official visit to the Booker Elementary School. The renowned 9/11 researcher and critic of the official narrative of 9/11, David Ray Griffin, points out that the first media *reports* of the crash of American Flight 11, Mohamed Atta's flight, into the North Towers occurred at about 8:48 AM, approximately two minutes *after* the crash had actually occurred. Yet, as the official narrative would have it, President Bush remained unaware of it for approximately another ten whole minutes.[108] This raises yet

---

[107] Jay Kolar, "What We Now Know about the Alleged 9-11 Hijackers," in Paul Zarembka, ed., *The Hidden History of 9-11*, 3-44, p. 24. Notably, unlike Hopsicker, who cites Sergeant Treanor as his source and quotes his remarks, Kolar does not give a source for his information.

[108] David Ray Griffin, *The New Pearl Harbor*, p, 57.

another set of uncomfortable questions about 9/11: what did the President know, and when did he know it?

Griffin points out that during a television interview, Vice President Dick Cheney committed a gaffe, admitting that within minutes of the strike against the North Tower of the World Trade Center, the Secret Service had established communications with the Federal Aviation Administration (FAA), and thus, that he, the FAA, and President Bush, were most likely aware that several airliner hijackings were in progress. As Griffin also points out, the official narrative also acknowledges that President Bush's Press Secretary, Ari Fleischer, learned of the strike against the North Tower *while the Presidential motorcade was on the way to Booker Elementary School*, making it likely that at some point prior to the beginning of his appearance at the school, that the President knew as well.

Nonetheless, he initially referred to it as a "horrible accident."[109]

As was seen previously in this chapter, according to David Schipper's Pittsburgh interview, American intelligence not only was aware months ahead of time of impending attacks, it had intelligence concerning the specific target, dates, times, and methods of financing, and that *all of this had been blocked*. We have also noted that the Bush Administration actually backed the fast-tracking of visa issuance from the American consulate in Jeddah. All of this, of course, implies some degree of foreknowledge, and therefore, complicity, at the highest levels of government, up to and including Bush himself.

It is against this backdrop that President Bush's *initial* behavior during 9/11 must be weighed, for having likely known about the threat, he then proceeds, as if nothing at all was happening, with the photo-op for the next twenty minutes in the classroom of Booker Elementary School. Equally important, and equally suspicious, is the fact that with a clear attack under way, Bush himself, and the elementary school, were potential targets, and yet, the Secret Service does not evacuate him from the school.[110]

Griffin observes that one year after 9/11, the White House had changed its story after the President had been subjected to withering criticism for his anomalous behavior at the school. Bush's chief of staff, Andrew Card, put out the story that the President had politely excused himself to the teacher and her students, and left the room "within a matter of seconds." The trouble is, video of the elementary school

---

[109] David Ray Griffin, *The New Pearl Harbor*, pp. 57-58.
[110] Ibid., p. 59.

clearly revealed that the President remained firmly seated for a "mere" 700 seconds.

This is the now well-known video where Bush is seen listening to Andrew Card, who enters the classroom, bends down, and whispers into the President's ear, presumably informing him that the South Tower of the World Trade Center has been struck, making it clear that the country was under attack. Rather than "politely excusing" himself, Bush remained seated, and the children continued reading the story *My Pet Goat*, a fact not without its own dreary and dark significance, as we shall discover much later in this book. So the question recurs: why did the President, or even his security personnel, not remove him from the school, and thereby remove him—and the school—from being a potential target? "Might the answer be," asks Griffin, "that Bush knew that there was really no danger?"[111] The fact that the Secret Service did not scoop him up and rustle him out the door is itself suspicious, for it raises the same question with respect to the Secret Service; did their "failure" really reflect the fact that they already knew the school was not a target?

There is, however, a much more serious fact that indicates that there was likely *some* foreknowledge of the events of that day on the part of the President, foreknowledge that allowed him to remain so calm at the elementary school, calm in the knowledge he—*at that time at least*—and the school were *not* scheduled targets, according to the plan of the operation. Here it is best to cite Griffin extensively:

> Much attention at the time was given to the fact that once Air Force One became airborne at 9:55, President Bush remained away from Washington for a long time, perhaps, speculated some commentators, out of fear.

However, as was seen in the Preface, we now know that *Bush's and his security team's attitude changed completely by the time he returned to Air Force One, for by **that** time, the attackers had signaled their intentions to attack the President, and validated that threat by their demonstrations that they knew highly classified codes of various federal agencies, up to and including the presidency, codes which, moreover, indicated a possible penetration of the command structure of America's strategic thermonuclear forces, necessitating Bush's hasty flights to Barksdale and Offut Air Force Bases, headquarters for the command structure of those*

---

[111] David Ray Griffin, *The New Pearl Harbor*, p. 61.

forces, in order to reassert personal control over them, lest the Global Guardian exercise be flipped "live" by the attackers.

To put an even finer point on this, **Bush's behavior at Booker Elementary School is consistent with someone involved to some degree in the second level of the operation, and his behavior after departing on Air Force One for Barksdale and later Offut is consistent with Level Two realizing that their entire carefully planned operation had been co-opted by a completely different and unanticipated player, by "Level Three."**

With this in mind, we return to David Ray Griffin's statements:

Indeed, some reporters who criticized the president on that score lost their jobs—which may account for why the White House could later be confident that the news media would not challenge any of its fabrications. In any case, **the real question, the critics suggest, is why there was apparently no fear during the first hour.** The implied question is, of course, a disturbing one: Did the president and at least the head of his Secret Service detail know that he was *not* a target?

The idea that the Bush administration had advance knowledge of the attacks is further suggested by a statement later made by Bush himself: "I was sitting outside the classroom waiting to go in," he claimed, "and I saw an airplane hit the tower—the TV was obviously on—and I used to fly myself, and I said, 'There's one terrible pilot.'" Given the fact that according to the official story, Bush did not have access to a television set until at least 15 minutes later, this statement raised questions. An article in the *Boston Herald* said:

"Think about that. Bush's remark implies he saw the first plane hit the tower. But we all know that video of the first plane hitting did not surface until the next day. Could Bush have meant he saw the second plane hit—which many Americans witnessed? No, because he said that he was in the classroom when Card whispered in his ear that a second plane hit."

Pointing out that Bush had told this story several times, the writer asked: "How could the commander-in-chief have seen the plane fly into the first building—as it happened?"[112]

---

[112] David Ray Griffin, *The New Pearl Harbor*, pp. 62-63, boldface emphasis added, italicized emphasis in the original, citing the *Boston Herald* October 22, 2002.

Griffin concludes that the behavior of the President "reinforces the conclusion... that government and military officials at the highest level had advance knowledge of, and conspired to allow, the traumatic events of that day."[113]

The problem with this LIHOP view, of course, is the already-mentioned fact that 9/11 was planned with a detailed eye towards the numerous drills—some of which were mimicking aspects of the attack itself—that were simultaneously occurring on that day, and this means that planning of the 9/11 attacks could only have come from *within* the national security structure.

3. The Bush-Saudi-Bin Laden Connection

No study of the possibilities of the potential existence of a third level or player in the events of 9/11 that revealed itself to the American command structure, and which shocked President Bush from calm inaction to a rush to reestablish control over the American military's strategic forces, would be complete without a brief overview of the relationship of the Bush family to the Saudis, and more importantly, to the Bin Laden Construction Group, for of course, Osama bin Laden was already being touted as the favored mastermind—and patsy—of the operation within mere hours of the attacks.

Webster Griffin Tarpley notes that top Republican party power brokers, including the former Secretary of State James A. Baker under the administration of President George H.W. Bush, and G.H.W. Bush himself, were close financial allies and consultants to the Saudi Bin Laden Construction Group, via their involvement with the Carlyle Group.[114] The late Michael Ruppert noted that on the very day of 9/11, even as the attacks were occurring, "members of the bin Laden family (along with other key investors) were in Washington DC meeting with the Carlyle Group at the Ritz Carlton Hotel, just blocks away from the White House."[115] More to the point, however, is what the Carlyle Group actually *does*.

Ruppert minces no words: the Carlyle Group, he says, "buys and sells defense *contractors*."[116] In other words, the Carlyle Group is to

---

[113] Ibid., p. 64.

[114] Webster Griffin Tarpley, *9/11 Synthetic Terror: Made in USA,* fifth edition, p. 166. For a good review of the Bush-Bin Laden connection and how it came about, see also James Mann's essential study of Bush's post-9/11 "war cabinet," *The Rise of the Vulcans: The History of Bush's War Cabinet* (New York: Penguin, 2004).

[115] Michael C. Ruppert, *Crossing the Rubicon*, p. 129.

[116] Ibid.

defense industries what a solicitor, as distinct from an attorney or barrister, is in British law: it is the group that places certain defense industries in certain positions with certain groups of investors according to their needs. It is thus in a key position not only to be a potential interface between investors and the black technology world –a kind of "interface" or holding corporation for the breakaway civilization as it were—but as such, it is also in the perfect position to facilitate technology transfers via corporate agreements, and to profit from events like 9/11. Indeed, as Ruppert also states, the Bin Laden family had extensive investments and holdings in the group, and thus, when family member Osama ostensibly masterminded the 9/11 attacks, the Bin Laden family profited enormously from the expansion of the American defense budget after 9/11.[117]

Moreover, according to Ruppert, the Bin Laden group owns the Iridium satellite company, a company possessing over 72 low-earth orbit satellites that provide satellite phone coverage over the entire planet,[118] a fact made more disturbing by the fact that via its contacts with the international defense community, Saudi Arabia through the Bin Laden Group has been attempting to buy long range missiles, and to purchase nuclear weapons from Pakistan.[119] Finally, it was via his family connection and fortune via the Bin Laden Group that Osama bin Laden was able to pay for the training of fellow Muhajedin fighters in Afghanistan in the 1980s, when he functioned as a CIA asset in the country.[120]

Putting this point differently, the Bin Laden Group functioned, during this time, as a kind of corporate *militant order*, funding its own mercenary-terrorist army.

Why is all this important in the context of the emerging outlines of a third player possibly involved with the events of 9/11, a third player that announced its presence during that day as the events were unfolding? While it might be tempting to view Saudi Arabia and its vast financial connections as *being* that third player, in the final analysis, this seems unlikely, for as is evident, the desert kingdom must *purchase* virtually all its advanced technology, including its military hardware. Decades of Wahabbist fundamentalism have effectively rendered its general population incapable of sustaining an indigenous technological and scientific, advanced manufacturing infrastructure. It is therefore unlikely that the kingdom would risk cutting off its largest source of

---

[117] Michael C. Ruppert, *Crossing the Rubicon*, p. 131.
[118] Ibid., p. 128.
[119] Ibid., p. 141.
[120] Nefeez Mosaddeq Ahmed, *The War on Freedom*, p. 177.

supply for these technologies by turning on and attacking its American allies. If the desert kingdom is involved in any deep level planning and involvement in 9/11 beyond the connection to the hijackers themselves, it is more likely at level two, than at level three.

This, finally, leads us to the Patsy-in-Chief, Osama bin Laden.

4. Osama Bin Laden, the Plutocrat-Jihadist Patsy for the Pancake Theory

Oddly, it is Osama Bin Laden himself who symbolizes the probable existence of a "rogue network" within the American national security-military-intelligence complex that planned at carried out the attacks. Equally oddly, it is he who may also point very subtly to the existence of a *third* layer. The fact that Bin Laden's death was reported many times before his "real" and "final" death[121] is a signal that "almost everything about Osama Bin Laden remains uncertain, down to the question of whether he is dead or alive, free or in captivity, and whether he is one person or a group of doubles, *Doppelgänger*."[122]

Nothing signals Bin Laden's role as a patsy more than the supposed "confession" video that was aired by the American press on December 20, 2001. In this video Bin Laden praises the "martyrs" of 9/11. The problem, however, is that the White House and Pentagon translations of the Arabic each list different numbers of "martyrs" being praised by Bin Laden for their "participation" in the attacks. In the White House version, only one "martyr" is mentioned, the Pentagon version, three. But when German(!) and Saudi investigators examined the video, it was discovered that the American translations were deliberately manipulative of the facts, for the Saudis insisted that Bin Laden had actually named *nine* "martyrs", five of whom were still alive![123] As Kolar points out, "Bin Laden erroneously praising uninvolved men makes no sense. At the expense of embarrassing himself, bin Laden would also be proliferating propaganda in support of the US war effort. Most likely US intelligence moles created this video forgery for that reason."[124]

However, there is an entirely different possibility for the motivation behind the forgery. In the video, "Bin Laden"(for we must assume that it is either him, one of his doubles, or a complete imposter) also states that his whole diabolical, ingenious plan was to crash airplanes into the Twin

---

[121] Webster Griffin Tarpley, *9/11 Synthetic Terror: Made in USA*, fifth edition, p. 161,

[122] Ibid., p. 167.

[123] Jay Kolar, "What We Now Know about the Alleged 9-11 Hijackers," in Paul Zarembka, ed., *The Hidden History of 9-11*, 3-44, p. 10.

[124] Ibid.

Towers, in the hopes the resulting fires would weaken the towers sufficiently enough to lead to their collapse.

In other words, "Bin Laden" was used to endorse the government's own official narrative and its emerging "pancake theory" that the ultimate cause of the Towers' destruction was burning aircraft fuel, which sufficiently weakened the structures that the floors began to collapse one on top of the other, driving a "collapse" that proceeded at nearly free fall speed, a physical impossibility, and one, moreover, that would have left a much larger debris pile at Ground Zero than was in fact observed. It should also be pointed out that the real "Bin Laden" might have been unlikely to make any such statement in any case, since his access to the skilled engineers and architects in his own family construction business could easily have told him that his brilliant plan was almost certain to fail, if indeed the objective was to destroy the Twin Towers by an airplane-fueled pancaking-floor collapse theory.

In this respect, niceties of Arabic translation were unnecessary. All that *was* necessary was to plant the "airplane fuel pancake-collapse theory" into the public mind, straight from the "mastermind's" mouth itself. It was a clever means to divert the public's attention away from the incongruities and impossibilities of that model, and from examining the actual mechanisms of their collapse.

After all, those mechanisms—the actual murder weapon—might lead back to the real perpetrators themselves, and *if* those mechanisms moreover were not available to the level two perpetrators, but revealed the existence of a third level, unknown to them, and surprising them, then all the *more* reason to conceal them. Some mechanisms might implicate them, others might implicate an enemy they did *not* want to acknowledge. But even if the level three reading of the motivations behind the Bin Laden "confession video" are *not* true, his mention of the pancake theory was certainly enough for the level two perpetrators to create it. Either way, he was, as Webster Tarpley aptly opines, "a patsy of incalculable value."[125]

---

[125] Webster Griffin Tarpley, *9/11 Synthetic Terror: Made in USA*, fifth edition, p. 164.

2

THE PUZZLES OF THE PENTAGON AND PENNSYLVANIA

"They also kept insisting that a plane hit the building. They repeated this over and over. But I was there and I never saw a plane or even debris from a plane. I figure the plane story is there to brainwash people."
Pentagon 9/11 witness April Gallop[1]

UNTIL THE DISAPPEARANCE OF MALAYSIA AIR FLIGHT 370 on March 8, 2014, no civilian airliner disappeared as successfully and as completely as American Airlines Flight 77, the flight that the official government-sponsored 9/11 conspiracy theory says crashed into the Pentagon. And like Malaysia Air Flight 370, no flight has sponsored so much debate as American Flight 77, for in a very real sense, Flight 77 was where the official narrative of 9/11 began to unravel, and to unravel very quickly. In fact, one wonders whether the 9/11 truth movement, flush with success in challenging the Flight 77 aspects of the narrative, did not go overboard with respect to the *other* 9/11 flights, for it has now reached the point that the hypotheses being offering for the flights that struck the Twin Towers range from remote-controlled aircraft, to planes being *substituted* for the flights and firing missiles into the towers just before they impacted, to drones, and even to a theory that there were no planes at all, and that what was seen on television was a Hollywood production, never mind that people in New York City saw planes; what *they* saw were just "holograms". Here too, the official narrative has only fueled the theories, for the public is being asked to believe a lone hijacker's passport survived the inferno of the Twin Towers to be conveniently discovered on the streets below, while the huge jet engines and other aircraft parts were conspicuous by the lack of witness testimony or media reference to them.

There is, however, perhaps a better explanation for the proliferation of plane hypotheses, for the problems and problematics surrounding Flight 77 are so dense, and the critique of the official narrative so deep-cutting and effective, that conceivably the only way to deflect this criticism was to seed the 9/11 truth community with such ridiculous theories about the *other* aircraft that any critique whatsoever was tarred with the brush of irrationality. In this, the "rogue network"

---

[1] Jim Marrs, *Inside Job: Unmasking the 9/11 Conspiracies* (Can Rafael, California: Origin Press, 2004), p. 26.

demonstrates that it learned a thing or two since the Kennedy assassination; merely denouncing critiques and criticism of the official story is ineffective and only intensifies curiosity and skepticism concerning approved narratives. *Infiltrating* such research communities and obfuscating data, and pushing explanatory hypotheses into ridiculousness, or seeding possible hypotheses with irrational elements, or getting adherents of various interpretive hypotheses to denounce each other for methodological faults when one employs the same faults oneself—a phenomenon in sad abundance when we consider the mechanisms being proposed for the destruction of the Twin towers - is far better. And if all else fails, then the time-tested and trusted method of standing on credentials and that peculiar mixture of the *ad hominem* and arguments from authority can always be applied.

Along with President G.W. Bush's strange behavior at the Booker Elementary school, and more importantly, the existence of several drills paralleling exactly certain features of the 9/11 operation, Flight 77 is important for yet another reason, for in all the research uncovered by 9/11 investigators, it is also the part of the 9/11 narrative that reveals the existence of that second layer, the rogue network within the American national security state, that planned and executed the horrible events of that day. However, on careful and closer examination, the clues uncovered by 9/11 researchers hint, yet again, at the existence of a *third* layer, unknown to the second layer planners, that revealed itself on that day.

A. Puzzles at the Pentagon
1. Egyptian President Hosni Mubarak begins the Unraveling of the Narrative

It was French researcher Thierry Meyssan that first pointed out the problems at the Pentagon with a book whose conclusions soon went viral around the world, and that began the unravelling of the official 9/11 narrative: *9/11: the Big Lie.* Meyssan notes that on September 15, 2001, just four days after the attacks, then Egyptian President Hosni Mubarak, a former fighter pilot for the Egyptian Air Force, gave an interview to the 24 hour American news channel, CNN. In this interview, Mubarak let slip several key pieces of data, not the least of which was that Egyptian intelligence had become aware of the impending attacks several weeks previously, and that he himself conveyed the warnings directly to Washington.[2]

---

[2] Thierry Meyssan, *9/11: the Big Lie*, p. 25.

But Mubarak did not stop there. He went on to point out the extraordinary difficulty for a *skilled* pilot to execute the spiraling descent maneuver that Hani Hanjour is alleged to have achieved in crashing Flight 77 into the Pentagon:

> Not any intelligence in the world could have the capability in the world to say they are going to use commercial planes with passengers on board to crash the towers, to crash the Pentagon, *those who did that should have flown in the area a long time, for example.* The Pentagon is not very high, a pilot could come straight to the Pentagon like this to hit, *he should have flown a lot in this area to know the obstacles which could meet him when he is flying very low with a big commercial plan to hit the Pentagon in* **a special place.** *Somebody has studied this very well, some has flown in this area very much.*[3]

Mr. Mubarak's words cannot be lingered over too long, for he is very subtly suggesting that the story of a rank amateur like Hanjour being capable of performing the spiraling descent maneuver he is alleged to have executed is next to impossible. Additionally, note that Mubarak is also suggesting that the Pentagon was hit in "a special place." This will become a crucial consideration, as we shall eventually discover, that 9/11 *was* an inside job.

CNN was not oblivious to what Mubarak was implying, and followed this response up with a question that went to the heart of the matter, and again, Mr. Mubarak both diplomatically avoided answering directly, but also gently reinforced the focus of attention on the detail of the narrative—Hani Hanjour's "impossible maneuver"—that was the weakest link in the emerging 9/11 narrative:

> CNN: Are you suggesting it was an inside operation? I may ask, who do you think is behind this?
> Mubarak: Frankly speaking, I don't want to jump to conclusions, you in the United States when you catch somebody, some rumors about somebody, you say 'Oh no, it is not Egyptian, it is Saudi, it is Emirates... all this is inside any house of an Arab, the people say the Arabs are participating... you cannot foretell, it is better wait.' (sic) You remember Oklahoma... there came rumors immediately that the Arabs did it, and it was not Arabs, who knows... let us wait and see what is the result of the investigations, because *something like this done in the United States is not an easy thing for some pilots who*

---

[3] Theirry Meyssan, *9/11: The Big Lie*, p. 26, all emphases added.

had been training in Florida, so many pilots go and train just to fly and have a license, that means you are capable to do such a terrorist action? I am speaking as a former pilot, I know that very well, I flew very heavy planes, I flew fighters, I know that very well, this is not an easy thing, so I think we should not jump to conclusions for now.[4]

Given that the 9/11 official narrative by September 15th, the time of Mubarak's CNN interview, had already concluded that the hijackers were all Arabs, and that they had trained at various flight schools around the country, when one parses Murabarak's words closely, what he was *really* subtly pointing out was not only did the narrative make no sense, but that one should not too readily leap to endorse that narrative. Mubarak, in other words, *was* strongly implying that the events were an inside job, without directly saying so.

2. The Safest Airspace in the World:
Indications of a Third Player in the Timeline of Events

It is when one considers Mayessan's Flight 77-Pentagon investigations more closely that one discovers more hints that a *third* player might have been involved, one suddenly announcing its presence to the "rogue network" or level two planners of the American "deep state". Once again, the possibility of this "third, deeper level" has gone largely unmentioned—save in the research of Webster Tarpley—and hence, its interpretive possibilities have been largely ignored.

To appreciate this point, one must look at a basic *timeline* of the day more closely. Our guide here will be the extensive timeline of the events painstakingly pieced together by Paul Thompson and the Center for Cooperative Research:

1) *8:46 AM*: Flight 11 strikes the North Tower of the World Trade Center. At this moment, three of the F-16 fighters normally assigned to Andrews Air Force Base are on a training exercise in North Carolina. Thompson observes that F-16s are capable of a maximum speed of 1500 mph, and even at 1100 mph, some of these fighters would have been capable of returning to Washington DC's airspace to be on station against any threat against the capital by 9:00 AM.[5]

---

[4] Thierry Meyssan, *9/11: The Big Lie*, p. 26, emphasis added.
[5] Paul Thompson, *The Terror Timeline: Year by Year, Day by Day, Minute by Minute: A Comprehensive Chronicle of the Road to 9/11—and America's Response* (New York: Harper, 2004), pp. 371-372

2) *ca 8:46-8:55 AM:* President G.W. Bush's motorcade is en route to Booker Elementary School and hears of the first crash(Flight 11) but according to the official narrative, President Bush himself is still unaware of the crash, which is highly unlikely, as was seen.[6]

3) *8:46 AM:* President Bush, on the evening of 9/11, states that immediately upon the first attack, he ordered the implementation of the government's terrorism emergency contingency plans. However, a *Wall Street Journal* article of March 22, 2004 cites Bush as maintaining that he did not give any orders in response to the attacks until 9:55 AM.[7]

4) *8:46 AM:* According to the American television network MSNBC on September 16th, 2001, after Flight 11 struck the North Tower of the World Trade Center, the Federal Aviation Administration (FAA) opened a secure line to the Secret Service. This is based on a statement made by Vice President Dick Cheney during a television interview, who said "The Secret Service had an arrangement with the FAA. They had open lines after the World Trade Center was ⸺" At his point, Cheney stopped himself in mid-sentence, and did not finish.[8] This is a crucial point, for it indicates, firstly, that after the first target was struck, *and before any **others** were struck*, there was a clear and secure communications channel open between the Federal Aviation Administration and the Secret Service. Secondly, this in turn means it is most likely that everyone in the presidential party in Florida also knew at that moment, including the President himself, giving lie to the official narrative.

5) *8:50 AM:* The last radio contact with Flight 77 occurs, and Flight 175 heads toward New York City.[9]

6) *8:55 AM* Air Force Captain Deborah Loewer, director of the White House Situation Room, is traveling in the Presidential motorcade in Florida. As soon as the motorcade reaches Booker Elementary school, according to an Associated Press article of the 26th November, 2001, and a later *Catholic Telegraph* article of December 7th, 2001, Captain Loewer runs to inform President Bush of the attacks, once again contradicting the official narrative.[10]

---

[6] Ibid., p. 374.
[7] Ibid., pp. 374-375.
[8] Ibid., p. 375.
[9] Ibid., p. 378.
[10] Paul Thompson, *The Terror Timeline*, p. 381.

7) *ca. 8:57-9:05 AM*: Flight 77's transponder signal disappears and the flight disappears from radar. While the 9/11 Commission later maintains this was due to a technical problem with "the way the software processed radar information," this could be a deliberate obfuscation to disguise the possibility that the entire system had been co-opted from within.

8) *9:00 AM:* A drill at the National Reconnaissance Office, responsible for all of America's spy satellites and the analysis of their data, is cancelled. The drill simulated an accidental airplane crash into its office headquarters.[11] At the same time, Operation Northern Vigilance, yet another 9/11 drill *simulating several concurrent hijackings*, is cancelled. As a component of this drill, false radar blips were entered into the air traffic control system. These were allegedly purged at this time. However, as Thompson notes, exactly which air traffic control centers had such false blips as a part of the exercise has never been revealed. The mere existence of the exercise, however, mimicking the exact events of that day, means not only that this could have caused immense command and control confusion,[12] but it again points to the existence of the level two rogue network and the careful planning evident in the 9/11 operation.

We now skip ahead several steps in Thompson's meticulous timeline to notice some curious things:

9) *ca 9:03 AM*: Both Deputy Secretary of Defense Paul Wolfowitz and Defense Secretary Donald Rumsfeld remain in their offices on the *east* side of the Pentagon.[13] This behavior parallel's President Bush's nonchalant attitude in Florida. At this time, United Airlines Flight 175 crashes into the South Tower of the World Trade Center.[14]

10) *9:06 AM*: Andrew Card walks into the classroom at Booker Elementary, leans down, and whispers into the President's ear, purportedly telling him America is under attack. Bush continues to read "My Pet Goat" for the next ten minutes, and is told not to talk by Ari Fleischer, who is holding up a card saying "Don't say anything yet."[15] This raises the possibility that Andrew Card

---

[11] Ibid., p. 384.
[12] Ibid.
[13] Ibid., p. 394.
[14] Ibid., p. 390.
[15] Paul Thompson, *The Terror Timeline*, pp. 397, 398.

might have whispered something else entirely into Bush's ear, namely, "Stay put, and finish the story. We're in no danger."

11) *9:10AM*: National Security Advisor Condaleeza Rice and Vice President Cheney arrive at the White House Bunker. However, *other* accounts place the time of Cheney's arrival, under Secret Service escort, around 9:30 AM. Complicating the timeline are eyewitness reports of Cheney in the bunker by 9:27 AM, when he is notified that Flight 77 is 50 miles away from Washington.[16] To compound matters further, Transportation Secretary Norman Mineta arrives at 9:20 in the White House bunker, and claims Cheney was already there. The official 9/11 Commission, however, maintains that Cheney does not arrive until just before 10:00 AM.[17] Since the preponderance of actual eyewitness testimony has the Vice President in the White House bunker sometime between 9:00 and 9:27, for our purposes, we will maintain, for the sake of analysis, that the Vice President was in the bunker by the time that Mineta arrived.

12) *9:30 AM:* American counterterrorism tsar Richard Clarke contacts the White House Bunker, where National Security Advisor Condaleeza Rice and Vice President Cheney are already present, and states that Bush should not return directly to Washington from Florida, and indicates that a fighter escort should escort Air Force One when it departs Sarasota.[18] However, as indicated in the previous chapter, when Air Force One departed Florida, it did so *without* fighter escort. Additionally, as was also indicated in the previous chapter, sometime *after* Mr. Bush's appearance at the elementary school, his demeanor, *and the messages he was conveying changed completely*, indicating the possible presence of a *third* layer that had revealed itself. It is thus possible that while Bush's calm behavior at Booker Elementary was due to the fact that at some level he knew he and the school were not a target, a possibility implying *some* degree of inside knowledge, the security stripping that occurred in the denial of fighter escort may indicate that some element had now co-opted the command and control structure, and was preventing a fighter escort from being available. In support of this hypothesis, recall again that sometime between the attacks on the World Trade Center and

16 Ibid., pp. 399-400.
17 Ibid., p. 404. See also p. 409.
18 Ibid., p. 413.

the President's departure from Florida, the attackers revealed themselves, stated that Air Force One was next, and revealed their capability by revealing top secret codes.

13) *9:30 AM:* Air traffic controller Chris Stephenson at Reagan National Airport in Washington reports that he was notified by the Secret Service that "an unidentified aircraft is speeding toward Washington."[19] Looking out the tower window he sees an aircraft turning right and descending rapidly.

14) *9:33-9:37 AM:* It is now necessary to cite Thompson directly, for the following two timeline events provide stronger indications that an unexpected third player may have announced its presence:

Radar data shows Flight 77 crossing the Capitol Beltway and headed toward the Pentagon. However, the plane, flying more than 400mph, is too high when it nears the Pentagon at 9:35 A.M., crossing the Pentagon at about 7,000 feet up.[20] The plane then makes a difficult high-speed descending turn. It makes a "downward spiral, turning almost a complete circle and dropping the last 7,000 feet in two-and-a-half-minutes. The steep turn is so smooth, the sources say, it's clear there (is) no fight for control going on."[21] *It gets very near the White House during this turn.* "Sources say the hijacked jet...(flies) several miles south of the restricted airspace around the White House."[22] The *Daily Telegraph* later writes, *"If the airliner had approached much nearer to the White House it might have been shot down by the Secret Service, who are believed to have a battery of ground-to-air Stinger missiles ready to defend the president's home. The Pentagon is not similarly defended."[23]* White House spokesman Air Fleischer suggests the plane goes even closer to the White House, saying, "That is not the radar data that we have seen. The plane was headed toward the White House."[24] *If flight 77 passed within a few miles of the White House, why couldn't it have been shot down by the weapons on the White House?[25]*

---

[19] Paul Thompson, *The Terror Timeline*, p. 424.

[20] Thompson cites CBS News, Sept 21, 2001, and the *Boston Globe*, November 23, 2001, for this point.

[21] Citing CBS News, September 21, 2001.

[22] Again, citing CBS News, September 21, 2001.

[23] Citing *The Daily Telegraph*, September 16, 2001.

[24] Citing CBS News, September 21, 2001.

[25] Paul Thompson, *The Terror Timeline*, p. 417, emphasis added.

If the White House air defenses were not responsive to the flight on 9/11, there are two possibilities: firstly, no action was taken because shooting down an airliner in the middle of Washington DC on a work day, would have caused even more loss of life. This is by far the most likely explanation. The second possibility is that the command structure had by that point been co-opted by the *third* layer, and thus while a shoot down order may have been given, the order simply was countermanded by the third level, either by all the confusion of the drills taking place, or by use of the codes that the attackers revealed they possessed.

While the first explanation is likely, the problem is with the assertion about the Pentagon itself, which, according to the *Daily Telegraph*, had no such air defenses! Additionally, while the region surrounding the Pentagon is full of high rise buildings and hence presents an "obstacle" course for anyone attempting to attack it with airliners, as Egyptian President Mubarak suggested, the area *immediately* around the Pentagon is relatively open ground, and hence, *if* the Pentagon had air defenses, an order to shoot down the craft before it struck the Pentagon might have been given. The question is, why was it *not* given? We shall return to this point subsequently. For the present, however, it is important to note that *at approximately the same time that it was apparent that Washington DC and the Pentagon were under attack, President Bush departs Booker Elementary School, and **this** time, according to NBC television reporter Ann Compton who was with the presidential party, the motorcade was "a mad dash."* Bush's Chief of Staff Andrew Card later admitted that it was during the motorcade that they learned about the threat to the Pentagon and to Air Force One.[26]

We conclude, therefore, that even though the behavior of the President at the school *up until the time of his departure* is indicative of knowledge of the events at some level(and this will oddly become even more clear when we consider the *occult ritual* aspects of 9/11 in the second part of this book), and that while the operation could not have been carried out on the very day that there were so many drills mimicking exact aspects of 9/11 without detailed planning from within the American national security apparatus' "rogue network," the failures to defend Washington's target rich environment, and the President's *subsequent* behavior and addresses after departing

---

[26] Ibid., p. 419.

Florida, indicate that the "third level" had revealed its presence sometime during this period.

But are we to believe *The Daily Telegraph*'s statement that, while the White House had a surface-to-air missile defense capability, the Pentagon had absolutely none? Meyssan flatly contradicts *The Daily Telegraph* article, pointing out that the Pentagon was in fact protected by no less than *five* missile defense batteries.[27] This presents yet another problem, and yet another possible manifestation of level two, and perhaps, of level three, for Meyssan observes that

> Contrary to the Pentagon's claims, the military thus knew perfectly well that an unidentified vehicle was headed straight for the capitol. Yet the military did not react and the Pentagon's anti-missile batteries did not function. Why? The close-range anti-aircraft defenses at the Pentagon are conceived to destroy missiles that attempt to approach. A missile should normally be unable to pass. As for a big Boeing 757-200, it would have strictly no chance. Whether an airliner or a missile, an explanation needs to be found.
> Each military aircraft in fact possesses a transponder which... permit(s) it to declare itself in the eyes of its possessor as *friendly* or *hostile*.... An antimissile battery will not ... react to the passage of a friendly missile. It is not impossible that was what happened at the Pentagon on 11 September, 2001.[28]

That is to say, in the context of level two planning and execution, the transponder codes could have been supplied by the planners themselves, and additionally, the confusion of command and control during the day caused by concurrently running drills simulating actual aspects of the attack also enter into the equation, allowing the attack to be successful. Meyssan puts this problematic even more bluntly in *9/11: The Big Lie*: "...only a missile of the United States armed forces transmitting a friendly code could enter the Pentagon's airspace without provoking a counter-missile barrage. This attack could only be committed by United States military personnel against other U.S. military personnel."[29] But this is *not* the only possibility. If one grants the possibility of a penetrated operation at the second level, of a *third* level—of a rogue faction within the rogue faction —with access to top secret codes, the possibility also arises that any shoot down order

---

[27] Thierry Meyssan, *Pentagate* (London: Carnot Publishing, 2002), p. 112.
[28] Ibid., p. 216.
[29] Thierry Meyssan, *9/11: The Big Lie*, p. 28.

issuing from the national command and control structure, or even the rogue network itself, could be co-opted and countermanded.

3. Was the Pentagon Struck by an Airliner, or a Missile?
a. Anomalies: Eyewitness Statements, Debris and Lightpoles

It was Thierry Meyssan who pointed out the *principal* problem with the Flight 77 story, namely, that the damage seen was incongruent with the crash of a Boeing 757-200 airliner, an aircraft with a wingspan of 124 feet 10 inches and a length of 155 feet. The damage was also inconsistent with a terrorist strike, for if the objective of presumptive Islamicist terrorist radicals was to do as much damage as possible, then "the Boeing should have dived into the Pentagon's roof,"[30] and even then, should have picked a target designed to hit the high value targets on the east side of the structure close to the Secretary of Defense's office, or other similar high value target.

As it was, the place where Flight 77 struck was a portion of the building that was undergoing renovation, including reinforcement of the walls and installation of special thick glass, and which was home to the U.S. Navy's new command center, a fact that will become quite important in chapter six, when we examine the financial aspects of the operation. This fact means that on 9/11, when the Pentagon was attacked, Flight 77 struck at one of the most sparsely occupied parts of the building at that time, and most of the casualties were from the civilian workers that were part of the renovation crews. The fact that Flight 77 executed a steep descending spiral in order to attack the Pentagon—and recall that it was close to the White House and other potential terrorist targets in the target rich environment—*can only mean that this section of the Pentagon was a deliberate target, and that the motivation was not terrorism.*

That is, if it was an airliner that struck the Pentagon in the first place.

In this regard, Meyssan cites the Department of Defense's own initial statement, released just before 10:00 AM, approximately 20 minutes after the attack:

> The Department of Defense is continuing to respond to the attack that occurred this morning at 9:38 am EDT. There are no casualty figures currently available. Injured personnel were taken to several area hospitals. Secretary of Defense Donald H. Rumsfeld has expressed his concern for the

---

[30] Thierry Meyssan, *9/11: The Big Lie*, p. 19.

families of those killed and injured during this shameless attack and is directing operations from his command center in the Pentagon. All personnel were evacuated from the building as emergency response personnel from the Department of Defense and surrounding communities responded to fire and medical emergencies. Initial estimates of the damage are significant; however, the Pentagon is expected to be reopened tomorrow morning. Alternate worksites for those affected parts of the building are currently being identified.[31]

The statement is perhaps significant for what it neglects to mention, namely, that the Pentagon had been struck by a civilian airliner in a terrorist attack.[32]

b. A Brief Introduction to the Eyewitnesses Who See an Airplane

This problem was compounded when a Dulles International Airport traffic controller, Captain Lincoln Liebner(US Army) indicated he saw an American Airlines airliner flying low and fast, directly for the Pentagon.[33] Danielle O'Brien told the ABC News network that what she watched on radar was a craft of some sort, flying directly toward the White House and Capitol at a speed of 500mph, when it turned sharply right. "For O'Brien and her colleagues, there was no possible doubt: given its speed and manoeuverability(sic), it could not be a commercial airliner, but only a military aircraft."[34] There is another problem: at Reagan National Airport, which is close enough to the Pentagon for air traffic controllers to have seen Flight 77, no one actually saw any aircraft at all.[35]

---

[31] Theirry Meyssan, *9/11: The Big Lie*, p. 13. Meyssan notes that the announcement "was removed from the Department of Defense's Internet server. It can be consulted in the archives at the following University of Yale website: www.yale.edu.lawweb/avalon/sept_11/dod_brief03.htm." (p. 214, n. 1) As of this writing, the Yale link also appears broken.

[32] Ibid., p. 24.

[33] Jim Marrs, *Inside Job: Unmasking the 9/11 Conspiracies*, p. 29.

[34] Meyssan, op cit.., p. 27. David Ray Griffin quotes O'Brien's remarks: "The speed, the maneuverability, the way that he turned, we all thought in the radar room, all of us experienced air traffic controllers, that that was a military plane." David Ray Griffin, *The New Pearl Harbor*, p. 26, citing "Extensive Casualties in Wake of Pentagon Attack, *Washington Post*, Sept 11, 2001, in Thierry Meyssan's *Pentagate*, pp. 38-39.

[35] Peter Tiradera, *9-11: Coup Against America: the Pentagon Analysis* (North Charleston, South Carolina: BookSurge LLC, 2006), p. 165.

The problems multiply, for some eyewitnesses claim to have seen an airplane while others adamantly insist that whatever struck the Pentagon, it was not an aircraft. One eyewitness saw an aircraft from a 14th story apartment building in Pentagon City. The only problem was, the witness described the aircraft as only being able to hold between eight and twelve persons, hardly a large enough aircraft to be a Boeing 757. Moreover, this craft made a noise more characteristic of a military fighter plane than a commercial airliner.[36]

b. The Eyewitnesses that See and Hear Something Else

One witness, driving in his car close to the Pentagon described it as being more like a "cruise missile with wings" while Lon Rains, an editor for *Space News* stated "I was convinced it was a missile. It came in so fast it sounded nothing like an airplane."[37] Some eyewitnesses, while describing an aircraft, also describe the strike against the building itself in unusual terms, as "melting into the building" or "sort of disappearing" or "in the air one moment and in the building the next."[38] But the most significant witness who insisted she did *not* see an airplane, and insisted to the point of suing the federal government, was April Gallop.

(1) The April Gallop Case

Gallop worked inside the Pentagon, on the west side, on 9/11, preparing to take her infant son to the day care center before beginning work, when the building was rocked by an explosion. The well-known conspiracy researcher Jim Marrs devoted a good deal of attention to the Gallop case, more than some 9/11 researchers. And for good reason, for her statements are flatly contradictory to the official narrative:

> "I thought it was a bomb," Gallop recalled. "I was buried in rubble and my first thought was for my son. I crawled around until I found his stroller. It was all crumpled up into a ball and I was then very afraid. But then I heard his voice and managed to locate him. We crawled out through a hole in the side of the building. Outside they were treating survivors on the grassy lawn. But all the ambulances

---

[36] David Ray Griffin, *The New Pearl Harbor*, p. 26.
[37] Ibid.
[38] Kevin Robert Ryan, *Another Nineteen: Investigating Legitimate 9/11 Suspects* (No Place of Publication: Microbloom, 2013), pp. 171-172.

had left, so a man who was near the scene stepped up, put us in his private car, and drove us to the hospital. The images are burned into my brain."

Gallop said while in the hospital, men in suits visited her more than once. "They never identified themselves or even said which agency they worked for. But I know they were not newsmen because I learned that the Pentagon told news reporters not to cover survivors' stories or they would not get any more stories out of there. The men who visited all said they couldn't tell me what to say, they only wanted to make suggestions. But then they told me what to do, which was to take the (Victim Compensation Fund) money and shut up. *They also kept insisting that a plane hit the building. They repeated this over and over. But I was there and I never saw a plane or even debris from a plane.* I figure the plane story is there to brainwash people."[39]

Of course, since she was *inside* the Pentagon, Gallop may or may not have seen an approaching airplane. The important point is what she did *not* see: airplane *debris.* Gallop eventually did join a RICO anti-racketeering lawsuit against President Bush. The suit was eventually dismissed on April 27, 2011 by the 2nd Circuit Court of Appeals, one of whose judges just happened to be John Mercer Walker, Jr., a first cousin of former President G.H.W. Bush, with whom he shared the same grandfather whose daughter married Prescott Bush, G.H.W. Bush's father.[40]

d. The Problem of the Debris

Since the appearance of Meyssan's book, a number of civilian and commercial pilots have pointed out additional difficulties: the Boeing 757 was simply incapable of flying at speeds of 500 mph that close to the ground, and in any case, it would require a pilot of exceptional skill to fly an aircraft that large and avoid hitting the ground prior to hitting the Pentagon façade between the ground and first floors.

However, the real difficulty was that Meyssan's book included photos which were taken within a few minutes of the attack. These

---

[39] Jim Marrs, *Inside Job: Unmasking the 9/11 Conspiracies*, p. 26, emphasis added. See also his *The Terror Conspiracy: Deception, 9/11, and the Loss of Liberty* (New York: The Disinformation Company, Ltd.), p. 31.

[40] Rady Ananda, "April Gallup versus Dick Cheney: Court Dismisses 9/11 Suit against Bush Officials," *Global Research*, April 29, 2011, www.globalresearch.com.

photos showed an uncharacteristic *lack* of debris on the Pentagon lawn, and a breathtaking lack of collateral damage to the surrounding area. Some of these photos were taken by 24 year old Steve Riskus, who maintained he saw the aircraft—or whatever it was—pass directly over him and hit the Pentagon. He began to take photographs, posting them on the evening of 9/11 on a website.[41] Riskus' photographs were problematic to the official narrative which had begun to emerge by the end of the day, for not only was the Pentagon's nice green lawn almost perfectly intact, but they also "showed one highway lamppost knocked down but not others nearby it within the range of the plane's wing span."[42] The lack of debris and even of any convincing marks on the lawn of the structure was highlighted by the AP photo that Meyssan placed on the front of his book:

The AP- Tom Horan Picture of the Pentagon Attack, Minutes After[43]

---

[41] Jim Marrs, *Inside Job: Unmasking the 9/11 Conspiracies*, p. 27.
[42] Ibid.
[43] Thierry Neyssan, *9/11 The Big Lie*, cover photo, see also pp. 15, 19.

Another photo challenging the emerging Flight 77 narrative was captured by Jim Garamone:

The Jim Garamone Picture[44]

The problem of the lack of debris in initial photographs was compounded by the type of damage that *was* seen in them, and in later photographs that *did* show debris. Jim Marrs puts it this way:

> The Boeing 757 has a normal wingspan of 124 feet, 10 inches. The official version of the Pentagon crash states that a 757 entered the building at a 45-degree angle. This angle would increase the wingspan to 177 feet. Note that the overall height of a 757 is 44 feet, 6 inches and the exterior body width is 12 feet, 6 inches. Yet the hole in the Pentagon cited as the entry point, photographed before the walls collapsed, was only between 15 and 20 feet wide, barely enough to accommodate the width of the craft's body. And the hole height was less (than) two stories or about 20 feet, *less than half the height of the 757*.[45]

---

[44] Thierry Meyssan, *9/11 The Big Lie*, p. 21, citing Jim Garamone, American forces Press Service, www.defenselink.mil/news/Sept2001/ n09112001.200109114.html.
[45] Jim Marrs, *Inside Job: Unmasking the 9/11 Conspiracies*, p. 28, emphasis in the original.

The problem of the debris, or lack thereof, has been a point of contention of many 9/11 researchers, with the lack of debris indicating, to some, that no plane at all crashed, backed up by photos apparently showing this.

The problem here, as in so many other places of 9/11, is that the data is badly contradictory, for the U.S. government published its own photos of debris wreckage, many of which became evidence during the trial of 9/11 conspirator Zacharias Mousaoui:

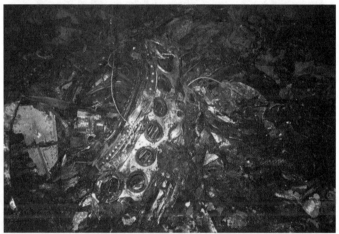

"Aircraft" Wreckage inside the Pentagon?

"Aircraft Wreckage"—Parts of Landing Gear—Inside the Pentagon?

Wreckage outside the Pentagon; note the apparent rotor to the left

Wreckage outside the Pentagon

*e. Back to the Eyewitnesses: A Compilation of Testimonies,
and Some Anomalies and Contradictions*

While many 9/11 researchers view this as conclusive that a commercial airliner did indeed strike the Pentagon, the conclusive case is provided by the fact that the overwhelming number of eyewitnesses did indeed describe a commercial airliner—many of them identifying it as an American Airlines flight—striking the Pentagon. While I personally am inclined to accept this as a *general* description of what happened, the mystery is not entirely dispelled by this appeal either, since when one compiles this evidence together and looks at it whole, a number of striking anomalies and contradictions occur. Eric Bart compiled the eyewitness testimony.[46] The following table summarizes the more important of these testimonies:

Witness	What He or She Saw
Steve Anderson	Hears jet aircraft from his office on the 19th floor of an office in Arlington, Virginia. Sees aircraft flying at treetop level and *sees aircraft's left wing drag along the ground.* Aircraft slams into the Pentagon
Deb Anlauf	Hears the loud roar of an aircraft from her 14th floor room at the Sheraton Motel west of the Navy Annex. Sees the aircraft outside her window and describes it as close enough to touch. Sees it fly into the Pentagon.
Gary Bauer	Driving into Washington DC close to the Pentagon when he and his passenger hear a jet engine. The plane is approaching behind them coming up the highway. It veers and strikes the Pentagon.
Paul Begala	Sees a bright orange fireball explode near the Pentagon. He says a witness informs him that a helicopter had crashed.
Richard Benedetto	Clearly sees an *American Airlines airplane* but did not see the impact. Benedetto, however, describes it as flying not level with, and low to, the ground, but as *heading straight down.*
Staff Sergeant Chris Braman	*Describes the Pentagon lawn as being littered with twisted pieces of aluminum.*

---

[46] Eric Bart, *Pentagon Attack Eyewitness Account Compilation,* at 911research.wtc7.net/pentagon/evidence/witnesses/bart.

Witness	What He or She Saw
Mark Bright	Sees an aircraft from his vantage point manning the guard booth at the main entrance. The plane is flying very low, and hears the aircraft power up just prior to striking the Pentagon.
"Campo"	Is mowing the lawn when he describes an "American Airways" plane, which he thinks is a passenger plane, screaming over his head.
James R. Cissell	Is caught in traffic, sees the blur of a commercial jet flying low and crossing over the highway.
Allen Cleveland	Is travelling on the Metro train to National Airport, sees a jet "heading down" to the Pentagon, which he and others on the train describe as a "silver passenger jet, mid-sized." Shortly after seeing the crash, within 30 seconds, Cleveland also states that he sees a C130 military cargo plane fly over the site, circle the mushroom cloud. Cleveland states his brother, who is also in the area, sees the same C130 following the airliner.
Scott P. Cook	Also sees the C130 plane flying low over the Pentagon.
Dan Creed	Creed and two colleagues from Oracle Software are in a stopped car near the Pentagon, at the Naval Annex, when they see a plane "dive down and level off" at no more than 30 feet above the ground. Creed describes the sound as "screaming" and "going full speed, going full throttle," with its wheels up.
"Damoose"	States that when one left the Pentagon and proceeded along Fort Meyer Drive, one could see "pieces of the plane."
Steve DeChiaro	Running *toward* the smoke from the Pentagon after the strike, DeChiaro sees a lightpost bent in half. More importantly, however, DeChiario testifies to the apparent *absence* of debris: **"My brain could not resolve the fact that it was a plane because it only seemed like a small hole in the building... No Tail. No wings. No nothing."** He also notes that the emergency crews were just arriving. In this DeChiaro is one of the few people whose testimony appears to corroborate the early photographs purporting to show a *lack of debris or damage to the Pentagon lawn.*

Captain Defina	States that the only way to tell that it was an aircraft inside was that pieces of the nose gear could be seen, apparently corroborating the government's later pictures showing what appears to be nose gear inside the building.
Mike Dobbs(Marine Corps)	Dobbs is inside the Pentagon on an upper level, looking out a window. He sees an *American Airlines 737 twin engine airliner* strike the building.
Bobby Eberle	Is riding in his convertible near the Pentagon and looks back and sees a jet airliner flying very low and fast.
Steve Eiden	Sees an airliner flying so low *"You could almost see the people in the windows."* The plane disappears behind a line of tress, "followed by a tall plume of black smoke."
Penny Elgas	Stuck in traffic, she hears a rumble, looks out her driver's side window, and sees the nose of an airplane coming straight for her. Elgas explicitly describes an American Airlines airplane, sees the windows and the color stripes. *Elgas also describes the aircraft as seemingly "floating" and rocking gently, and **slowly gliding** into the Pentagon. "At the point where the fuselage hit the wall, it seemed to simply melt into the building. It appeared as a smoke ring that encircled the fuselage at the point of contact and it seemed to be several feet thick. I later realized that this was probably the rubble of churning bits of the plane and concrete. The churning smoke started at the top of the fuselage to the underside, where the coiling rings crosses over each other and coiled back to the top. Then it started over again—only this next time, I also saw fire, glowing fire in the smoking ring. At that point, the wings disappeared into the Pentagon. And then I saw an explosion and watched the tail of the plane slip into the building."*
Walker Lee Evey	Evey is a construction manager overseeing the Pentagon renovation project. Evey sees an aircraft approaching the Pentagon approximately six feet off the ground. It clips a light pole, car antenna, a construction trailer and emergency generator before striking the building itself.

Witness	What He or She Saw
Walker Lee Evey, continued.	Additionally there are no large debris pieces, only smaller debris pieces. *Evey also states that the resulting fire was so intense that it liquefied window glass, which spilled down the walls and pooled on the ground.*
Mark Faram	Sees small pieces of aircraft debris, no bigger than a half dollar coin, scattered over the highway.
Don Fortunato	Parks his car on the highway after the building is struck, and notes that next to him is a taxicab with its windshield smashed by "pieces of lampposts". Like Faram, Fortunato also sees debris scattered over the highway.
Kat Gaines	Traveling south on Route 101 near the Pentagon, sees a low-flying jetliner striking the tops of telephone poles.
Joe Harrington	Was inside the Pentagon installing new furniture and was called outside to the parking lot moments before the crash to confer about security. Two minutes later, one of his crew pointed "to an American Airlines airplane 20 feet high over Washington Blvd." The aircraft, Harrington states, *"made impact just **before** the wedge,"* i.e., **struck the ground before hitting the building.**
Albert Hemphill	Was meeting in an office of the Navy Annex, with windows and a good view of the Pentagon. He hears the approaching roar of the aircraft, and also *hears it powering up.* He then sees the aircraft fly overhead towards the Pentagon. *He describes this as a Boeing 757 or an Airbus* traveling between 250 and 300 knots, with the "left wing down." The plane was also ***flying at a sharp downward angle of attack.***
Nicholas Holland	Worked on the Pentagon renovation project in the reinforcement of the walls, ***installing a blast wall directly at the place the aircraft struck.***
Tom Hovis	Expressed disbelief that the aircraft did not hit other aircraft close to Reagan National Airport. Also described *the wings coming off the aircraft as it struck the building, leaving a hole a little larger than the width of the fuselage.*
Will Jarvis	Working inside the Pentagon, smells aviation fuel.

Witness	What He or She Saw
Will Jarvis, continued.	When leaving the building however, *sees no tail or wing debris, saying "there was just nothing left* and describes seeing "little bits of silver falling from the sky."
Representative Mark Steven Kirk (R-Illinois)	Went to the Pentagon after learning two friends had perished there. He notes the smell of aviation fuel
Charles H. Krohn	Krohn, the US Army's Deputy Chief of Public Affairs, states *one of the aircraft's engines somehow ricocheted out of the building. People exiting the Pentagon hear **a loud secondary explosion approximately ten minutes after the strike.***
William LaGasse	Sees the aircraft approximately 80 feet above the ground, traveling 400 miles per hour, in full flight trim: the landing gear and *flaps are not down.* LaGasse also states he is close enough to see the passenger windows, and **states that the blinds are down.**
Captain Lincoln Liebner, US Army	Racing to the Pentagon in his truck after watching the south tower of the World Trade Center being struck on television, Liebner sees a "large American Airliner passenger jet coming in fast and low". As he came to the entrance of the building, he turned as saw the aircraft *diving* toward the building, and states "I was close enough that *I could see through the windows of the airplane.*" It goes into the building "like a toy into a birthday cake."
"M.K."	Hears a low flying plane in his office, looks out the window, and sees it strike the Pentagon. "..it was in the air one moment and in the building the next."
David Marra	Is traveling on I-395 west of the Pentagon when he sees an American Airlines set coming in, its wings wobbling, about 50 feet above the ground with "the throttle completely floored." One wing **clips the ground near the helicopter pad, and the plane cartwheeled into the Pentagon."**
Lt. Col.(Ret.) Tom McClain(No service branch mentioned)	Sees remains of the engines in the North parking lot, and **melted aluminum** and other debris.

Witness	What He or She Saw
Elaine McCusker	Crossing the 14th Street bridge into Washington DC, she looks up, and sees "a very low-flying American Airlines plane" that was accelerating.
Fr. Stephen McGraw, St. Anthony Parish, Falls Church, VA	Hears the aircraft right above his car, which he estimates passed about 20 feet above his car, clipping a light pole just before it reached him. He hears an explosion, feels the impact, and the resulting fireball.
Lt. Col. Kenneth McClellan, Pentagon Spokeman (No Service branch named)	Confirms the reports of a C130 military cargo aircraft that was instructed by air traffic controllers to spot Flight 77 and "let us know where it is going." After 9/11, all reports of the C130 were classified by the Air National Guard.
Terry Mitchell	*Sees a debris pile, but states it is all metal from the Pentagon itself, and none of it was from an aircraft.*
Terry Morin	Was a former United States Marine Corps aviator, and working as a contractor in the old Navy Annex. He hears a very loud rumbling and seconds later sees what he describes as a silver body with red and blue stripes on the fuselage, which he believes to be a Boeing 737 American Airlines airliner, flying between 350-400 knots. Morin states explicitly that the aircraft **did _not_ strike the ground first or "skip" into the building.**
Vin Narayanan	Is locked in a traffic jam alongside the Pentagon when he looks up and sees "an American Airlines jet flying right at me." The jet flies overhead, clearing his car at an estimated 25 feet. He described the winders as being dark, and the tail of the aircraft clipping the overhanging exit sign. The aircraft is flying "at a ferocious speed." Additionally, he states that as the aircraft slams into the Pentagon, that "**the Pentagon wall held up like a champ. It barely budged as the nose of the plane curled upwards and crumpled before exploding into a massive fireball.** *The People who built that wall should be proud. Its ability to withstand the initial impact of the jet probably saved thousands of lives."*
John O'Keefe	Was traveling in his car when he sees a silver

	plane which he recognizes as an American Airlines jetliner. He also sees the C130 following it, which executes a turn over the Pentagon.
Mary Ann Owens	A journalist with Gannett News Service, Owens was driving alongside the Pentagon, when she hears the aircraft engines screaming. Looking up, she can only see the underside of the craft. She described its angle as so sharp, and its altitude as being 50 feet, and thinks the craft will not make it as far as the Pentagon. The wings are wobbling. She sees *the left wing scrap the ground near the helipad, and then the nose strikes the Pentagon.*
Steve Patterson	Was in his apartment in Pentagon City on the 14th floor, and sees a "silver commuter jet" fly past his window about 150 yards in the distance, and about 20 feet off the ground. Because it was flying so fast he could not see any writing, but *describes a much smaller aircraft, one only holding about 8-12 people.*
Don Perkal	Was in his office in the Pentagon, where he worked as Deputy General Counsel for Washington Headquarters Services of the Office of the Secretary of Defense. He heads people shouting in the corridor **that a bomb had gone off, and he smells the odor of cordite. "Then I knew explosives had been set off somewhere."**
Christine Peterson	Was stopped in traffic next to the helipad at the Pentagon, and looked out her left window and sees an airplane flying so low she thinks it will hit her car. As it passes over her car, *it shakes.*
Frank Probst	A former US Army officer, was working on the renovation project, and claimed he was walking outside to attend a meeting at the parking lot, when he sees flight 77 approaching. Its wings sheer off light poles, and the flight is so low Probest thinks he is going to die. Probest claims he dives to his right, and the aircraft's engine passes by him about six feet away. The starboard engine hits a low cement wall and blows apart, "just vaporizing."
Lt. Willis Roberts, U.S. Army	As part of the rescue team, Roberts states that the heat inside the Pentagon wedge where the strike occurs is about *"3,000 degrees inside."*
Jack Singleton	An electrical contractor, was outside the building,

	and saw the aircraft approaching, with its left wing down.
"Skarlet"	Webmaster for punkprincess.com, sees "a huge jet. Then it was gone." She goes on to state ***"Buildings don't eat planes. That plane, it just vanished. There should have been parts on the ground. It should have rained parts on my care. The airplane didn't crash. Where are the parts? … There was a plane. It didn't go over the building. It went into the building…. I want to see footage of the crash. I want to make it make sense. I want to know why there's this gap in my memory, this gap that makes it seem as though the plane simply became invisible and banked up at the very last minute…"***
Joel Sucherman	Was multimedia editor for USAToday.com, and states that he saw a large plane about 20 feet off the ground, flying quickly *but not at a steep angle, and "almost like a heat-seeking missile (that) was locked onto its target and staying dead on course."*
Jim Sutherland	Was a mortgage broker on his way to the Pentagon when he sees a white 737 twin-engine plane, flying approximately 50 feet above ground, striking the building.
Tony Terronez	Traveling away from the Pentagon near the helipad, he hears a loud screech and looks into his rearview mirror, and sees the side of the Pentagon explode. He hears the "pitter-patter of pebbles and concrete" striking his car. At the time, Terronez thinks he has seen *a missile strike.* As he drove frantically away from the building, he sees "tons of stuff on the ground, big pieces of metal, concrete, everything…and there was this huge piece of something—I mean it was big, it looked like a piece of an engine or something—in the road."
Tim Timmerman	A pilot, Timmerman was looking out of his 16th story apartment window hearing a jet that was too loud. He sees the aircraft travel down interstate 395, fly close to the Sheraton Hotel, and then hears the plane throttling up. The aircraft disappears momentarily behind a building, reemerges, and ***strikes the ground, as he sees the wings fly forward.***

Mike Walter	A reporter for *USA Today*, was stuck in northbound traffic on route 27 when he saw an American Airlines jet, flying low "like a cruise missile with wings", and slamming into the Pentagon.

This list is significant, for it clearly shows that *most* witnesses *do* describe seeing a plane, and many describe seeing *debris*, and in some cases, this is debris from an aircraft of some sort. Many witnesses are also clear that they saw a large commercial airliner, and some specify that it was an American Airlines airliner.

But here, agreements stop and problems multiply, for *some* witnesses describe the flight apparently coming in at a sharp angle; others describe the flight as being in cruising trim, with landing gear up and flaps not down, which some pilots have disputed as even being possible at such low altitude. This highlights a further difficulty, for most of the witnesses describe the aircraft as flying so low that it should be expected that they would have also described at least *some* effects from the wash of the aircraft's powerful engines shaking their cars, yet, only one witness describes this. To compound matters, some witnesses describe the left wing (or *a* wing) of the aircraft striking the ground, and one witness describes the aircraft as *cartwheeling* into the Pentagon, while yet another describes the reinforced walls of the structure holding up very well against the impact, while the nose of the craft crumples upward. However, another witness, a trained pilot, describes the aircraft as impacting the ground *outside* the Pentagon, dissipating most of its energy *prior* to impact with the building.

Some workers inside and outside the building described the odor of aviation fuel with its distinct kerosene smell, while one important witness inside the structure described the smell of *cordite*, i.e., of an actual military grade explosive, while yet another rescue worker described intense heat of around 3,000 degrees!

And finally, one witness—"Skarlet"—even describes having a gap in her memory!

All of this means one is in the presence of a genuine mystery that transcends any simplistic explanation. Airplanes, when impacting and exploding, do not smell like cordite. And they leave at least *some* recognizable debris. But only missiles, or demolitions explosives or perhaps even ordnance of some sort, will leave a smell resembling "cordite." These are important points, for many in the 9/11 truth community, responding to the earliest research and the photos purporting to show a lack of debris, have offered the theory that Flight 77 did not cause the damage to the Pentagon, but that a missile did.

Adding fuel to *this* theory is Secretary of Defense Donald Rumsfeld's statement to *Parade* magazine, during an interview on October 12, 2001; Rumsfeld referred to "the missile used to damage this building." As David Ray Griffin quips, "Was this a revealing slip?"[47] If it was, then how does one account for the photographs of apparent aircraft debris used in Zacharias Mousaoui's trial, which included what was apparently a compressor from a jet engine? This, however, as Webster Tarpley notes, may have been that of an A3 Skywarrior.[48]

Obviously, from this survey, it is evident that there are serious problems, even if one grants that Flight 77 *was* the "missile" referred to by Secretary of Defense Rumsfeld in his *Parade* interview. Nor can these dilemmas—was there a plane, wasn't there a plane, what kind of plane was it, &c., - be easily resolved without recourse to the various security camera tapes. These, of course, were confiscated by the FBI minutes after the crash, and they were not released by the 9/11 Commission.[49] The flight data recorders and cockpit voice recorders have never been released, "under the claim that they were rendered inoperable by the fire"[50] which resulted after the crash, a claim that, on the face of it, is ridiculous, since the "black boxes" are *designed* to withstand crashes.

What *has* been released is the now famous video tape from a Pentagon guard house, where any clear picture of what struck the building is impossible to determine. Some maintain frames have been removed. The release of this video spurred speculations that what had struck the Pentagon was not an airliner, but a much smaller craft, possibly even a cruise missile.[51] Advocates of this theory also point out that the alleged pilot of Flight 77, Hani Hanjour, executed a descending spiral turn that even experienced pilots would find difficult. Supposedly, Hanjour learned this at flight schools only training in Cessnas and Piper Cubs, and when this story failed to gain traction by dint of its obvious nonsensical nature, the narrative was quickly adjusted to maintain that in addition flight school training, Hanjour and the other hijackers trained on flight simulators, an assertion that Stan Goff (a critic of the official narrative of 9/11) stated was "like saying you prepared your

---

[47] David Ray Griffin, *The New Pearl Harbor*, p. 48.
[48] Webster Griffin Tarpley, *9/11 Synthetic Terror: Made in USA*, fifth ed, p. 255.
[49] Ibid., p. 256.
[50] Ibid., p. 257
[51] Ibid. Most 9/11 researchers believe that this implicates the FBI in an on-going cover-up, but it is equally possible that the release of this provocative tape was an attempt to *combat* the cover-up, by releasing footage which, on its face, seems to contradict the official narrative.

teenager for her first drive on I-40 at rush hour by buying her a video driving game."[52] Worse, Hanjour's flight instructors viewed him as "an especially incompetent" pilot.[53]

Three basic theories have been advanced to handle these difficulties: (1) What struck the Pentagon was not a commercial airliner, but a smaller aircraft, perhaps a drone or a missile, (2) what struck the Pentagon *was* Flight 77 itself, though it was under remote control and not under the control of Hanjour at all. Some advocates of this theory point to the presence of the C130 as being perhaps the aircraft *controlling* Flight 77; and (3) whatever *did* hit the Pentagon may have been accompanied by simultaneous detonations of munitions or demolition changes in the building itself.

Whichever of these theories one adopts, however, they all have two very important things in common. The first, and most obvious, is that they all reject the official narrative. The second, and much more important one, is that regardless of what struck the Pentagon, *they all assume that there is a second level—a rogue network—executing the attack as an inside job.* In this instance, the Pentagon component of the 9/11 operation is somewhat the reverse of the World Trade Center-Twin Towers component, for the important question is not so much the mechanism, the "means" or "murder weapon" itself, but the *motivation.*

Why was the Pentagon struck in a relatively *evacuated* part of the structure, one moreover that had recently been renovated and its walls reinforced, when terrorists would presumably strike at a part of the Pentagon that was a more target rich environment where there were not only *more* people, but higher value targets, such as the Offices of the Secretary of Defense, the Joint Chiefs of Staff? And why attempt such a difficult maneuver in any case, a maneuver that risked hitting the ground—as some witnesses reported—and hence jeopardize the operation? One of the most provocative examinations of this question is given by Kevin Robert Ryan in an important, and unjustly neglected, book of 9/11 research, *Another Nineteen: Investigating Legitimate 9/11 Suspects.*

4. Kevin Robert Ryan and the Pentagon Renovation Problem

Ryan begins by noting both his methodology, and the questions posed both by the official narratives of 9/11, and by the results of 9/11

---

[52] David Ray Griffin, *The New Pearl Harbor*, p. 41, citing Stan Goff, "the So-Called Evidence is a Farce," Narco News #14, October 10, 2001, www. Narconews.com.
[53] Ibid., p. 41.

truth community research. It is essential to cite him in his own words and at length, for the issues are crucial to the thesis of this book that there were *three* levels involved in the operation, not just two, an insiders' layer, and an "insiders' insiders" layer:

> Considering means, motive, and opportunity might allow us to propose a possible insider conspiracy while maintaining much of the official account as well.

In other words, what Ryan is dealing with in his reconstruction of events at the Pentagon is what we have been calling "level two." Continuing:

> A few of the more compelling unanswered questions are as follows.

1. How could American Airlines Flight 77 have hit the building as it did, considering that the evidence shows the alleged hijacker pilot, Hani Hanjour, was a very poor pilot?
2. Why did the aircraft make a 330-degree turn just minutes before hitting the building?
3. Why did the aircraft hit the least occupied one-fifth of the building that was the focus of a renovation plan and how was it that the construction in that exact spot just happened to be for the purpose of minimizing the damage from a terrorist explosion?
4. *Why was the company that performed the renovation work, just for that one-fifth of the building, immediately hired in a no bid contract to clean up the damage and reconstruct that area of the building?*(Note: The same company was also immediately hired to clean up the WTC site within hours of the destruction there.)
5. What can explain the damage to the building and the aircraft debris or lack thereof?
6. Why were the tapes from the surveillance videos in the area immediately confiscated by the FBI and never released?

> These questions should be considered along with the fact that U.S. military and "Homeland Security" expenditures since the 9/11 attacks have totaled approximately $8 trillion. This paints a picture that calls for an in-depth investigation into the people running the Pentagon, to see if they might have had the motivation and ability to plan and execute the attack.
>
> What happened during the Pentagon renovation project should be of great interest. A preliminary investigation raises the possibility that the work done during that time could have provided the cover for an effective insider conspiracy. We should

examine the people involved in planning the renovation project in order to begin answering the question of who might have benefited from the attack.[54]

It is precisely at the point of the renovation, the point of attack at the Pentagon on 9/11, that one sees a pattern emerge.

The Pentagon renovation was begun during the Administration of President G.H.W. Bush, under then Secretary of Defense Dick Cheney.[55] As planning for the renovation proceeded, in order to make the construction and renovation more secure, ownership of the massive building was transferred from the General Services Administration directly to the Department of Defense.[56]

In the earliest stages of the renovation, direct oversight of the project was by the Deputy Secretary of Defense John Deutch, whose earlier career had included stints in the Department of Energy, and the defense contractor, Mitre Corporation. Ryan also observes that in 1999, when Deutch was with Mitre Corporation, that the corporation was involved with PTech, another company which was looking at the systems compatibility and inoperability issues of coordination between the Federal Aviation Administration, the North American Air Defense Command (NORAD), and the US Air Force, in cases of emergency. It was PTech software that was used to coordinate the FAA, NORAD, and Secret Service on 9/11.[57]

But there is another Deutch connection to the corporations that form a part of the USA's "military-industrial complex," and this connection, in this author's opinion, may be one of the Rosetta stones of the 9/11 events that indicates a potential "third level" player; Duetch, notes Ryan, was also connected to the well-known, and secretive, Science Applications International Corporation, or SAIC.[58] Here one must pause to take a brief detour into the subject of SAIC, former NSA director Admiral Bobby Inman, and UFOs.

---

[54] Kevin Robert Ryan, *Another Nineteen: Investigating Legitimate 9/11 Suspects*, pp. 152-153, emphasis added.

[55] Ibid., p. 153.

[56] Ibid., p. 154,

[57] Ibid.

[58] Ibid.

The Puzzles at the Pentagon and Pennsylvania

a. A Brief Foray into SAIC, Admiral Bobby Inman, and UFOs

One of the most bizarre twists in the tangle of 9/11 is precisely the presence of SAIC, Science Applications International Corporation, and its relationship to the UFO question. SAIC is not the only corporation with "weird technological interests" among those companies represented in the 9/11 event.

SAIC's entry into this high strangeness is an interview purportedly conducted by Bob Oechsler, a former NASA technician and UFO researcher, and Admiral Bobby Ray Inman, a former director of the National Security Agency and of the Office of Naval Intelligence, a former Deputy Director of the CIA, and at one point, President of the SAIC corporation, whose goal, as its name suggests, is the practical application of science and technology, just the sort of corporation some believe would be involved in advanced black technology projects, including the reverse engineering of UFOs and the possible weaponization of their technologies.

Inman's resume is that of the consummate military-intelligence "insider" of the highest level. In 1974 Inman, a rear admiral, became director of the Office of Naval Intelligence (ONI)—an agency that will figure prominently in the 9/11 operation—and remained at this post until 1976 when he was promoted to vice admiral. Inman then was director of the Defense Intelligence Agency (DIA) for a year, whence he moved to the National Security Agency as its Director until 1981, when he was again promoted to full admiral and became a deputy director of the Central Intelligence Agency (CIA), where he remained until his ostensible retirement from all government service in 1982. In 1990 he became a member of President G.H.W. Bush's Foreign Intelligence Advisory Board.[59]

Oechsler himself had his own strange connections, joining the U.S. Air Force in 1968, eventually winding up at Wright Patterson Air Force Base in Dayton, Ohio, where he remained until 1972. Wright Patterson is, of course, the air force base rumored in ufology to be the home of a number of "crashed and retrieved" UFOs and the bodies of their occupants, and *was* the home to a number of postwar Operation Paperclip Nazi scientists and engineers.

In any case, on May 13, 1988, Oechsler, at the behest of British UFO researcher Timothy Goode, approached Admiral Inman at the ground-breaking ceremony for the NSA's supercomputer facility for the

---

[59] Timothy Goode, *Alien Contact: Top Secret UFO Files Revealed* (New York: William Morrow, 1993), p. 215.

Institute of Defense Analysis. Oechsler approached Inman, gave him his business card, and later made contact by phone with Inman and conducted the following interview:

> **Oechsler**: Yes, Thank you very much for returning my call.
> **Inman:** You're most welcome.
> **Oechsler:** Do you remember who I am?
> **Inman:** Unfortunately I do not, I apologize.
> **Oechsler:** OK, well we met at the University of Science, University of Maryland Science and Technology ...
> **Inman:** I do pull out, now, thank you.
> **Oechsler:** I wanted to, for one thing, on behalf of myself I was looking for some guidance that I hoped you might be able to afford me ...
> **Inman:** OK.
> **Oechsler:** ... in giving me some kind of direction in how I can assist in this project. I've been spending a great deal of time researching the phenomenon and technologically I think I might have some very interesting things to offer ...
> **Inman:** Uh huh.
> **Oechsler:** ... Probably not nearly as much as it was, what you probably already know. But I certainly would like to get some guidance in a number of different areas. It's probably a situation where I would like to at some point get together with you, and get an overview of what direction I might take in which I might be able to help in. On behalf of Admiral Lord Hill-Norton and Mr. Good (sic et passim), the best I can do there is I have no idea what the level of security crossing countries happens to be. And I really don't want to get too much involved in that end of it, I'll leave that to your discretion.
> **Inman:** What is Peter Hill-Norton doing now?

At this juncture, it is worth nothing that (1) Inman indicates he knows British Admiral Peter Hill-Norton, and (2) that Hill-Norton in turn was greatly interested in the subject of UFOs. In other words, the likelihood is that Inman, especially given his intelligence background, knows what the real subject of Oechsler's phone call is concerned with:

> **Oechsler:** What is he doing right now?
> **Inman:** Yeah.
> **Oechsler:** As far as I know he is working in the background of things. He has worked extensively with Timothy Good in a publication he has put out, *Above Top Secret,* which you may or may not be aware of, out by William Morrow out of New York.
> **Inman:** I am not aware of it.

Again, we must pause to note that Goode's book, *Above Top Secret*, about the subject of UFOs, had been published, and that Inman professes not to know the work.

Oechsler: OK, in any case he is working, they are more or less working together, Timothy Good as a consultant. Admiral Lord Hill-Norton is, as the way he's expressed it to me, quite furious with his inability to gain knowledge on the issues.

Inman: (Muffled acknowledgement)

Oechsler: And he in fact sent Timothy Good here on a tour hoping to find out more information. There was a conference in Las Vegas at the end of June (and) the first couple days of July, where he had hoped to pick up some contact information. And I had suggested to him that the only individual I knew that possibly would be able to help him, if it was indeed possible to gain any information across country boundaries would be through you. And I suggested that that contact be made.

Inman: What is the general area of interest?

Oechsler: Two things, one, it's my feeling from my research that there is a dichotomy of sorts, one in which there seems to be an indoctrination program to educate the public to the realities that are involved here. The other must be a problem relating to security measures and the need to know level. I have the ability to control the influence and understanding and acceptability of a great, great mass of the public. I have a nation-wide radio broadcast, regular radio broadcast on the subject matter. I'm well written amongst all of the publications. I am connected with all the major organizations. I've investigated, I spent 18 months investigating, including field investigations involving the Gulf Breeze situation. I know all the internals on that. And I have focused a great deal on the technological end of the technologies, and I've studied a great deal of the things that have been going wrong along in the Chesapeake Bay, in connection with the Electromagnetic Continuity Analysis Center and with the EMP projects.

Inman: All of those are areas in which I am vastly out of date. When I made the decision to retire seven years ago, I made a conscious decision to sever ongoing ties with the U.S. Intelligence Community. I have had some exposure on limited occasions, to some areas of activity over the succeeding seven years when I did the Embassy Security Survey as a consultant to the Defense Science Board. But overwhelmingly my efforts in these seven years have been focused on industrial competitiveness ...

Oechsler: Right.

Inman: ... *on the application of science and technology in the commercial world.*

Oechsler: I am aware of that.

Inman: *So for many of the things, at least as I sort of infer from the conversation of the interest of Mr. Goode and Peter Hill-Norton, they are areas where while I had some expertise,* it's now, you know, seven years old.

Note that at this juncture of the conversation, Inman professes knowledge of the subject matter of interest for Hill-Norton and Goode, namely, UFOs, and that "they are areas" where he had "some expertise."

Oechsler: I see.

Inman: And the pace at which things move in that field, the odds of my being accurate are increasingly remote, in understanding those things.

Observe now that Inman is acknowledging that things in the field of interest of Hill-Norton and Goode—again, meaning UFOs—"move quickly."

Oechsler: Is it your understanding that there is a cultural dialogue going on, (long pause) today?

Inman: Well I guess I'd have to ask with whom? Between what parties?

Oechsler: Well, between any of the parties that presumably are behind the technology in the crafts.

Inman: I honestly don't know. Have no exposure at all. So I haven't a clue whether there are any ongoing dialogues or not. I'm trying to think who there in the Washington area that is at least much closer to the issues that might be able to at least give you some guidance.

Oechsler: That's what I am looking for. I'm not looking to step on any toes. I think I have some things to offer and I would like to participate. And to be frank with you, you are essentially the only one I would feel safe in getting guidance from at this point...

Inman: Uh huh.

Oechsler: ... Based on the more I know...

Inman: Yeah

Oechsler:... the more concerned I become with how I should handle what I know.

Inman: The Deputy Director for Science and Technology at CIA is named Everett Hineman. He is in fact getting ready to retire in the very near future. That may make him somewhat more willing to have dialogues than he otherwise would have had. When I knew him in the period seven to ten years ago, he was a person of very substantial integrity and just good common sense. So as a place to start he would clearly be high on the list. In the retired community of those who nonetheless were exposed to the intelligence business and stayed reasonably close to it, *there is a retired Rear Admiral, a former director of Naval Intelligence, named Sumner Shapiro*, who has been a Vice President of BDM. I think he just retired.

Oechsler: VDM?

Inman: BDM. It's a corporation there in the McLean area. His level of competence again is very high, his integrity is very high. Whether he has any knowledge in the areas you are working on I don't have a clue, because I don't have any ongoing dialogue with him. But those are at least two thoughts for you that are there in the area where you are located. And who have a prospect of still having some currency. I don't know that they do. In my case I don't have any.

Oechsler: Do you anticipate that any of the recovered vehicles would ever become available for technological research? Outside of the military circles.

Inman: Again, I honestly don't know. Ten years ago the answer would have been no. Whether as time has evolved they are beginning to become more open on it there's a possibility. Again, Mr. Hineman probably would be the best person to put that kind of question to.

Oechsler: OK.

Inman: Well good luck to you.

Oechsler: OK, and also Louis Cabot has become quite interested in ...

Inman: Good.

Oechsler: ... some of my findings, so you may hear from him.

Inman: OK, he's a good man.

Oechsler: OK.

Inman: Thank you.

Oechsler: Very good, thank you for calling.

Inman: Bye.

Oechsler: Bye-bye."[60]

Timothy Goode states that after this interview, Oechsler eventually met with Rear Admiral Sumner Shapiro, as suggested by Inman. Shapiro, like Inman, had connections to the Office of Naval Intelligence, having worked as its Deputy Assistant Chief of Staff at its London branch from 1967 to 1969, and then beginning in 1976, as Deputy Director for ONI, becoming its Director from 1978 to 1982.[61] Shapiro allegedly told Oechsler that UFOs had been retrieved, and that they were built in a

---

[60] "Exclusive Bob Oechsler Interview with Admiral Bobby Inman, www.theoutpostforum,.com/tof/showthread.php?1772-Exclusive-Bob-Oechsler-Interview, all emphases added.

[61] Timothy Goode, *Alien Contact: Top Secret UFO Files Revealed,* p. 221.

modular fashion requiring them to be disassembled and reassembled in a particular order.[62]

In any case, what now has emerged, if one takes the Oechsler-Inman interview at face value, is that SAIC, the corporation heavily involved in the Pentagon renovations on 9/11, is also connected to Admiral Bobby Inman, who had deep connections to American intelligence in virtually all its major aspects, to the UFO problem, as is evident from the interview, and who served as a President of SAIC. *It is also worth noting that until 2013, SAIC was an entirely employee-owned corporation, and thus free of most forms of regulatory scrutiny. Additionally, it is deeply connected to the Defense Advance Research Projects Agency, and is even involved in the voting machine business!*[63]

Admiral Bobby Ray Inman, Official CIA Photograph as Deputy Director, CIA

As noted, the SAIC corporation's "exotic technology" interests will figure again in our investigations, but for the moment, we may now return to Kevin Robert Ryan's investigation of the Pentagon attack and its relationship to the Pentagon renovation.

---

[62] Ibid., p. 222.
[63] See "Admiral Bobby Ray Inman", at Democratic Underground.com

5. White, Hamre, and More Mitre and SAIC Corporation Connections

Ryan notes that the Pentagon renovation project was overseen by the office of the Deputy Secretary of Defense, and after the departure of John Deutch, this was held by John White, a former Marine Corps officer, who later joined Deutch and Global technology Partners, "an exclusive affiliate of Rothschild North America."[64] The project was then "turned over to White's successor, John J. Hamre" in 1997. Hamre after leaving the office of the Deputy Secretary of Defense, Hamre became a director for Mitre corporation and SAIC.[65]

6. The Renovation Project and Walker Lee Evey:
Satellites, Boeing, and Saudis

In the aftermath of the Oklahoma City Bombing, the Pentagon renovation project mandated five changes to the structure of the building: firstly, the outer walls were to be reinforced with steel, and secondly, these walls were in turn to be backed with Kevlar "to minimize shrapnel effect." Thirdly, blast-resistant windows were to be installed along with, fourthly, the addition of fire-doors and an automatic sprinkler system, and fifthly and finally, the addition of a building-wide operations and control center.[66]

During his tenure as Deputy Secretary of Defense, Hamre also created an entirely new position to deal with the renovation, the Pentagon Renovation Program Manager, which was given to Walker Lee Evey, a man with little experience in construction management, but who had been involved in an Air Force black projects program involving satellite communications that would allow them to communicate directly with each other without a ground station. "Theoretically," notes Ryan, this project "could have been used on 9/11 to communicate changes to the flight plans of the hijacked aircraft."[67] Ryan also notes that at the time of the 9/11 attacks, the American aerospace and defense corporation Boeing—whose aircraft were used in the attacks themselves—was involved with project Peace Shield, a joint project with the Saudi government for an airspace control system.[68]

---

[64] Kevin Robert Ryan, *Another Nineteen: Investigating Legitimate 9/11 Suspects*, pp. 154-155.
[65] Ibid., p. 155.
[66] Ibid., p. 155-156.
[67] Ibid., p. 156.
[68] Kevin Robert Ryan, *Another Nineteen: Investigating Legitimate 9/11 Suspects*, p. 156.

On the day of the 9/11 attack, the *only* area of the Pentagon where the renovation project had been completed was precisely the area where Flight 77 allegedly struck.[69] The actual construction was handled by the British construction firm AMEX, a firm that also had close ties to the giant Saudi oil company Aramco. It was AMEX that was hired not only to clean up the damage at the Pentagon and to reconstruct the stricken wedge of the building, but also the damage at Ground Zero of the World Trade Center.[70]

7. Pentagon Witness Frank Probst Again:
Remote Piloting Systems and the Presence of Level Two at the Pentagon

As was noted previously in this chapter, Frank Probst was one of the *closest* eyewitnesses to the attack on the Pentagon, claiming to have been outside and to have lunged away from the approaching flight to avoid being struck.[71] Probst, it will be recalled, claimed that one of the airplane's engines passed within a mere six feet of him. Ryan notes the problem that was pointed out earlier: "It is amazing," he says, "given this account, that Probst wes not injured by the turbulence from the wake of the aircraft. Such aircraft wakes are known to be highly dangerous."[72] Indeed, the wakes from large commercial airliners can easily toss cars several feet, let alone a human being.

According to Probst's own story, he was inside the Pentagon mere minutes before Flight 77 struck, commenting on the attacks on the World Trade Center to co-workers that the Pentagon itself would be a good target.[73] He then left the building to go outside to check equipment in a construction trailer. "His presence in the building just before it hit, then in the construction trailer a few minutes later, and then just below the aircraft as it impacted the building, does not seem to be

---

[69] Ibid., p. 159.

[70] Ibid., pp. 159-160. Yet another strange connection of AMEX was the head of a corporate subsidiary of the AGRA Corporation in Toronto. The head of this office was one Peter Janson, who also was the CEO of the Swiss-Swedish engineering firm ABB, which also numbered Donald Rumsfeld as one of its directors during the 9/11 attacks. ***ABB's corporate predecessor was the Swedish firm of ASEA, which included directors Gerhard Cromme of the Thyssen-Krupp combine, and Jürgen Dormann, a CEO of the German chemicals firm Hoechst, one of the parent, and successor, companies comprising the I.G. Farben cartel.*** (p. 160)

[71] Ibid., op. 162.

[72] Ibid., p. 163.

[73] Kevin Robert Ryan, *Another Nineteen: Investigating Legitimate 9/11 Suspects*, p. 163.

accidental."[74] Further raising the suspicion meter into the red zone, Probst is one of only four Pentagon witnesses that the Department of Justice on whom it put severe restrictions for interviews. Probst could only be interviewed with five days' warning and only under the conditions that a Department of Justice attorney be present. Additionally, no records of any kind could be made or kept.[75]

One possibility that we have noted as an explanation for the strange descending spiral of Flight 77 is remote piloting systems. There were two such systems available at the time, one, the Wide Area Augmentation System (WAAS), allowed aircraft to navigate on autopilot, or via remote control. These systems were developed by Boeing and Raytheon during the 1990s.[76] For close maneuver and remote landing control, the Joint Precision Approach and Landing System (JPALS), was developed by Raytheon, and designed to be an all-weather, unjammable system. This system required a transmitter antenna about two times the height of a human being, and a receiver "the size of a camera tripod."[77]

Ryan thus proposes an intriguing scenario, one coupling the chronological account of Flight 77, with Probst's own movement to the outside construction trailer to check on equipment, which may have been final adjustments in a JPALS system. This, coupled with the use of explosives inside the building rigged to blow at the moment of impact, might account for why so little of the plane remained in the form of debris, and why it appeared to simply "melt" into the building.[78]

Why is this scenario important?

Because when one adds up all that has preceded—the conflicting eyewitness accounts suggesting data obfuscation, the smell of "cordite", the selection of a sparsely populated part of the building rather than high value targets on the opposite side of the building—*plus the fact that Flight 77 struck at the new "renovated" offices of the Office of Naval Investigations*—suggests that the real motivation for the strike at that precise place had nothing to do with terrorism, and everything to do with something else, utilizing technologies in the form of missiles or remotely guided aircraft and possibly explosives, *that only level two would have had access to.*[79]

---

74 Ibid., p. 164.
75 Ibid., p. 164.
76 Ibid., p. 167.
77 Ibid., p. 168.
78 Ibid., pp. 168-171.
79 It is worth noting that Jim Marrs states that the German national airline, *Lufthansa* was well aware of remote electronic capture of airplanes, and had stripped the flight control systems out of its American-built airliners in the early

The hypothesis of remote controlled aircraft raises the possibility that the hijackers may have simply thought they were part of a drill. As was seen, Atta himself has all the earmarks of an intelligence operative, not a terrorist. Additionally, Jay Kolar points out that several pilots, including a 35 year pilot veteran of PanAm and United Airlines, Russ Wittenberg, maintain that Flight 77's Boeing 757 simply could not have performed the spiraling descending turn ascribed to it.[80] Wittenberg maintains that such a maneuver would have stalled the aircraft. Wittenberg also challenged air traffic controller O'Brien's assertions that she saw the aircraft execute such a maneuver on her radar, an impossibility, since Flight 77s transponder had been turned off.[81] Another possibility here, however, is that O'Brien saw exactly what she claimed to have seen, since *insertion of false radar blips on radar screens was a part of the hijacking "Amalgam Virgo drill on 9/11.* [82]

8. The Problem of Delta Flight 1989:
Cleveland Airport, Delta 1989, and Flights 77 and 93

Before one can conclusively reject the idea that what struck the Pentagon was a missile, or that Flight 93 indeed was shot down in Pennsylvania, one has to contend with the very different theory of an independent German journalist writing under the pseudonym Woody Box, who investigated Delta Flight 1989, thought to be a *fifth* hijacked aircraft during 9/11. "Box" based his theory on Internet reports that were circulated on 9/11, as well as on articles from the *Akron (Ohio) Beacon Journal,* and the *Cleveland Plain Dealer* from September 11th and 12th, 2001.[83]

"Box" began by noting that Cleveland Airport was evacuated at 10:00 AM, and that this "had to do with the rumors that a hijacked plane was going to land."[84] After the emergency landing of this aircraft, Cleveland Mayor Michael White held a televised press conference at 11:00 AM, during which he indicated the plane had been hijacked and that there may have been a bomb on board. However, during the course

---

1990s. See Jim Marrs, *The Terror Conspiracy: Deception, 9/11, and the Loss of Liberty,* p. 135.

[80] Jay Kolar, "What We Now Know about the Alleged 9-11 Hijackers," in Paul Zaembka, ed., *The Hidden History of 9-11,* 3-44, p. 19.

[81] Ibid., p. 20.

[82] Ibid., pp. 20-21.

[83] Michael Ruppert, *Crossing the Rubicon: The Decline of the American Empire at the End of the Age of Oil,* p. 587.

[84] Ibid.

of the day, the story changed, for in the very middle of the press conference, he informed the audience that the flight that had made an emergency landing at Cleveland Airport had *not* been hijacked. Later that day, White stated no bomb had been found on the airplane.[85]

"Box" then goes on to state that five parameters will be examined for the Cleveland Airport component of the 9/11 story:

> 1. The moment of landing;
> 2. The begin (sic) of the evacuation of the passengers;
> 3. The number of passengers;
> 4. The place the passengers were interviewed after the evacuation;
> 5. The exact location of the grounded plane.
>
> We will see that there are two different sets of data for every parameter, suggesting that we are dealing with two different planes.[86]

With this in hand, "Box" notes that the Associated Press and the two Ohio newspapers reported a landing at the Cleveland airport at 10:45 AM. But Delta Airlines operations stated that one of its planes had landed at 10:10 AM, and Cleveland firefighters, dispatched to the airport, indicated a landing prior to 10:30.

Because Delta had not lost track of its own flight, "Box" maintains that the 10:10 landing was in fact Delta flight 1989, and this meant that "by definition" the landing at 10:45 AM was another flight, "Flight X."[87] Adding to the possibility that there was an unknown flight "X" that landed at Cleveland, "Box" points out that the *Akron Beacon Journal* stated that passengers were released from the flight at 11:15 AM. However, a passenger from Delta Flight 1989 stated that the passengers on that flight were held "more than two hours in the plane before the FBI started to search it" and to remove passengers for questioning. "Box" then notes that the *Cleveland Plain Dealer* gave the passenger evacuation time as 12:30 PM, which confirmed the Delta Flight 1989 passenger's statement. Thus, *it had to have been Delta Flight 1989 that was evacuated ca. 12:30 PM*. And this in turn meant that whatever plane as was evacuated at *11:15* had to have been a different flight, flight "X", which landed at 10:45. [88]

Adding grist to the mill of a mystery flight at Cleveland airport, "Box" observes that the first news reports of the *number* of passengers

---

[85] Ibid., p. 588.
[86] Ibid.
[87] Ibid.
[88] Michael Ruppert, *Crossing the Rubicon*, p. 588.

released varies. The initial reports, and Mayor White's news conference itself, mentioned 200 passengers. But the passenger of Delta 1989 mentioned "60 or so" passengers, which later reports confirm. Given that the previous two parameters suggest that *two* flights landed at Cleveland—Delta 1989 and the mystery "flight x"—"box" concludes there are two releases of passengers, the "60 or so" from Delta flight 1989, which indeed carried only 69 passengers, at 12:30PM, and the "200 passengers" at 11:15AM.[89]

But why bother with planes that are so on the periphery of 9/11? The astonishing answer—and the "high octane speculative possibilities" that it brings with it—are to be found in the fourth and fifth parameters, and here it is necessary to cite "Box" extensively:

4. The Place the passengers were interviewed after the evacuation

The (sic) most reports say that the passengers were brought *into a nearby NASA facility. This is the NASA Glenn Research Center located near the west end of the airport.* It was already evacuated. The passenger of Delta 1989 however tells us that *she was taken into a "secure building at the airport." This is confirmed by a report that the Delta 1989 passengers were interviewed in the FAA headquarters.*

Surely the FAA headquarters is not located in the NASA facility.

We can conclude that Delta 1989 landed at 10:10, and at 12:30 the 69 passengers were taken into the FAA headquarters. Flight X landed at 10:45, and at 11:15 the 200 passengers were taken into the evacuated NASA Center.

5. The exact location of the plane

This is the final proof that we have to do with (i.e., we are dealing with) two different planes. Both planes were sitting on a runway, but miles away from each other. One plane was at the west end of runway 28/10 near the NASA center... This is confirmed by Associated Press and an eyewitness. The other plane was sitting at the south end of runway 18/36 near the I-X-Center, also confirmed by two eyewitnesses. The geographic conditions on the airport suggest that the passengers at the west end were taken to the NASA Center and the passengers at the south end to the FAA headquarters.[90]

---

[89] Ibid., pp. 588-589.
[90] Michael Ruppert, *Crossing the Rubicon*, p. 589, boldface emphasis in the original, italicized emphasis added.

Based on "Woody Box's" article, some 9/11 researchers concluded that the mysterious Flight X at Cleveland may have been, in reality, Flight 77, whose passengers deplaned into the evacuated NASA Center.

However, regardless of what the mysterious flight X may have been, the whole episode raises a series of implications that have no easy or pleasant resolutions, for in the case of either plane, why have no witnesses stepped forward to confirm the story? One answer, of course, is that they were warned not to talk about anything, and in the post-9/11 surveillance state, their movements and communications would have been relatively easy to monitor in order to ensure compliance to such orders. But the evacuation of the mysterious Flight X's passengers—whether those of Flight 77 or otherwise—to an evacuated NASA facility suggests an uneasy and disturbing alternative scenario, namely, that they were simply "disappeared" into some black world of hidden projects and facilities, possibly having to do with space, and were never seen again. This is not, as will eventually be seen, the only strange appearance of "space" in relationship to 9/11, and we have already witnessed the bizarre appearance of the SAIC corporation and all its intelligence-UFO connections. This is, in other words, a possible and very subtle indicator that one might be dealing with yet a third level to the 9/11 events.

Before leaving this topic, it is also worth noting that Paul Zarembka thoroughly studied the evidence relating to the four 9/11 hijacked airplanes, and concluded that while there was enough evidence to conclude that American Airlines flight 11, United Airlines flights 175 and 93 where hijacked, there was less confirmation for flight 77.[91]

But before we leave the Pentagon for Pennsylvania, there is...

9. One Final Pentagon Oddity

Researcher and investigator Jim Marrs states that prior to the attacks on 9/11, at approximately 7:30 AM, many people in and around the Pentagon reported seeing bomb-sniffing dogs and their camouflaged handlers.

Finally, Marrs also points out that an explosion apparently destroyed the Secretary of Defense's underground hardened Counterterrorism Command Center,[92] This one point alone indicates

---

[91] Paul Zarembka, "Initiation of the 9-11 Operation, with Evidence of Insider Trading," in Paul Zarembka, ed., *The Hidden Historyof 9-11*, 47-74, pp. 49-56,

[92] Jim Marrs *The Terror Conspiracy.*, p. 32.

that Flight 77—or whatever struck the Pentagon—was not the only thing in play at that site on that day. And if one assumes that the strike against Wedge One on the West side of the Pentagon, targeting the Offices of Naval Investigations, was the work of level two, one might reasonably suspect that the explosion in the counterterrorism unit might be the work of that level, or perhaps level three showing its hand, for as we have seen in the two previous chapters, and thus far in *this* chapter, there is abundant evidence that 9/11, in some respects, is an inside job. But as we have also noted, at some time close to or after the Pentagon attack, the situation changes, and the conspirators may have realized that they themselves were the victims of a coup attempt, and the bombing of the Defense Secretary's command center may be another indication of this.

B. Flight 93 and the Problems in Pennsylvania
1. Secretary of Defense Donald Rumsfeld's Curious Statement, and the Debris Field from Flight 93

On Christmas Eve, 2004, Secretary of Defense Donald Rumsfeld made a surprise visit to American troops in Iraq, which of course by that time had been invaded over the now well-known and notorious fabrication that Saddam Hussein was producing weapons of mass destruction, and that any minute, he could rain down a nuclear, biological, or chemical apocalypse on the West. No one seemed to have noticed, in all the war hysteria, that Hussein was not a terrorist nor was his government (corrupt and brutal though it was) a radical Islamist government. Rumsfeld's remarks, however, were so embarrassing that the Pentagon had to explain that his statements were simply a misstatement, "not some sort of Freudian slip of the tongue."[93]

What Rumsfeld said, however, that required the Pentagon to qualify it as a misstatement, could not be so easily dispelled, for he stated that "...the people who did the bombing in Spain or the people who attacked the United States in New York, shot down the plane in Pennsylvania and attacked the Pentagon..."[94] The reason Rumsfeld's remarks could not simply be shrugged off as a mere "misstatement" was pointed out by researcher Jim Marrs:

---

[93] Jim Marrs, *The Terror Conspiracy*, p. 143. The words are Marrs' explanation, not a direct quotation of Secretary Rumsfeld's remarks.

[94] Ibid., p. 142. These are Rumsfeld's words.

According to the official story, Flight 93 barreled into the ground at close to five hundred miles per hour. Yet, wreckage was strewn for up to eight miles, including paper mail, personal belongings and even magazines and newspapers the plane was carrying. One engine, which weighs in excess of one thousand pounds, was found more than two thousand yards from the crash scene, indicating that it came loose prior to the ground impact.[95]

This, of course, raised the issue of whether the aircraft had suffered some sort of catastrophic event in flight, such as being shot down.

2. Did Vice President Cheney Order a Flight 77 Shoot Down "Stand Down"? More Evidence of a Deliberate Obfuscation of Data, and of a Level Two Insider MIHOP Operation

As noted previously in this book, the strike against the Pentagon occurred sometime 9:32 and 9:38 AM. In this respect, the testimony of Transportation Secretary Norman Mineta "throws crucial elements" of the 9/11 Commission's official narrative "into doubt."[96] Testifying to Commission member and former congressman Lee Hamilton, Mineta indicated that he was with Cheney in the White House's Presidential Emergency Operations Center ca. 9:20 AM. Mineta relates how a "young man" repeatedly entered the room, informing Cheney that the aircraft– Flight 77–approaching Washington DC was fifty, then forty, then thirty, twenty, and finally ten miles out, at which point he asked Cheney if "the orders still stand?" According to Mineta, Cheney "whipped his neck around and said 'Of course the orders still stand. Have you heard anything to the contrary?'"[97] Many have assumed that the "order" being discussed was a shootdown order. But it is much more likely that the order was an order to "*stand* down" and *not* to shoot down the aircraft.[98] As we have already seen, many of Washington DC's fighter security cover had been stripped due to the "drills" being run concurrently with the attacks themselves, and were thus out of the immediate operational theater. Any such shoot down *or* stand down orders thus were more likely intended for the presumed missile defense

---

[95] Ibid., p. 143.

[96] Bryan Sacks, "Making History: The Compromised 9-11 Commission," in Paul Zarembka, ed., *The Hidden History of 9-11,* 229-252, p. 237.

[97] Bryan Sacks, "Making History: The Compromised 9-11 Commission," in Paul Zarembka, ed., *The Hidden History of 9-11,* 229-252, p. 237.

[98] Ibid., p. 239.

batteries around the Pentagon. Since shoot down orders *were the normal operational parameters for such situations*, the extraordinary nature of Cheney's orders, which the aid is repeatedly checking and verifying, indicate they must have been orders of an extraordinary nature, i.e., orders to stand down. *Consequently, this is yet another indicator that level two was in play, and that what was happening was MIHOP scenario.* Not surprisingly, Mineta's troublesome testimony was excised from the record of the 9/11 Commission.[99]

3. Flight 93 and Its Apparent Shoot Down

The problem posed by Flight 93 is that while the official narrative maintains that the passengers of the flight regained control over the aircraft briefly before its crash, in the ensuing struggle between the hijackers and the passengers, the latter lost control and the plane crashed near Shanksville, Pennsylvania. Again, however, the apparent lack of debris at the alleged crash site, plus the fact that debris *was* scattered over an eight-mile long area, suggests rather that the aircraft was shot down in midair.

This sad circumstance has problems of its own, and these again point to the presence at the Pentagon and in Pennsylvania of "level two" in the events. David Ray Griffin puts these problems very aptly:

> The main problem raised by the first three flights—aside from the question of the identity of the aircraft that hit the Pentagon—was the fact that aircraft that *should* have been shot down were *not*. The fate of [United Airlines] Flight 93, say critics, presents us with the opposite problem: A plane that should *not* have been shot down *was*.[100]

This raises in its turn the questions of motivations, means, and opportunity, and points us once again to the presence of a level two player. *Why* was Flight 93 shot down, according to some 9/11 researchers?

United Airlines flight 93 departed Newark, New Jersey at 8:42 AM, fully forty-one minutes *later* than its scheduled departure. Then, at 9:27 AM, passenger Tom Burnett called his wife and informed her that his flight "had been hijacked, and that she should call the FBI, which she

---

[99] Ibid.
[100] David Ray Griffin, *The New Pearl Harbor*, p. 49.

did."[101] At 9:54, Burnett again called his wife and told her that he and other passengers, which included a professional pilot and a flight controller, were going to attempt to regain control of the airplane.[102] At 9:58, another passenger on Flight 93, on the phone with her husband, said "they're doing it! They're doing it!" This was following by a "whooshing sound, a sound like wind" and more screaming, after which all contact was lost.[103]

It is significant that it was only after 9:56 AM that orders finally came through that all fighter jets were to shoot down any aircraft under control of hijackers. But what this effectively meant was that *only Flight 93 was susceptible to being shot down, since the other three flights had already crashed into their targets.*[104] Equally significantly, a military aide informed Cheney that Flight 93 was "eighty miles out" and asked him "should we engage." Cheney answered "yes" and an F-16 fighter pursued Flight 93, during which time Cheney was asked two more times to confirm the shoot down order, which, again, he did.[105] As Griffin points out, the presence of a second smaller white aircraft near Flight 93 and its crash site was confirmed by numerous witnesses, including one woman who insisted that the craft was military.[106]

4. Paul Thompson's Theory about the Motivation behind the Shoot Down of Flight 93

As previously indicated, Flight 93 had aboard a professional pilot, and a flight controller, as passengers. Thus, had the passengers of Flight 93 managed to regain control of the flight, it is conceivable that they might have successfully restored communications with air traffic control and landed the flight safely. Investigator Paul Thompson, whose meticulous timeline research has already been referred to, has a unique, and in my opinion, probable theory on why Flight 93 was apparently shot down, a theory that Griffin summarizes in this way: it was necessary to shoot down Flight 93, but not because there was a danger that the flight was going to reach its target. Rather, Thompson

---

[101] Ibid.

[102] Ibid., p. 50.

[103] Ibid.

[104] Ibid., p. 51. This of course assumes that Flight 77 *did* crash into the Pentagon, and not a smaller aircraft, drone, or missile.

[105] Ibid.

[106] Ibid., pp. 51-52.

Asks why fighter pilots were given authorization to shoot down hijacked airplanes only after Flight 93 was the only one left in the sky. This is, of course, the disturbing question raised by the evidence Thompson presents about this flight. His implicit answer, given the evidence that the passengers were successfully wresting control of the plane away from the hijackers, is that this was the one plane that was likely to be landed safely—*which would, among other things, mean that there might be live hijackers to be interrogated.* Thus interpreted, the evidence about Flight 93 provides further reason to conclude that the failure to shoot down the previous three flights was *not* due to incompetence. This evidence suggests that when the authorities wanted a flight shot down, they were not hindered by lack of either competence or coordination.[107]

Potentially live hijackers might have exposed significant portions of the deeper layers of the 9/11 operation, i.e. might have exposed level two, and the flight therefore had to be eliminated.

When one considers the evidence of this chapter, and it is by no stretch of the imagination a complete survey of all the aspects of Flights 77 and 93, one is confronted with the unavoidable fact that a second level, deeply embedded in the American state apparatus, was operative in the events of that day. And as has been seen, there are subtle indicators of yet another level, a level that will now become much more apparent, when one considers the Problem of the Prescience.

---

[107] David Ray Griffin, *The New Pearl Harbor*, p. 53, emphasis in the original.

The Plain Dealer | Wednesday, September 12, 2001   A11

TERROR HITS HOME

Plane diverted to Cleveland triggers alarm

FBI finds nothing aboard flight to L.A.

PATRICK O'DONNELL
Plain Dealer Reporter

A plane diverted to Cleveland Hopkins International Airport yesterday morning was kept sitting on a runway for a couple hours and its passengers were interviewed by FBI agents. But suspicions that the plane had been hijacked or had a bomb on board turned out to be unfounded.

Delta Flight 1989 made an emergency landing at Hopkins about 10:45 a.m., nearly two hours after the World Trade Center towers were hit by two hijacked planes.

Delta ordered the plane to land in Cleveland, according to Cleveland FBI Special Agent Robert Hawk.

He said airline officials wanted the Boeing 767 down because it was traveling from Boston to Los Angeles, the same flight path as two of the planes that crashed into the World Trade Center.

At one point, Hawk said, there was confusion about whether there had been an incident on the plane. Delta, he said, told the Federal Aviation Administration there was a problem with the flight.

Delta spokeswoman Cindi Kurczewski declined comment.

In a televised news conference at 11, Mayor Michael R. White first said there was an unconfirmed report that the plane might have been hijacked or was carrying a bomb. But in the middle of the news conference, he reported that it had not been hijacked, and later in the day he said no bomb had been found.

White's office later said that the plane landed as a precaution.

The plane sat on airport property between the terminal, the NASA Glenn Research Center and the International Exposition Center for about two hours. About 12:30 p.m. baggage cars and shuttle buses approached the

plane. The 69 passengers and nine crew members then walked down a portable staircase and onto the buses, which took them to FAA headquarters nearby.

Hawk said the FBI did not want to let the passengers into the terminal because agents needed to interview them and search the plane before releasing

them. The delay, he said, was needed to set up an interview site and arrange for buses and emergency crews.

All the passengers were re-

CHUCK CROW / THE PLAIN DEALER

Delta Flight 1989 — with 69 passengers and a crew of nine — was grounded at Cleveland Hopkins International Airport yesterday. It had left Boston en route to Los Angeles. There had been rumors a bomb was on board, but none was found.

leased after none reported seeing anything unusual on the flight.

Contact Patrick O'Donnell at: podonnell@plaind.com, 216-999-4818

The Cleveland Plain Dealer Article about Delta Flight 1989:
"Terror Hits Home: Plane Diverted to Cleveland Triggers Alarm: FBI finds
Nothing Aboard flight to LA" by Patrick O'Donnell,
Cleveland Plain Dealer,
September 12, 2001

3

THE PROBLEMATICS OF THE PRESCIENCE

"Warnings were also reportedly given by Jordan, Egypt, and Israel."
David Ray Griffin[1]

"...The world's foreign ministries.... soon learned the German, Egyptian, French, Israeli and Russian intelligence services had all alerted in vain their American counterparts as to what was being prepared..."
Thierry Meyssan[2]

I T MAY SEEM TO BE A HIGHLY IRREGULAR OR PECULIAR PROCEDURE to begin a chapter by reviewing the ones that preceded it, but in this case, that review forms the essential context from which to view the information presented here, and also in the next chapter. The fact that there *were* numerous warnings to the U.S. government, both from other governments, and from its own foreign and domestic intelligence gathering operations, has constituted a key element of the argument that there was a "rogue network" within the American government that helped plan, and execute, the 9/11 attacks. For most of the "9/11 truth movement," the "problematics of the prescience" have pointed to the existence of this level of the operation, "level two."

However, when one adds what has preceded, a slightly different picture begins to emerge. For example, we have seen that sometime during the morning of 9/11, President G.W. Bush's behavior, and that of his staff traveling with him in Florida, is suggestive of the fact that they initially did not think they, the President, or the children of Booker Elementary School were potential targets of an attack. The reasons for this might rationalized in a number of ways, but they reduce to three basic possibilities: (1) either they had performed an *ad hoc* threat assessment and concluded that there was no threat, an unlikely consideration given the confusion and events taking place, or (2) they knew, at some level, that they were not targets because of the intelligence they had received, or (3) they knew they were not targets because at some level they were involved, or made privy to, some aspects of the planning of the operation. Buttressing the latter two possibilities are the strange facts surrounding the Pentagon and Pennsylvania components of 9/11, for regardless of whether one assumes an aircraft or a missile struck the Pentagon, all best

---

[1] David Ray Griffin, *The New Pearl Harbor*, p. 70.
[2] Thierry Meyssan, *9/11: The Big Lie*, p. 67.

interpretations suggest a degree of access to technologies and planning that could have only come from within the "rogue network," i.e., from within level two. And with the alleged shoot-down of Flight 93 over Pennsylvania, the possibility arises that the perpetrators may have ordered the shoot-down, to avoid the nasty questions that surviving hijackers and their victims would have presented.

As was also seen, however, sometime between President Bush's appearance at the Booker Elementary School, and his departure from there to Air Force One, the situation—and the behavior and statements—changed completely. The movements of Air Force One, and President Bush's own statements, were the types of movements one might expect during the institution of Continuity of Government Operations, and more importantly, as was seen in the preface and as Webster Tarpley has suggested, these movements and statements became the types of movements one would expect as responses to an attempted coup d'etat. The President's statements no longer made any mention of terrorist attacks but of "attacks" and "tests". Only upon his return to Washington was the terrorist narrative restored.

Thus, there are subtle indications of an entirely new level, a "rogue network" or "faction" within the "rogue network" or "faction," a *third* level. The suggestions of the existence of this level have also already been encountered in chapter one, with the mysterious connections of Mohammed Atta, presumed "ring leader" of the hijackers, not to other "radical Islamicists," but to a bevy of Dutch, German, and French persons, and to the *Carl Duisberg Gesellschaft* and its disturbing overtones and connections to the notorious I.G. Farben "military industrial complex" of the Nazi war machine of World War Two.

It is in the context of all these things that we must now examine more closely the "problematics of the prescience," the forewarnings of the 9/11 attacks, for here again, if one examines the record *and its implications* closely, the indications of a third level becomes disturbingly clear.

A. Internal American Counter-Intelligence Warnings

With respect to the intelligence forewarnings and the "coincidental" occurrence of so many military drills mirroring actual aspects of the 9/11 operation, one figure in the upper echelons stands out as combining in his person aspects of both, and therefore, as a powerful indicator that at the *second* level, 9/11 may have been an inside job:

1. In May 2001 Dick Cheney was placed directly in charge of managing the "seamless integration" of all training exercises through the federal government and military agencies by presidential mandate.
2. The morning of 9/11 began with multiple training exercises of war games and terror drills, which Cheney, as mandated by the president was placed in charge of managing.
3. Cheney was in charge of the war game known as Tripod 2, an exercise set up in downtown New York that set up a command and control center on 9/11 that was configured exactly like the one lost that morning in WTC 7.
4. *Dick Cheney was one of the main government officials deciding that such extensive drills would take place on 9/11, in spite of (or because of) the intelligence warning that terrorists would hijack aircraft and crash them into targets during the week of September 9th, 2001.*[3]

In other words, at the very minimum, Cheney's role in 9/11 points clearly to the LIHOP scenario, and possibly to the MIHOP scenario, for in either case, he had a hand in the planning and coordination of the drills taking place on that day, and this in spite of—or "because of"—the intelligence warnings. This is a clear indication that there was a second level to the operation beyond that of the hijackers.

1. Deliberate Dissembling by Condaleeza Rice? Or an Attempt to Draw Attention to Something?

The national security establishment wasted no time trying to cover-up the existence of this second level, for as David Ray Griffin points out, President G.W. Bush's national security advisor Condaleeza Rice, in May of 2002, stated "I don't think anybody could have predicted that these people would take an airplane and slam it into the World Trade Center, take another one and slam it into the Pentagon, that they would try to use... a hijacked airplane as a missile."[4] But as Griffin also points out, in 1995, Georgia Democratic Senator Sam Nunn, at the time the Chairman of the Senate Armed Services Committee, in an article in *Time* magazine "described a scenario in which terrorists crash *a radio-controlled*

---

[3] Four Arrows, a.k.a. Don Trent Jacobs, "The Military Drills on 9-11: 'Bizarre Coincidence' or Something Else?" in Paul Zarembka, ed., *The Hidden History of 9-11*, pp. 130-131, emphasis added.

[4] David Ray Griffin, *The New Pearl Harbor*, p. 67, citing Rice's press statement of May 16, 2002, which was reported by the *Washing Post* of May 17, 2002.(See p. 223, n. 1.)

airplane into the US Capitol building,"[5] a scenario that many 9/11 researchers believe was operating on 9/11 both with respect to the Pentagon attack and the attacks on the World Trade Center twin towers. Rice, as national security advisor, could hardly have been ignorant of the studies of such scenarios, nor of the intelligence warnings that something was going to happen that day. Was she therefore deliberately dissembling? Or was she deliberately trying to draw attention to the ludicrousness of her claims and statements in hopes that something else might be exposed?

2. Historical Precedents and Other Indications:
Even the Media is Prescient

Howsoever one might answer those questions, the scenario itself was not unknown to Senator Nunn, and indeed to any educated person (including Condaleeza Rice), for both the Germans and Japanese had used suicide planes during World War Two, and high security precautions were put into place around Atlanta, Georgia, against suicide planes during the 1996 Atlanta summer Olympic Games.[6] The Pentagon itself had commissioned a study in 1993 to "investigate the possibility of an airplane being used to bomb national landmarks" under the direction of retired U.S. Air Force Colonel Doug Menarchik.[7] Additionally, in December 1994 members of the Algerian terrorist group, the GIA or Armed Islamic Group, commandeered an Air France flight while it was on the ground in Algiers, planning to crash the aircraft into the Eiffel Tower. The operation was "cancelled" when French special forces made some "last minute scheduling adjustments" to the GIA's plan.[8]

Events such as this, and the trial of Pakistani Ramsi Yousef, the ring leader for the 1993 World Trade Center attacks, uncovered plans and plots on Yousef's computer to use aircraft as suicide bombers against a variety of American targets, including CIA headquarters in Langley, Virginia.[9] These plans were dutifully reported by the press around the world.

---

[5] David Ray Griffin, *The New Pearl Harbor*, p. 68.
[6] Nafeez Mosaddeq Ahmed, *The War on Freedom*, p. 86.
[7] Ibid., p. 81.
[8] Ibid., p. 82.
[9] Ibid., p. 83.

3. A Brief Survey of Internal Federal Government Intelligence Warnings:
The FBI, State Department and Other Internal Warnings

When one turns to consider the specific prescience of the 9/11 events, it becomes clear that many, if not most, elements of the American national security-military-intelligence apparatus had received numerous warnings, some via human intelligence contacts, others by concerned citizens trying to warn the government, and some via electronic signals intercepts. The intercepts, in particular, afforded a rich cache of information that something was going to happen:

> Shortly before 9/11, the FBI reportedly intercepted messages such as "There is a big thing coming" and "They're going to pay the price." On September 9, a foreign intelligence service reportedly passed on to US intelligence an intercepted message from bin Laden to his mother, in which he told her "In two days you're going to hear big news, and you're not going to hear from me for a while." And the next day, September 10, US intelligence reportedly obtained electronic intercepts of conversations in which al-Qaeda members said "Tomorrow will be a great day for us." One of those intercepts was reportedly made by the National Security Agency (NSA), which had monitored a call during the summer between Mohamed Atta and Khalid Shaikh Mohammed, believed to be one of the architects of Project Bojinka, the 1993 bombing of the WTC, and the bombing of the *USS Cole*.[10]

We shall have more to say about "Project Bojinka" below; for the moment, note that if these reports are true, then Atta himself becomes an even more significant figure, for not only does he interface with a peculiar group of Dutch, French, and Germans, as well as with the *Carl Duisberg Gesellschaft*, but also with the al-Qaeda terrorist network. In Atta's case, in other words, there is a radical Islamist terrorist connection, and a peculiar Nazi one via the Duisberg Society and its symbolic connection to I.G. Farben.

In any case, these warnings were apparently strong enough to cause a variety of high-ranking Pentagon officials to cancel their traveling

---

[10] David Ray Griffin, *The New Pearl Harbor*, pp. 72-73, citing *Newsweek*, October 2, 2001, *NBC News*, October 4, 2001, *USA Today*, June 4, 2002, *The Los Angeles Times*, December 22 and 24, and August 1, 2002.

plans for 9/11.[11] San Francisco mayor Willie Brown was also warned the Monday night prior to 9/11 about security risks. He was booked to fly to New York City on the morning of 9/11, and cancelled his flight; this is another indicator that "certain high-level U.S. security authorities anticipated some sort of grave danger, and believed it to be urgent, threatening, and certainly real enough to inform a U.S. City Mayor about to catch a flight to New York—but not the general public."[12]

The Willie Brown warning is also a salient indicator that there was a significant "LIHOP" *attitude* within the American national security structure, for it knew something was going to happen, warned certain "important" people, and let the events unfold without warning the general public. However, this is not the only indicator that there was vast internal knowledge of the impending attacks. Given the fact that there were exposed plots to use airliners as suicide missiles to attack targets—particularly in the "Project Bojinka" case as we shall see— there was an increased FBI monitoring of flight schools where, according to the *Washington Post*, the bureau had been keeping careful watch for potential danger since *1996!*[13]

The military-national security-intelligence complex was not the only element of the U.S. federal government to issue warnings about an impending event during the week of September 9, 2001, for on September 7th, the U.S. Department of State issued a *global* alert that that Americans might be the targets of an al-Qaeda-sponsored terrorist attack.[14]

4. The Earliest Interpretations of the Internal Warnings:
a. The LIHOP and "Rogue Network" Scenarios

As early 9/11 researchers such as David Ray Griffin and Nafeez Ahmed—and many others—contemplated these facts, it became evident that at the minimum, the LIHOP or "Let It Happen On Purpose" scenario was operating on 9/11:

According to established procedures by which the CIA keeps U.S. decision-makers informed, President Bush and other key members of his Cabinet would have received CIA intelligence assessments on the imminent Al-Qaeda operation, This seems to lend significant

---

[11] Davir Ray Griffin, *The New Pearl Harbor.*, p. 73, citing *Newsweek*, Sept 24, 2001. See also Nafeez Mosaddeq Ahemd, *The War on Freedom*, p. 125.

[12] Nafeez Mosaddeq Ahmed, *The War on Freedom*, p. 125.

[13] Ibid., p. 85, citing *The Washington Post*, September 24, 2001.

[14] Ibid., p. 116.

weight to the conclusion that the CIA, the DCI, the State Department, the President, and key figures around him in the White House, were ultimately responsible for doing *nothing* in the face of the mounting evidence of an impending threat to U.S. national security.

...

Thus, from both a statutory and an organizational standpoint, the argument of incompetence or bureaucratic blocking is extremely weak. *Even to argue that elements of the Bush administration had significant knowledge of what would happen, but not enough detail to take measures to prevent the attacks, is based on a very shallow appraisal of the nature and number of intelligence warnings received. As evidenced on public records, these warnings were not only extremely detailed, but also extremely specific as to probable perpetrators, methods, targets, and dates.*[15]

Even the prestigious British *Janes's Intelligence Review's* editor, Alex Standish, concluded that the 9/11 attacks were not an intelligence failure, but rather the result of a deliberate political decision not to act.[16]

b. Reports of Bin Laden in an American Hospital Mere Weeks Prior to 9/11

One crucial component to the 9/11 operation—and a component whose significance for the hypothesis of a third level is seldom correctly appreciated—is a story that was reported on October 31, 2001, in the French press, by *Agence France Presse, Radio France International*, and by France's premier newspaper, *Le Figaro*.[17] According to Webster Griffin Tarpley, *Agence France Presse's* version of the story documented an ongoing CIA relationship with Osama Bin Laden, long after the latter had become *publicly* been declared a number one enemy of the USA:

Bin Laden Underwent Treatment in July at Dubai American Hospital
Osama bin laden underwent treatment in July at the American Hospital in Dubai where he met a US Central intelligence Agency (CIA) official, French daily *Le Figaro* and Radio France International reported. Quoting "a witness, a professional partner of the administrative management of the hospital," they said the

---

[15] Nafeez Mosaddeq Ahmed, *The War on Freedom,* p. 129, emphasis added.
[16] David Ray Griffin, *The New Pearl Harbor*, p. 76.
[17] Alexandra Richard, *"La CIA recontré Ben Laden à Dubaï en juillet"*, *Le Figaro*, October 31, 2001, Webster Griffin Tarpley, *9/11 Synthetic Terror: Made in USA*, fifth edition, p. 170.

man suspected by the United States of being behind the September 11 terrorist attacks had arrived in Dubai on July 4 by air from Quetta, Pakistan. He was immediately taken to the hospital for kidney treatment. He left the establishment on July 13, *Le Figaro* said.

During his stay, the daily said, the local CIA representative was seen going into bin Laden's room and "a few days later, the CIA man boasted to some friends of having visited the Saudi-born millionaire."

Quoting "an authoritative source," *Le Figaro* and the radio station said the CIA representative had been recalled to Washington on July 15. Bin Laden has been sought by the United States for terrorism since the bombing of the US embassies in Kenya and Tanzania in 1998. But his CIA links go back before that to the fight against Soviet forces in Afghanistan.

Le Figaro said bin Laden was accompanied in Dubai by his personal physician and close collaborator, who would be the Egyptian Ayman al-Zawahiri, as well as bodyguards and an Algerian nurse. He was admitted to the urology department of Doctor Terry Callaway, who specializes in kidney stones and male infertility. Telephoned several times, the doctor declined to answer questions. Several sources had reported that bin Laden had a serious kidney infection. He had a mobile dialysis machine sent to his Kandahar hideout in Afghanistan in the first half of 2000, according to "authoritative sources" quoted by *Le Figaro* and RFI.[18]

The U.S. government and the CIA, of course, quickly denounced these claims, and the American Hospital in Dubai also denied the notorious al-Qaeda leader was a patient.[19]

The French were not buying the denials, however, and pointed out that bin Laden's CIA connections were well known since his Mujaheddin days fighting the Soviets in Afghanistan. Nor was the French press backing off any of its claims.

Radio France International stuck to its guns and followed up on its story with further details about bin Laden's CIA handler and case officer, Larry Mitchell: "The local representative of the CIA who visited Osama bin Laden last July 12 at the American Hospital in Dubai is called Larry Mitchell. If his visiting card specifies that he is a 'consular agent,' everyone in Dubai knows, especially in the small

---

[18] *Agence France Presse*, Wednesday, October 31, 2001, 2:04 PM, cited by Webster Griffin Tarpley, *9/11 Synthetic Terror: Made in USA*, p. 171.

[19] Tarpley, op. cit., p. 171.

expatriate community, that he is working under cover. To say it openly, Larry Mitchell belongs to the 'big house', otherwise known as the CIA. He himself does not hide it." RFI went on: "An expert in the Arab world and especially in the Arabian peninsula, Larry Mitchell is a colorful personality who livens up the somewhat drab evenings of the expatriates of Dubai. One of his friends likes to say that his natural exuberance often gets into classified matters. That is perhaps one of the reasons why he was called back to the United States last July 15. About twenty days after the September 11 attacks, in a statement dated October 5, the CIA dismissed as baseless rumors the story that the agency had had contacts with bin Laden and his group in the past, especially at the time of the war against the USSR in Afghanistan. It happens that this communiqué of the CIA is in complete contradiction with the earlier official statements of several representatives of the US administration itself."[20]

But how does this point to a potential *third* layer?

c. The Bush-Bin Laden-Carlyle Group Connections

The answer to this question lies in the well-known Bush family connection to the Bin Ladens. That relationship was so deep and is so troubling for any serious 9/11 investigator, that the observations of Michael Ruppert are apropos to the question of a *third* level of the 9/11 operation, a third level that turned the whole operation *against* whatever "rogue network" that might have planned it inside the American national security structure:

> Osama bin Laden is probably the last witness the United States would like to have interrogated. There is a compelling case to be made that Osama bin Laden has long been a well-cultivated, protected, and valued asset of US and British intelligence. It is also possible that he has been used.
> The bin Laden family of Saudi Arabia is vastly different from what has been described in the American press. Much of its wealth, power, sophistication, and political and economic influence has been overlooked. A close examination leads directly to US economic and intelligence interests. And this does much to explain

---

[20] Webster Griffin Tarpley, *9/11 Synthetic Terror: Made in USA*, pp. 171-172.

why American corporate media has avoided discussing it in detail.[21]

The power and influence of the Bin Laden family leads to a virtual warren of rabbit holes of implications for the hypothesis of a *third* level to the 9/11 operations beyond that of a "rogue network" operating inside the American deep state that helped plan the operation.

For example, the *Wall Street Journal* very shortly after 9/11 ran a story which raised the whole issue of the Bush family's connection to the wealthy Saudis:

> If the U.S. boosts defense spending in its quest to stop Osama bin Laden's alleged terrorist activities, there may be one unexpected beneficiary: Mr. bin Laden's family...
>
> Among its far-flung business interests, the well-heeled Saudi Arabian clan—which says it is estranged from Osama—is an investor in a fund established by Carlyle Group, a well-connected Washington merchant bank specializing in buyouts of defense and aerospace companies. Through this investment and its ties to Saudi royalty, the bin Laden family has become acquainted with some of the biggest names in the Republican Party. In recent years, former President Bush, ex-Secretary of State James Baker and ex-Secretary of Defense Frank Carlucci have made the pilgrimage to the bin Laden family's headquarters in Jeddah, Saudi Arabia. Mr. Bush makes speeches on behalf of Carlyle Group...[22]

President G.W. Bush himself had indirect ties with the Carlyle Group and the bin Laden family via his friend James R. Bath, one-time investment counselor for the Bin Laden family, and who had helped fund Bush's Arbusto Energy company to the tune of fifty thousand dollars.[23]

The connections between the Bush family and the Bin Ladens thus runs through the Carlyle Group in two ways, (1) via former President G.H.W. Bush's relationship to Carlyle, and (2) through Bush family ally, James Baker, who, let it be noted, was the attorney-of-choice to represent G.W. Bush in the U.S. Supreme Court hearings over the Florida "presidential election irregularities" in 2000 that saw G.H.W. Bush's son G.W. Bush win the White House. The third connection is via Bin Laden

---

21 Michael C. Ruppert, *Crossing the Rubicon: The Decline of the American Empire at the End of the Age of Oil*, p. 123.

22 Nafeez Mosaddeq Ahmed, *The War on Freedom*, p. 180, citing Daniel Golden, et al., "Bin laden Family Could Profit from a Jump in U.S. Defense Spending Due to Ties to U.S. Banks," *The Wall Street Journal*, 27 September 2001.

23 Michael C. Ruppert, op cit., p. 131.

investment counselor James R. Bath, a financier to some of G.W. Bush's early corporate ventures.

These deep connections—and these are only a few, more will be uncovered in a subsequent chapter—suggest that there may have been deep factors at work behind the numerous evasions of Osama Bin Laden from capture during the 1990s, when American intelligence was given specific information his location by the Sudanese government, which was then rebuffed and warned not to apprehend him![24] Indeed, on August 22, 2001 FBI agent John O'Neill, one of the federal government's counter-terrorist experts and expert on Osama Bin Laden and Al-Qaeda resigned from his post resigned from the FBI, complaining that the White House, now occupied by G.W. Bush, had obstructed his investigations, and had done so at the behest of corporate oil interests anxious to conceal the deeper Saudi role min 9/11, beyond that of the fact that the majority of the hijackers were Saudi. For O'Neill and other investigators, the head of Al-Qaeda's global network lay in Saudi Arabia.[25]

Fueling the idea of a deeper Saudi role than that of just providing some of the hijackers was an interview given by a captured Saudi Arabian Al Qaeda operative, Abu Zubaydah, who was captured in Pakistan toward the end of March, 2002.

> The interrogation, aided by thiopental sodium (Sodium Pentothal), was carried out by two Arab-Americans pretending to be Saudi Arabians. Relieved to be in the presence of men he believed to be fellow countrymen, Zubaydah became very talkative.
>
> Hoping to save himself, Zubaydah claimed that he, as a member of al-Qaeda, had been working on behalf of senior Saudi officials. Encouraging his interrogators to confirm his claim, he told them to call one of King Fahd's nephews, Prince Ahmed bin Salman bin Abdul-Aziz (chairman of a huge publishing empire and founder of the Thoroughbred Corporation, which produced Kentucky Derby winner War Emblem). Zubaydah even gave them Prince Ahmed's telephone numbers from memory. When his interrogators said that 9/11 had surely changed everything, so that Prince Ahmed would no longer be supportive of Al-Qaeda, Zubaydah told them that it would not have changed anything, *because Prince Ahmed had known in advance that America would be attacked on 9/11.* Zubaydah also gave from memory the phone numbers of two other relatives of King Fahd's who could confirm his claims: Prince Sultan

---

24 Michael C. Ruppert, *Crossing the Rubicon*, p. 125.
25 David Ray Griffin, *The New Pearl Harbor*, p. 78.

bin Faisal bin Turki al-Saud, and Prince-Fahd bin Turki bin Saud al-Kabir.

Less than four months later, events occurred that suggested... that Zubaydah's testimony may have been true. Within an eight-day period, all three of the named Saudis died.[26]

Moreover, as is now known, the G.W. Bush administration exerted pressure on the 9/11 commission not to release some 28 heavily redacted pages indicating the scope and nature of deep Saudi involvement in 9/11, and U.S. intelligence investigators other than John O'Neill complained that they were told to "back off" any investigations of the Bin Laden family after G.W. Bush became president.[27] As British investigative reporter Gregory Palast put it, what 9/11 was, was not an intelligence failure, "it was a directive."[28]

What is the significance of all of this?

Consider all that has preceded:

1) President G.W. Bush's behavior, and that of his staff, prior to departing Booker Elementary School, is one of calm, suggesting they knew that they were not targets of any attack;
2) Ordinary intelligence briefing protocols would certainly have alerted the President and his national security council of an elevated threat level;
3) *This could have been confirmed through the* **private** *Bush family connections to the Bin Laden group and hence to the upper echelons of Saudi power previously mentioned*;
4) Vice President Dick Cheney was authorized by presidential directive to coordinate the various exercises occurring on 9/11;
5) Sometime after leaving the elementary school and departing on Air Force One, the situation changes, and Bush's statements and flights to Barksdale and Offut Air Forces bases, indicate that a coup attempt may have been in progress, and that it had to be forestalled, requiring his personal presence at strategic nuclear forces command centers.

The argument here is a subtle one, and many people may not understand it: *whatever deep operation as may have been planned and executed by the Saudis, with or without the knowledge (or obstruction) or planning by elements of the American Deep State, something beyond*

---

[26] David Ray Griffin, *The New Pearl Harbor*, pp. 78-79, emphasis in the original.
[27] Ibid., p. 79.
[28] Ibid.

terrorist strikes and even deep Saudi participation had shown its hand, for the Bush connection to the structures of Saudi power may have conceivably given them more or less complete knowledge of the terrorist strikes disguised in the "drills" taking place that day. The motive of the operation of 9/11, to create a false flag event to project American power into the Middle East (notably against target nations hated by the Saudis) had to go forward, while a coup attempt had to be forestalled.

In effect, if this reading be true, the level two perpetrators of 9/11 had been "pinned" in a classic chess move: they had to go forward, in full knowledge there was another player on the scene that had turned the whole operation inside out. And this means that at whatever deeper level the Saudis may have been operating, they too were simply pawns in a much larger scheme. Lauren Guyénot reaches similar conclusions, again suggesting a "third level" *unexpected by the planners of level two:*

> The idea of a conspiracy emanating from inside the Bush administration, which is the common wisdom of the 9/11 Truth movement, faces a major contradiction: *if the responsibility of Osama bin Laden is a prefabricated lie, so are the elements that are potentially embarrassing for the Saudi state, and indirectly for the Bush family.* The involvement of the Bush clan in the planning of the September 11th scheme (and not only in its cover-up) is plausible, but the choice of bin Laden as a patsy does not seem very wise, especially if the objective was to divert suspicion away from the Bush family. *This paradox can be resolved if we consider that a complex operation like 9/11, designed to change dramatically the course of world history, necessarily involves several powerful networks, whose long-range interests do not necessarily coincide, and who hold each other hostage after the operation.*
>
> It is impossible, at this stage, to know exactly who knew what and who did what on 9/11, but it is conceivable that the Bush clan was outsmarted by the real masterminds, the President believing he had allowed a limited and harmless false flag attack (involving for example only two virtual planes and an explosion in the Pentagon) for the limited purpose of invading Afghanistan and (to) get the UNOCAL project going,[29] *while the master plotters raised the stakes by adding two fake planes into the WTC,* and then forced Bush into the Iraq invasion that his father had refused them in 1991,

---

[29] UNOCAL project: i.e., the oil pipeline project through Afghanistan that US leaders were trying to negotiate with the Taliban prior to the 9/11 attacks.

bullying even Colin Powell to support it by who knows what blackmail.[30]

While this author does not share Guyénot's theory that the planes involved at the WTC were only "virtual" planes, *I do maintain the possibility that the **destruction** of the Twin Towers may not have been an objective of the level two planners, and thus, both with their destruction and perhaps with the **manner** of their destruction, level three revealed itself and its capabilities to the level two planners and plotters very clearly, in addition to revealing itself via the use of highly classified federal agency code words, as was noted in the Preface.*

In order to see what Prime Minister Tony Blair's unnamed "global network," or what we have called "level three" might be, a deeper look at the *structure* behind that purported "global network" is required, and this in turn requires a look at *where* the foreign warnings were coming from.

B. Foreign Warnings and their Global Extent:
1. The "Project Bojinka" Warnings and the Philippines

One of the earliest warnings about the use of airliners as "suicide missiles" came from the Republic of the Philippines in 1995, and here it is worth citing Nafeez Ahmed's summary of this forewarning extensively:

> Rafael M. Garcia III, Chairman/CEO of the Mega Group of Computer Companies in the Philippines, who often works with the National Bureau of investigation (NBI) in his field of expertise, was involved in the intelligence operation that uncovered Project Bojinka. Garcia was responsible for the decoding of (Ramzi) Yousef's computer. "This was how we found out about the various plots being hatched by the cell of Ramzi Yousef. First, there was the plot to assassinate Pope John Paul II," he observes. "Then, we discovered a second, even more sinister plot: Project Bojinka, or a Yugoslav term for a loud bang. This was a plot to blow up 11 airlines over the Pacific Ocean, all in a 48-hour period. The planes would have come from Seoul, Hong Kong, Taipei, Tokyo, Bangkok, Singapore, and Manila....
>
> "Then we found another document that discussed a second alternative to crash the 11 planes into selected targets in the United States instead of just blowing them up in the air. These

---

[30] Laurent Guyénot, *JFK-9/11: 50 Years of Deep State*, pp. 140-141, emphasis added.

included the CIA headquarters in Langley, Virginia; the World Trade Center in New York; the Sears Tower in Chicago; the TransAmerica Tower in San Francisco; and the White House in Washington, DC... I submitted my findings to NBI officials, who most certainly turned over the report (and the computer) either to then Senior Superintendent Avelino Razon of the PNP(the Philippine National Police) or to Bob Heafner of the FBI... I have since had meetings with certain U.S. authorities and they have confirmed to me that indeed, many things were done in response to my report."[31]

Lest it be missed, the mention of an assassination plot on Pope John-Paul II may be significant in terms of its suggestions about the structure of Blair's "global network," for the actual assassination attempt on the Pope that had been *previously* carried out in 1981 by Turk Mehmet Ali Agca is rife with its own strange connections to the militant pan-Turkish fascist group, the Gray Wolves, of which Agca was purportedly a member.[32]

These warnings from the Philippines resulted in intensified US intelligence monitoring and surveillance efforts, to the extent that by July 2001, it became clear to intelligence analysts that Project Bojinka-like preparations were under way for an imminent attack on American symbols.[33]

---

[31] Nafeez Mosaddeq Ahmed, *The War on Freedom*, pp. 83-84.

[32] The attempt by the West to place the blame for the attempt on Pope John-Paul II's life quickly on the Soviets and their satellites ran into trouble, once the connection of Agca to the Grey Wolves was known. See "Pope John Paul II Assassination Attempt: Grey Wolves," en.wikipedia.org/wiki /Pope_John_Paul_II_ assassination_attempt #Grey_Wolves. In response to growing "pan-Turkish" sentiments surrounding the Russian intervention in Syria, Russia's *Sputnik* ran an internet article, "Turkish Grey Wolves: Forgotten Story of Cold War-Era Paramilitary Group," on November 12, 2015. The Grey Wolves were, as the article notes, founded in 1969 by Turkish Colonel Alparsian Turkes, which group "widely used translations of Nazi texts and formed a Nazi-like credo 'the Turkish Race above all others.'" The Grey Wolves, notes the article, "also established close ties with the Anti-Bolshevik Bloc of Nations (ABN), backed by the Central Intelligence Agency (CIA). The ABN was an umbrella organization for anti-Communist emigres—former Nazi collaborators—formed in 1943 by the Organization of Ukrainian Nationalists (OUN). Headed by the infamous Nazi collaborator and OUN member Yaroslav Statsko, the organization brought together a wide range of Eastern European émigration groups."

[33] Ahmed, op. cit., pp. 88, 92.

2. A Strange Catalogue of Warnings: Even the Taliban!
a. Israel, Odigo, and the "Art Student" Network

The catalogue of nations warning the USA of imminent attacks on its soil reads like a Who's Who of geopolitical powers and players. The London *Daily Telegraph* stated that the Israeli Mossad had warned the USA of imminent attacks, actually sending two counter-terrorism experts to Washington in August 2001 to brief the CIA and FBI about "the existence of a cell of as many (as) 200 terrorists said to be planning a big operation," and linking this cell to Osama bin Laden.[34] Clearly, Israel knew that *something* was going to occur, because the Israeli newspaper *Ha'aretz* stated that an Israeli electronic communications firm, Odigo, which had offices in lower Manhattan, received anonymous warnings about the attacks two hours prior to their occurrence,[35] warnings that fueled speculations that the Mossad, in addition to warning its American intelligence counterparts, was warning Jewish people to stay away from the center.

Also fueling speculations about deeper Israeli involvement was the strange story of the Israeli "art student" spy ring. A report of the Drug Enforcement Agency from 2001 stated that an Israeli spy ring of no less than 120 agents was operating in the USA, posing as "art students." These agents operated primarily in Hollywood, Florida, close to the Venice, Florida Huffman Aviation flight school attended by Atta, in San Diego, and Phoenix, all places where "many of the 9/11 hijackers had lived and trained." The *modus operandi* of the "art students" was to go door to door, selling "art works" as a cover for conducting surveillance. The DEA report also noted that the "art students" were also interested in the offices of the DEA and other Federal agencies, and the homes of their employees.[36]

The "art student" spy ring story was broken on the FOX news network by the late Britt Hume, who, according to Michael Ruppert's unnamed sources, learned of the investigation of the Mossad spy ring from no less than Vice President Dick Cheney at a Washington cocktail party "about two months after the attacks."[37]

But this was not all:

---

[34] Nafeez Mosaddeq Ahmed, *The War on Freedom*, p. 114.
[35] Thierry Meyssan, *9/11: The Big Lie*, p. 37. See also Michael C. Ruppert, *Crossing the Rubicon*, p. 262.
[36] Michael C. Ruppert, *Crossing the Rubicon*, p. 262.
[37] Ibid.

The FOX stories raised interesting questions about two Israel-owned companies in the US. One of them, Amdocs, handles almost all telephone billing records in the United States and thus was in a position to provide invaluable intelligence information about who was being called from what phones anywhere in the country. The second company, Comverse, has multiple contracts to handle sensitive wiretap operations for government agencies, and FOX reported that the Comverse systems included a "back door" for outside parties with access to it to overhear monitored conversations. This is reminiscent of the back door in PROMIS software.[38]

While explorations of the famous—or, depending on one's lights, infamous—case of the PROMIS software system will have to await a subsequent chapter, it is worth pausing to ponder the implications of these revelations.

At one level, that both of "human intelligence" (or "humint", to use the professional intelligence jargon), and that of "signals" intelligence or electronic intelligence (or "elint" or "sigint"), the "art student" spy ring affair may indicate that the Mossad's warnings to the US intelligence community stemmed from these two types of sources. But at a deeper level, the deep intelligence penetration of Israeli companies into sensitive signals intelligence operations and roles within the USA, plus the fact that the "third level" of the 9/11 operation revealed its presence by the use of highly classified code words, as was noted in the preface, may also indicate that the Israeli deep state is implicated or involved at that third level. The focus of intention on embarrassing the Bush family and its deep relationship with the Bin Ladens and the Saudis would tend to corroborate such a view, as would the fact that Atta, it will be recalled, was fluent in Hebrew.[39] Additionally, the Israeli-American shipping firm, Zim, broke its lease to move its offices out of the World Trade Center just one week before the attacks.[40]

Against this view, however, are some little known facts that cast an Israeli role at the deepest, third level of the 9/11 operation into a doubtful light:

---

[38] Michael C. Ruppert, *Crossing the Rubicon*, p. 262.

[39] Daniel Hopsicker, *Welcome to Terrorland,* p. 84. It should also be noted that Atta's father maintained that Atta was recruited by the Mossad.

[40] Ruppert, op. cit., p. 257. Guyénot states that the federal investigation of the art student spy ring also included actual arrests of the Israeli spies, and that among their possessions were phones paid for by a former Israeli vice counsel. The arrests apparently *increased* after 9/11, but all were eventually released on orders of Bush's attorney general, John Ashcroft. (Guyénot, *JFK-9/11: 50 Years of Deep State*, p. 179).

A leaked Federal Aviation Administration memo written on the evening of September 11 contains disturbing revelations about American Airlines Flight 11, the first to hit the World Trade Center. The "Executive Summary," based on information relayed by a flight attendant to the American Airlines Operation Center, stated "that a passenger located in seat 10B shot and killed a passenger in seat 9B at 9:20 a.m. The passenger killed was Daniel Lewin, shot by passenger Satam al Suqami." The FAA has claimed that the document is a "first draft," declining to release the final draft, as it is "protected information", noting the inaccuracies in reported times, etc. The final fraft omits all mention of gunfire. Lewin, a 31-year-old American-Israeli citizen was a graduate of MIT and Israel's Technion. Lewin had immigrated to Israel with his parents at age 14 and had worked at IBM's research lab in Haifa, Israel. Lewin was a co-founder and chief technology officer of Akamai Technologies and lived in Boston with his family. A report in Ha'aretz on September 17 identified Lewin as a former member of the Israel Defense Force Sayeret Matkal, a top-secret counter-terrorist unit, whose Unit 269 specializes in counter-terrorism activities outside of Israel.

This particular story raises a multitude of questions. Guns were on the hijacked flights? How did they get there? Why have they not been mentioned? What was someone with Lewin's background doing sitting in front of one of the hijackers on the day of the hijackings? Was he still active? Mere coincidence is nearly impossible here. So the question becomes: did the hijackers—all nineteen of them—plan their activities to kill Lewin, or was Lewin following the hijackers even into the gates of death? Did they have to kill him to complete their mission? Who had penetrated whom, and who had compromised Lewin's presence on the planed hijacked by Mohamed Atta?[41]

Given these indications of deep Israeli knowledge of, and perhaps involvement in, the 9/11 operation, it should come as no surprise that an Israeli company, ICTS, was contracted to provide security at Boston's Logan airport, from which American Flight 11 and United Airlines Flight 175, the two flights that struck the World Trade Center Twin Towers, originated, and "through subsidiaries it had contracts at every other airport where planes were hijacked on 9/11."[42]

---

41 Michael C. Ruppert, *Crossing the Rubicon*, pp. 256-257.
42 Michael C. Ruppert, p. 259. Ruppert also notes that "the same company was apparently well aware that alleged shoe bomber Richard Reid was connected to al

b. Other International Warnings

Taken alone, these indicators might suggest Israeli complicity in the events of 9/11, but in point of fact, the warnings coming to US intelligence did not come solely from the Mossad. In an interview given on the American MS-NBC network, Russian President Vladimir Putin indicated that he had warned the USA "in the strongest possible terms for several weeks prior" to the attacks. These warnings were specific enough to note that approximately 25 hijackers would be involved in flying civilian airliners on suicide missions against prominent American targets.[43] One can only assume that the Russian warnings were based on a similar mixture of intelligence coming from signals surveillance and human intelligence sources.

The French DST intelligence service also issued a warning to the USA, stating that attacks on American targets would be worldwide, would include attacks on US soil, and that the "order to attack was to come from Afghanistan."[44] Egypt's President Hosni Mubarak, as was seen earlier, also warned the US government twelve days prior to the 9/11 attacks.[45]

Moreover, we know for a fact that President Bush *did* receive intelligence warnings of impending attacks, for a *British* memo warning of attacks involving al-Qaeda hijacking several airplanes was included in his intelligence briefing on August 6, 2001. This was disclosed by CBS News on May 15, 2002, and required some sort of response from the Bush Administration. National Security Advisor Condaleeza Rice "tried to dismiss its significance by saying that it was 'fuzzy and thin,' consisting of only a page and a half."[46] However, media reports indicated the British memo was actually eleven pages long, and the U.K.'s *Guardian* newspaper stated that the memo indicated that the hijacked airlines were to be used as suicide missiles against targets on American soil.[47] Jordan and Germany also reportedly warned the USA, and even the Taliban's Foreign Minister warned that "Osama bin laden

---

Qaeda, and yet they still allowed him to board the Paris-US flight he tried to blow up. If the UPI story about a gun on Flight 11 is correct, then this might help to explain how it got through screening." (p. 259). It might also explain why the Bush administration reacted by creating the Department of Homeland Security.

[43] Nafeez Mosaddeq Ahmed, *The War on Freedom*, p. 114.

[44] Ibid., pp. 114-115.

[45] Ibid., p. 115.

[46] David Ray Griffin, *The New Pearl Harbor*, p. 71.

[47] David Ray Griffin, *The New Pearl Harbor*, p. 71.

was planning a 'huge attack' inside America that was imminent and would kill thousands."[48]

Before proceeding to one final country from which warnings came, it would be helpful to note what countries *did* warn the US government of the impending attacks, as this consideration will become crucial in the analysis which concludes this chapter. According to the 9/11 Truth community's own researchers, the foreign governments which warned the US government were:

1) Afghanistan's Taliban regime;
2) Egypt;
3) France;
4) Germany;
5) Great Britain;
6) Israel;
7) Jordan;
8) The Philippines;
9) Russia

Notably *absent* from the list of "warners" was Saudi Arabia.

But there's one more country to add to the list, and the circumstances of the warning emanating from there may be the strangest of them all.

3. Canada and the Strange Case of Delmart Vreeland
a. Michael Ruppert's Involvement

It was the late Michael Ruppert who uncovered an aspect of the 9/11 operation that continues to be ignored by most of the 9/11 truth community. This was the strange case of Delmart Vreeland, a case so strange, quips Ruppert, that "gravity seems to go up, and where red means go, and green means stop."[49] Nothing is normal about this case,

---

[48] Ibid., p. 70. According to Jim Marrs, there were actually *two* attempts by the Taliban leadership to warn the US government. See Jim Marrs, *Inside Job*, p. 54. For the warning from Germany, see Meyssan, *9/11: The Big Lie*, p. 67. Meyssan also notes that the European members of NATO met in a closed door meeting during which some members states expressed the "thought that (the) attacks could have been ordered from within the American state apparatus and refused to commit themselves to a '*war on terrorism*' whose objectives and limits were badly defined." (pp. 68-69)

[49] Michael C. Ruppert, *Crossing the Rubicon*, p. 175.

but it is included here simply for the sake of completeness; the reader must make up his or her own mind about it.

Well did Ruppert complain about the affair, and of his personal involvement with it, for Vreeland finally ended up being arrested in Franklin County, Iowa on October 20, 2004. His rap sheet included running an identity theft ring in Michigan, and eventually Vreeland was convicted in Colorado in 2008 of "inducement of child prostitution, sexual assault, sexual exploitation of children and distribution of cocaine", and was sentenced to 336 years to life in prison.[50]

Here it is best to allow Ruppert to present the story and how he became involved with it, in his own words:

> Before I ever met Vreeland's attorneys or published a word about the case, Bill Tyree called me from his prison cell and warned, "They're going to turn Vreeland into a 'honey pot'" A honey pot, in intelligence jargon, is a tempting source of information or "dangle" that is set out to lure intended victims into a trap. Ultimately the honey pot is violently and maliciously discredited so as to destroy the credibility of anything stuck to it by association. In some cases the honey pot is an innocent victim. But in many other cases, victims are a willing part of the plot, serving covert interests in order to cut a deal for themselves.[51]

Given the fact that Ruppert's book was published in 2004, the year of Vreeland's arrest, and four years prior to his conviction in Colorado, Ruppert's words may have been prophetic. Continuing with Ruppert's story, however, reveals just how strange the Vreeland case really was:

> As early as November of 2001, I started getting e-mails about a case in Toronto concerning a man who was claiming to be an officer in what was traditionally called the Office of Naval Intelligence and who had forewarned of the attacks of 9/11. I had been sent a copy of an October 23 *Toronto Star* story, by a reporter named Nick Pron, that described the basics of the case. The man, Delmart "Mike" Vreeland, had been held in jail since December of 2000 and was fighting extradition to Michigan on charges of credit card fraud. *According to Pron's story, Vreeland had written a sealed warning of the attacks a month before 9/11 and handed it to his jailers. The note had been opened on September 14.*

---

50 "Delmart Vreeland," *Wikipedia*, en.wikipedia.org/wiki/Delmart_Vreeland.
51 Ruppert, op. cit., p. 184.

Pron's story was about a 35-year-old man who claimed to have been part of a special US Navy undercover unit investigating both organized crime and drug smuggling and who had recently returned from a secret mission to Moscow. Pron described what I took to be a cover story concerning Vreeland's claims that he had been dispatched to retrieve or examine documents concerning the Star Wars missile defense system. He returned from Russia only to be jailed, almost immediately, on the fugitive warrant from Michigan. Right off the bat I suspected that this was the tip of a tiny tail fin on the back of the Loch Ness monster. If Vreeland was for real he was making the most common mistake I have seen made in such cases. He was trying to serve two masters by simultaneously trying to prove his credentials while also attempting to prove his loyalty to a system that had written him off.[52]

The case became stranger almost at once.

Persuaded by Vreeland's counsel, Rocco Galati, to visit a hearing in the Vreeland Crown court case while visiting Toronto in January 2002, Ruppert notes that security was unbelievably tight around the hearing, with all of the items in his pocket and briefcase inspected individually.[53] Ruppert began to take notes of the proceeding, and observed that the Crown Solicitor made a significant point when he pointed out the unlikelihood that Vreeland was sent to Russia to examine top secret documents relating to the Star Wars missile defense system, since the US government monitored anyone with such technical expertise very closely. A dispute then ensued between the Crown Solicitor and Vreeland's lawyer, Galati, regarding the state of Vreeland's military records, with the Crown maintaining Vreeland had only been in the US Navy for a few months, and Galati maintaining that Vreeland's service records were actually over 1,200 pages long, and showed evidence of alteration.[54]

"Then," according to Ruppert, "about 15 minutes later, I heard the Crown Solicitor step through the looking glass into the parallel universe." The "parallel universe" in question appeared to be not only contradictory claims from the Crown about Vreeland, but specific foreknowledge of the 9/11 attacks, and a financial crime of an almost unbelievable size. The Crown Solicitor, Ruppert states,

---

[52] Michael C. Ruppert, *Crossing the Rubicon*, pp. 184-185, emphasis added.
[53] Ibid., p. 186.
[54] Ibid., p. 187.

...was rebutting the claim that Vreeland's other lawyer, Paul Slansky, had previously made a phone call from the (open) courtroom to the Pentagon switchboard. And in that phone call a Pentagon operator had confirmed Vreeland's rank as a naval lieutenant (impossible for someone who only served a few months) and provided Slanksy with an office number and a direct dial phone number. To counter this claim the Crown Solicitor then suggested that Vreeland, who had been held without bail for more than a year on a non-capital offense, had somehow hacked into the Pentagon's computer system from his jail cell and altered the Pentagon's database.

Galati was vibrating with frustration from his chair as the Crown Solicitor also suggested that "Vreeland-the-Idiot" had somehow translated documents in Russian and Albanian and then had them posted on a secure and unknown website. Galati was quick to point out to the court that Vreeland didn't speak Russian or Albanian and he was wondering why the Crown Solicitor was so quick to have Vreeland be both a village idiot and a criminal mastermind at the same time.[55]

This exchange caused Ruppert to realize that any potential personal involvement in the case on his part hinged upon two key questions: (1) was there any explicit proof that Vreeland's alleged note warning of the 9/11 attacks *before* they occurred actually existed, and was there any proof that it was indeed sealed *before* the events, and (2) did the note actually explicitly and unmistakably refer to the events of 9/11, and not something else?[56]

Putting these questions directly to Vreeland's attorneys, Ruppert notes that "They stated that they knew of a certainty that Vreeland had written the note in mid-August, a month before the attacks, that it could be proven, and that they were even then trying to get the court to do just that. They were also absolutely certain that Vreeland had been referring specifically to the attacks of 9/11 when the note was written."[57] Moreover, Vreeland's attorneys told Ruppert there was no doubt in their minds that Vreeland had some connection to American naval intelligence and the CIA. Both attorneys had been followed; Galati had found a dead cat hanging on his porch; Slansky's rear car window had been smashed and his car burglarized. And both insisted that they had tried to warn Canadian and American authorities of the impending

---

[55] Michael C. Ruppert, *Crossing the Rubicon*, p. 188.
[56] Ibid.
[57] Ibid., p. 189.

attacks based on Vreeland's information.[58] It was because of this that Vreeland and his lawyers hit upon the idea of writing out a detailed description of the attack in a handwritten letter, which was then placed into Vreeland's personal property, inaccessible to him, prior to the attack.

This was then opened by the Canadian authorities on September 14, 2001. The contents of the letter were forwarded to Ottawa "while the letter itself was submitted as Exhibit 'N' in Vreeland's case on October 7th,."[59] The Canadian authorities did not begin to dispute the fact that Vreeland's note had been sealed into evidence "until the summer of 2002".[60] When Ruppert was eventually able to examine the note, which he reproduces in his book, the results astounded him. The brief note mentioned not only Osama bin Laden, but the World Trade Center and the Pentagon.

> It also mentioned other things that had been prominently in the news right after the attacks: Sears Towers, water supplies, the White House, the Navy pier, and several Canadian targets.
>
> Two chilling sentences appeared in the top half: "They will paint me crazy and call me a liar"; and "let one happen—stop the rest!!!" The last phrase was the most important item on the note. It directly implied that US intelligence services had achieved complete penetration of al Qaeda cells involved in the attacks. This was something I had suspected.
>
> The lower half of the note was filled with a variety of names that had little immediate significance. I did recognize the name "Ulista Petrovka" as being a street or place in Moscow not far from Red Square. Upon returning to L.A., I checked a few of the names to see what I could find quickly. One in particular was Chalva Tchigirinsky, (Vreeland had misspelled it) who was connected somehow with money. It did not take long for me to confirm that Tchigirinski was a Russian oil executive who had business relationships with BP and Gazprom, the company that had been trying to build the trans-Afghan gas pipeline from Turkmenistan....
>
> Later on a talented researcher named Nico Haupt was to forward me a detailed background on Tchigirinski, which elaborated further on his oil, real estate, and business ventures, including a deal signed in early 2002 with Halliburton. Tchigirinski was an oligarch.[61]

---

[58] Michael C, Ruppert, *Crossing the Rubicon*, p. 189.
[59] Ibid., p. 190.
[60] Ibid.
[61] Michael C. Ruppert, *Crossing the Rubicon*, p. 191.

In addition to this, Vreeland's note mentioned a "Dr. Haider," which Ruppert discovered was the alias of one Abu Doha, the leader of an Algerian terrorist cell operating in Afghanistan in association with Bin Laden. As Ruppert points out, this inconvenient point "certainly begs the question of how a jailed man with limited access to computers could know such an obscure detail?"[62]

None of this, however, was the most sensational thing Vreeland claimed to know, for in July 2002, Ruppert was to learn via a cache of documents disclosed by Vreeland that demonstrated "that trillions of dollars had been stolen out of the United States Treasury over a period of years and that some of the biggest names in American politics had been involved. These included the Bushes, the Clintons, Federal Reserve Chairman Alan Greenspan, and the heads of many major banks and government agencies."[63] While we shall investigate the financial aspects of 9/11 more in depth in a subsequent chapter, it is important to note that in Vreeland, the aspects of 9/11 as a terror operation, and as a financial crime, all meet in an individual *who claimed to work for the Office of Naval Investigation.*

The documents that are referred to are another bizarre part of the Vreeland saga of 9/11. The Canadian court records of his case maintain that

> Vreeland brought back from Moscow intelligence documents in a sealed pouch in December 2000. He said he was simply a courier and was to hand over the documents to a contact in Toronto but the contact failed to arrive.
>
> "The meeting didn't go as planned. I didn't like it, so I basically scanned and copied everything. I opened everything," Vreeland recalled in a June 5, 2002, radio interview. He said that when he returned for a second meeting he was arrested.[64]

---

[62] Ibid., p. 195.

[63] Ibid., p. 295. As Ruppert was investigating these strange Vreeland financial allegations in 2002, he notes that he "received a postcard sealed in an envelope. The envelope had been postmarked in Venice, Italy. On the face of the postcard was a print from a European fairy tale, *The Queen and the Trolls*. The picture showed the Queen. The message read: 'Attn to Michael Ruppert Good Work!—To Mr. Vreeland for SSST... Change lawyer not in Canada, not in USA is his place—Help Him—by Casanova from PIOMBI.'" (p. 297)

[64] Jim Marrs, *Inside Job*, p. 81.

One of the targets, according to Vreeland, was the Three Mile Island nuclear plant,[65] and he maintained during another telephone interview from Canada that this was the target of Flight 93, and that it was "shot down by American fighters to prevent completion of its mission,"[66] an important allegation in the context of the scenario outlined by Webster Tarpley, and reviewed in the Preface, that American nuclear forces were on full alert status, and that President Bush rushed to Offut Air Force base in a likely attempt to assert personal control over the strategic command structure, for if indeed Three Mile Island *had* been struck by Flight 93, it would have constituted a *nuclear* attack on the USA, and perhaps demanded a nuclear response. This puts the scenario advanced in so many 9/11 truth quarters of Vice President Cheney ordering the shoot down into yet a different light, for it again tends to confirm that the American deep state was responding to a threat of a very different nature than that of simple terrorism.

b. Back to Russia and Russian Intelligence's Actual Assessment: The Global Network Once Again

Vreeland's assertions involved a Russian angle to the story that indicates a possible *deeper* knowledge of the 9/11 operation. As has already been noted, Russian President Vladimir Putin gave interviews to American media after the 9/11 attacks, in which he indicated that Russian intelligence had warned the US government in the strongest possible language about the attacks, and included specific information about the size of the operation, its method(suicide hijackings of airliners), and the potential targets. Ruppert writes:

> Russian news stories had proved even more revealing about how much the Russian government knew beforehand.
> One story from *Izvestia* was to subsequently *have a key paragraph removed but not until after my staff had archived the story for safekeeping.* I made sure to obtain two different translations to make sure that the wording was correct.... Portions in bold were subsequently deleted from the *Izvestia* website:
> "September 12, 2001 (14:15) Yesterday at the headquarters of Central Intelligence Service in Langley a confidential meeting between one of the Deputy Directors of CIA and a special messenger of Russian intelligence Service took place. According to NewsRu sources he delivered to his American colleagues some

---

[65] Ibid.
[66] Ibid., p. 82.

documents including audiotapes with telephone conversations directly relating to terrorist attacks on Washington and New York last Tuesday. **According to these sources, Russian Intelligence agents** *know the organizers and executors of these terrorist attacks.* ***More than that, Moscow warned Washington about preparations to these actions a couple of weeks before they happened.***

"Russian Intelligence Service states that behind the terrorist attacks on Washington and New York stands the organization of Usama bin Laden, Islamic movement of Uzbekistan and Taliban government. According to our intelligence agents among terrorist there were at least two Uzbeks, natives of Fergana, who arrived in the U.S.A. on forged documents about ten months ago. A terrorist group which realized actions against the U.S.A. consisted of at least 25 people. All of them had a special training on the territories of Afghanistan and Pakistan including piloting of an aircraft."[67]

Note carefully what the implications of the omitted passage in the *Izvestia* story are: the Russian government knew "the organizers and executors of these terrorist attacks," yet the article goes on in the *next* paragraph to specify various terrorists and their training and mentions Osama bin Laden in this connection. Yet, this latter information has *not* been redacted from the *Izvestia* article.

The implication, in other words, of the deleted passage is *either* (1) it was deleted simply out of editorial considerations, as being redundant and non-specific, since the following paragraph specifies who the "organizers and executors of these terrorist attacks" were, or (2) *it was deleted because the statement implies that some **other** group of people was actually involved in the planning and execution of the attacks.* There are other indications from Russian sources close to President Putin and his advisory circle that the *second* interpretation is in fact the case:

Dr. Tatyana Koryagina, a senior research fellow for the Institute of Marcoeconomic Research under the Russian Ministry of Economic Development and reportedly close to President Putin's inner circle... *said that the 9/11 attacks were not the work of nineteen terrorists but (of) a group of extremely powerful private persons seeking to reshape the world. This group, she added, has assets of*

---

[67] Michael C. Ruppert, *Crossing the Rubicon*, pp. 185-186, boldface emphasis added by Ruppert to show the paragraph subsequently deleted on the *Izvestia* site, italicized emphasis added.

about $300 trillion, which it will use to legitimize its power and create a new world government.[68]

Koryagina's story appeared in *Pravda* on July 12, 2001, as yet another prediction of dire events that would befall the United States in August 2001.[69]

In other words, *Russia had precise knowledge of Mr. Blair's "unnamed global group," and precise* **financial** *knowledge of its assets.* This implies something equally important for our analysis, for it means that not only did Russia know of a *deeper layer* than simply a "rogue element" within the American national security state, it also strongly suggests the possibility that Mr. Putin's government *communicated this information to the Bush administration prior to the 9/11 attacks.* Given that there is evidence suggesting *some* involvement of the Bush administration in the planning of the drills behind which mirrored aspects of the 9/11 attacks, we posit *that the Russian intelligence information may in part be behind the realization on the part of the Bush Administration that a coup attempt was in progress, and that it had to be headed off.* The allegations of Dr. Koryagina also imply something else, and equally significant: *the global group must have had detailed inside financial knowledge and connections, which the Russians also knew.*

c. The Strange Prescience of the Domain Names

These considerations form the backdrop for yet another strange indicator of foreknowledge of the 9/11 attacks, for prior to the attacks, unusual domain names were registered on the Internet, names like

1) attackontwintowers.com
2) worldtradetowerattack.com
3) attackamerica.com
4) horrorinamerica.com
5) horrorinnewyork.com
6) nycterroriststrike.com
7) pearlharborinmanhattan.com
8) worldtradecenter929.com
9) worldtradetowerstrike.com; and finally,
10) terroristattack2001.com,

---

[68] Jim Marrs, *Inside Job*, p. 57, emphasis added.

[69] Ibid., p. 57. See also "Russian Economist Predicted Strikes on America, Says Shadow Power Planning More," November 1, 2001, www.apfn.org/thewinds/201/11/prediction, for excerpts from the *Pravda* interview.

all of which domain names were allowed to lapse. No one knows who registered the domain names.[70]

These registrations suggest the possibility that in addition to huge financial assets, the global network outlined by Dr. Koryagina also had either a great deal of cyber-expertise, or that it had access to sophisticated software that allowed such names to be registered without recording the owners of the domain names. We shall explore the "software" aspects of 9/11 in Part Two. For the moment, it is now time to look more closely at the outlines of "level three" suggested by the "problematics of the prescience."

C. Implications: The Structure behind the Warnings Indicative of a Level Three Operation

When summing together all the facts outlined in this chapter, the first thing indicated by the fact that so many countries *did* warn the US government is that *the network was truly global*. In Russia's case, the indications are that this network itself was known to them, and that it constitutes a genuine *third level* to the events of 9/11, since the Russians were also aware of the existence of military and other drills concurrent with the 9/11 operation and mirroring crucial aspects of it, for as was noted in the Preface, the Russian military was monitoring those drills in real time. Thus, *the 9/11 events could only have been planned and executed by some level or rogue network operating inside the US national security-intelligence-and military command structure.*

However, this element could only constitute a *level two* nature, for as the behavior of Bush and Cheney indicate, the initial attitude displayed was one of non-chalance. This *changed* prior to the Pentagon strikes and the destruction of the Twin Towers when it became clear— perhaps on the basis of the information communicated by the Russians—that some element within the 9/11 planning structure had turned against the rest of level two, indicating a *penetrated operation*. The Russians additionally implied that they had detailed information about the financial structure of this global network. *The sheer scale of the financial assets indicated in Dr. Koryagana's statement, and the international extent of the network, as suggested by the forewarnings themselves, means that this network is **not** identical to any of the level two players, neither the US rogue group, the Saudis, the Israelis, or any other single nation. One is thus looking at "level three."*

---

[70] Jim Marrs, *Inside Job*, p. 83.

Yet, when one considers other evidence, three things stand out about the possible composition of this network: (1) it may have some connection to Israeli intelligence, (2) it may have some connection to Fascist ideology and networks, as suggested strongly by Mohamed Atta's association to the *Carl Duisberg Gesellschaft*, and (3) it may have some connection to Saudi Arabia, as is suggested by the fact that the Saudi role in sponsorship of terrorism and the events of 9/11 was censored and obstructed from public view by the Bush Administration.

In view of the fact that the Bush-Bin Laden-Saudi connection was already well-known, however, the censorship of these connections by the Bush Administration may have served an entirely different purpose, namely, to cloak the presence in the 9/11 of this international fascist group, with its own deep historical connections to radical Islamicist groups, connections that may have unraveled if too much attention were paid to the Saudi and Bush connections. After all, the Bush family patriarch, Senator Prescott Bush, was well known to have had connections to Fritz Thyssen, financial backer at one time of Adolf Hitler, and Prescott Bush's Union Bank was seized by the Roosevelt Administration after the American entry into World War Two under the trading with the enemies act.

I have suggested in previous works the deep historical and organizational connections of postwar Nazism to radical Islamicist terrorist groups and also to deep and large systems of "hidden finance". These connections will be explored more completely in Part Two, but it is worth mentioning here, for by maintaining that level two was infiltrated by yet a third level which announced its presence *and break* with level two on 9/11, we must infer that the American national security apparatus was deeply hollowed out and penetrated, thus making Bush's flights to Barksdale and Offut Air Force bases necessary.

The question is, is there any evidence that suggests that level two was involved in planning 9/11, and that it in turn was penetrated by level three?

To answer this question, we must have a closer look at the "dilemma of the drills" and the "conundrum of the codes."

4

THE DILEMMA OF THE DRILLS
AND THE CONUNDRUM OF THE CODES

"The principle directly at stake here is that state terrorists wishing to conduct an illegal terror operation often find it highly advantageous to commandeer the government military/security bureaucracy with the help of an exercise or drill that closely resembles or mimics the illegal operation. Once the entire apparatus is set up, it is only necessary to make apparently small changes to have the exercise go live, and turn into a real hecatomb."
Webster Griffin Tarpley[1]

RESEARCHERS OF THE TERRIBLE EVENTS OF 9/11, such as Jim Marrs, Thierry Meyssan, Nafeez Ahmed, Webster Tarpley and many others, very quickly discovered that numerous military and civilian drills or scenario-games were occurring on 9/11, and that many of these drills mirrored or closely paralleled the components of the terrorist operation itself. These findings led to an intriguing progression of explanatory hypotheses in the chronology of the challenges to the official narrative, for just as the numerous forewarnings of the events from various domestic and foreign intelligence sources led to the elaboration of the "Let It Happen On Purpose" or LIHOP hypothesis relatively early in the development of the 9/11 truth movement, so the later determination that a number of imitative drills led to the later elaboration of the "Made It Happen On Purpose" or MIHOP hypothesis. The presence of so *many* such drills all occurring concurrently with the terrorist attacks implied that at some level, the planning for 9/11 occurred within the American national security apparatus itself. This in turn implied the existence of a "rogue network." The closer the 9/11 truth movement looked, the more 9/11 looked like a classic intelligence covert operation, *requiring* the expertise and planning of a major power with significant financial resources:

> This pattern of doubling, together with evidence of patsies, cut-outs, national security overrides, protected hijacker activities, and of the hands of controller-moles pulling the strings from inside the government, all suggest the entire 9-11 scenario was a covert US intelligence operation. The double-agent status of Mohamed Atta

---

[1] Webster Griffin Tarpley, *9/11 Synthetic Terror: Made in USA*, fifth edition, p. 282.

would require an entire book to address, as Hopsicker has shown, in order to do justice to the complexities of Atta's nefarious connections to off-line CIA (sic), an underworld of drug-trafficking and gun-running figures like super-billionaire Khashoggi, and others with ties to government elites.[2]

While we have yet to confront the mysterious presence of billionaire Adnan Khashoggi squatting like a toad in the middle of the 9/11 attacks, this will have to wait until our investigations of the *financial* aspects of 9/11 in a later chapter.

For the present, our focus is on the pattern of drills, doubles, and patsies. We have already had occasion in chapter one to stress the apparent "doubles" at work among the hijackers with particular focus on the indications of possible doubles for Mohamed Atta, and to note the resemblance of this pattern to the pattern of doubles employed for Lee Harvey Oswald in the Kennedy assassination. But a brief closer look is in order, for "doubling" occurs not only with respect to the *drills* and the actual events of 9/11, but also with respect to the *perpetrators and patsies* of 9/11.

A. A Brief Look at the Question of Doubles and National Security Overrides

Jay Kolar, whose invaluable essay "What We Now Know about the Alleged 9-11 Hijackers" has already been cited, summarizes the general problem of the 9/11 doubles in the following way:

> Attention to the timelines of the locations and movements of the hijackers reveals their role in 9-11 is not simply a question of stolen identity, but more importantly of doubles at work. For example, neighbors at the Parkwood Apartments witnessed that Hanjour, al-Hazmi, and al-Mihdhar all remained in San Diego through the month of August up to September 8, 2001. However, these eyewitness accounts are contradicted by other August sightings of them on the opposite coast, obtaining drivers licenses in Falls Church, Virginia, crossing back to Las Vegas, returning across country to Baltimore, and then spending ten days in Newark. How could they be holed up in San Diego while simultaneously crisscrossing the US for the whole month preceding the attacks? Short answer: doubles.[3]

---

[2] Jay Kolar, "What We Know About the Alleged 9-11 Hijackers," in Paul Zarembka, ed., *The Hidden History of 9-11*, 3-44, p. 5.

[3] Ibid., p. 21.

It is to be noted that both al-Hamzo and al-Mihdhar, in addition to Hani Hanjour, were allegedly on Flight 77 that attacked the Pentagon in such an unusual and "non-terroristic" manner.

Another equally suspicious and strong case for doubling occurs with Ziad Jarrah, one of the hijackers on the shot-down flight 93 over Pennsylvania. In January 2001, Ziad Jarrah #1 had been detained in Dubai at the airport, and interrogated for four hours. During this interrogation, Jarrah #1 stated he had spent the previous two months in Pakistan and Afghanistan.[4] These statements should have placed the name "Ziad Jarrah" on a watch list.

The difficulty was that during the period that Jarrah #1 was being interrogated, researchers were able to confirm that a Ziad Jarrah was indeed in Pakistan and Afghanistan. The only problem was, *another one*, Jarrah #2, was attending the flight school of Rudi Dekkers associate Arne Kuithof in Venice, Florida until mid-January of 2001, the same period Jarrah #1 was in Afghanistan and Pakistan.[5]

While the presence of doubles is a strong indicator of the involvement of level two working to create the legends of the patsies, and even stronger indicator of the presence of this level is the fact the some of the alleged nineteen hijackers were the subjects of numerous overrides and permitted their free travel. Kolar notes that on March 5, 2000, a cable was "sent to CIA headquarters announcing the presence of accused hijacker al-Hamzi in the US" and that according to the Joint Intelligence Committee Inquiry of September 20, 2002, this was marked "'Action Required' followed by a space that was routinely filled in 'None.'"[6] Webster Tarpley also points out that hijackers Atta and Shehhi had also been flagged with national security overrides. This is a virtual certainty especially in Mohamed Atta's case, for as has been noted, Atta shared the same name as the 1986 Israeli bus bomber, and thus his entry into the USA from Hamburg, Germany almost certainly required an override.[7]

---

[4] Jay Kolar, "What We Now Know about the Alleged 9-11 Hijackers," in Paul Zarembka, ed. *The Hidden History of 9-11*, 3-44, p. 22.

[5] Ibid., p. 22.

[6] Ibid., pp. 30-31. See also Webster Griffin Tarpley, *9/11 Synthetic Terror: Made in USA*, **fourth** edition, p. 174.

[7] Webster Griffien Tarpley, *9/11 Synthetic Terror: Made in USA*, **fourth** edition, p. 174.

B. The Other Example of Doubling: The "Mirroring" Drills
1. The Number and Covert Operations Use of Drills

However, the strongest indications of a deep rogue network within the American national security structure planning and enabling the attacks of 9/11 are the numerous drills taking place on that day. While many researchers began to point this out, including Jim Marrs, Michael Ruppert, Thierry Meyssan, no one has done the yeoman's work of assembling all the data on these drills more than Webster Griffin Tarpley, whose work we shall review here.

Tarpley states that approximately 46 drills exist—"depending on how we wish to count them"—that either closely preceded, ran concurrently with, or occurred soon after 9/11, or that "bear on 9/11 in some other direct way."[8] From the sheer numerical scale of such drills, one must conclude both that there was a rogue group inside the American national security structure that planned and executed the event, and that "the 9/11 terror events were largely camouflaged, assisted, conducted, and bootlegged through these drills."[9] Notably, Tarpley points to the classical example of the *modus operandi* of using drills as a means of camouflaging actual events and coups-d'etat as being the anti-Hitler "bomb plotters" of July 1944 using the Nazi regime's contingency plans to maintain power in Berlin against any potential coup, Operation Valkyrie, as a means of disguising the actual coup attempt.[10]

2. The Purposes of the Drills vis-à-vis the 9/11 Operation

According to Tarpley, when one examines these various drills closely, it becomes immediately evident that they serve a number of purposes:

---

[8] Webster Griffin Tarpley, *9/11 Synthetic Terror: Made in USA*, fifth edition, p. 288. Tarpley lists all these drills on pp. 335-338 of the fifth edition of his book. The detailed discussion of these drills occurs from pp. 275-338. This discussion is invaluable to any serious 9/11 research.

[9] Ibid.

[10] Ibid., p. 285. It should also be pointed out that Tarpley, almost alone of the 9/11 researchers, understands that there is some sort of international fascist connection transcending that of the Anglo-American financiers of the City of London and "Sullivan and Cromwell crowd." In this respect, he points to the relationship of Prescott Bush and his Union Bank to Nazi financier and corporate cartelist Fritz Thyssen.

1) In certain drills preceding 9/11, the purpose of the drill is to "secure control over certain key military facilities, a number of them in the Washington DC area," by imposing stricter entry and egress controls on these bases.[11] Pointing out that in Stanley Kubrik's now classic dark comedy *Dr. Strangelove*, the demented American general Jack D. Ripper, in order to close off attempts to countermand his orders for a nuclear strike on the Soviet Union, closes off his military base, that ordering anyone approaching or attempting entry—including US personnel—be met with armed resistance. In this respect, it should be recalled that on the day of 9/11, America's strategic nuclear and thermonuclear forces were in the highest state of alert, and conducting nuclear warfare drills, that forced President Bush to reassert personal command and control over the command centers of those forces at Barksdale and Offut Air Force bases. Among the bases affected by such drills prior to 9/11, were Forts Hamilton, Meade(the headquarters of the National Security Agency), Ritchie, Belvoir, Myer, and McNair.[12]

2) Some drills were designed for the purpose of *security stripping* response resources out of the theater of the impending 9/11 attacks. In particular, a joint FBI-CIA counter-terrorism drill was being conducted in Monterrey, California, on the day of 9/11, thus removing those assets from Washington DC![13]

3) Other drills were designed specifically to suppress the air defense of the theater of operations of the 9/11 events, the air corridor from Washington DC to Boston. A variety of drills were used to accomplish this objective via a variety of means, from hijacking drills (!) inserting *false radar blips* into the air traffic control and NORAD systems, to drills that actually reassigned American fighter aircraft from the corridor to overseas bases in Turkey and Saudi Arabia to enforce the "no fly zone" over Iraq.[14] Effectively, this set of drills amounted to the "security stripping"

---

[11] Webster Griffin Tarpley, *9/11 Synthetic Terror: Made in USA*, fifth edition, p. 288.

[12] Ibid., pp. 288-289.

[13] Ibid., p. 289.

[14] Ibid., p. 290. Tarpley notes that "Operation Northern Watch" removed six fighters from Langley Air Force Base in Virginia, rebasing them to Incirlik air base in Turkey, and that "Operation Southern Watch" rebased elements of the 174th Fighter Wing of the New York Air National Guard to the Sultain Air Base in Saudi Arabia, while Operation "Vigilant Guardian" was the operation injecting false radar blips into the air traffic control and NORAD systems of "hijacked airplanes", thus sowing confusion in the command and control structure. (See pp. 290-291).

of actual military assets away from the 9/11 theater of operations, while simultaneously using a "hijacking drill," Vigilant Guardian, to cause confusion in the command and control structure of North American air defenses. One other such drill enumerated by Tarpley is worth mentioning. This involved the hijacking of a Japanese airliner and then threatening to explode it over a city. This, observes Tarpley, may have been a component of Vigilant Guardian,[15] but it should also be noted that this is precisely one element of the Project Bojinka plot uncovered by the Republic of the Philippines.

4) Drills were used as a cover by which to procure command approval for operations that were later "flipped live." The key drill here, according to Tarpley, was Amalgam Virgo, which involved hijacked airliners and even a cruise missile being used to attack targets in the USA. Under the cover of preparations for the drill, a drill with command approval, the rogue network actually prepared for a real attack.[16]

5) Drills were used to blind American space assets, for on the day of 9/11 itself, a drill was being conducted involving the hijacking and crash of an aircraft into the headquarters building of the National Reconnaissance Office, the agency handling all of America's spy satellite data and its initial analysis. In the drill, the offices of the NRO *had to be evacuated* because of the "threat" in the drill. The real question is, *Why would America's spy satellites have to be blinded?* Tarpley offers one speculative answer: the National Reconnaissance Office and its spy satellites might have been "able to follow the movements of airliners without recourse to radars of any kind. With the help of Global hawk drone technology, it could also *steer* these airliners by remote control. This drill was under the command of John Fulton, the chief of the NRO's strategic war gaming office, and his CIA cohorts. The organizers claim that 'as soon as the real world events began, we cancelled the exercise,' and the NRO's 3,000 personnel were told to go home—an extremely unlikely scenario for a country supposedly under foreign attack."[17] However, this is not, as we shall see in a subsequent chapter, the

---

[15] Webster Griffin Tarpley, *9/11 Synthetic Terror: Made in USA*, fifth edition, p. 294.

[16] Ibid., p. 204.

[17] Webster Griffin Tarpley, *9/11 Synthetic Terror: Made in USA*, fifth edition, p. 307.

only possible interpretation for why it was necessary to blind US space assets.[18]

In addition to all these purposes and types of drills, there were also the "Positive Force" drills, run from April 17-26, 2001, which gamed various scenarios of Continuity of Government operations, from cyber-attacks, attacks on the power and railroad grids, and attacks on America's land based, maritime, and aviation transport. Such Continuity of Government contingency plans have "long been suspected of providing a cover story for the installation of a military regime or other dictatorship."[19] The fact that there are strong indicators that such operations *were* instituted on 9/11 in response to the attacks provides more compelling confirmation that at some point on that day the Bush administration began to act in a manner precisely consistent with efforts to *prevent* a coup d'etat, as we have seen.

Finally, there were a number of other odd exercises occurring prior to and during 9/11. For example, drills were conducted in May 2001 in New York City involving airplane crashes and collapsing buildings![20] During the week of 9/11, Operation "Northern Vigilance" was yet another drill that effectively "security stripped" the northeastern corridor of air defenses, as assets were sent to northwestern Canada and Alaska to counter a Russian drill involving its strategic bombers.[21] This is significant, for as was seen in the Preface, on 9/11, the US strategic forces were running two drills—Global Guardian and Amalgam Warrior—involving all of the USA's strategic nuclear forces (Global Guardian) and air intercept and defense against a "foreign attack"(Amalgam Warrior), in addition to the "Apollo Guardian" space command exercise noted above.[22] On top of all of this there was the Global Guardian Computer Network Attack exercise, which 'involved a

---

[18] Tarpley also mentions the mysterious "Apollo Guardian" space command exercise, apparently more or less concurrent with the 9/11 attacks, but that nothing further is known about this exercise. If, however, such an exercise *was* being run on 9/11, then it implies that there may be a hitherto unknown *space component* of the events of 9/11. Our "high octane speculations" about what this may have been, and why it was necessary to blind the National Reconnaissance Office, will be reviewed in chapter seven.

[19] Ibid., p. 305.

[20] Ibid., p. 308.

[21] Ibid., p. 297.

[22] Webster Griffin Tarpley, *9/11 Synthetic Terror: Made in USA*, fifth edition, p. 318.

STRATCOM[23] red tem '*bad*' *insider with access to a key command and control system.*"[24] This involved "red team" members who were simulating attempts "to penetrate the Command from the Internet to a '*bad insider with access to a key command and control system.*" Tarpley notes that this whole drill "suggests that if the simulated bad insider called for by the drill had turned into a really bad insider, a putchist plant working for some 'other organization,' namely the rogue network, missiles might actually have been launched. Here was the invisible government's back door to worldwide thermonuclear escalation if that had been necessary on 9/11."[25]

Note that Tarpley views this drill as one of the strong indicators for the existence of the rogue network—level two—operating within the American command structure. But as will be seen momentarily, this may be a better indicator of *level three* than of level *two.* In this respect, it is worth noting that America was not the only nation conducting significant strategic military drills on 9/11. Great Britain was conducting large scale naval maneuvers in the Sea of Oman with "one of (its) most important fleet deployments since the Falklands War and massed its troops off the shores of Pakistan," while yet another drill, Bright Star, saw 40,000 NATO troops taking part in wargames in Egypt. "Thus, the Anglo-American forces were already pre-positioned" in the Middle East prior to the 9/11 attacks.[26]

At this juncture, it is essential to understand that Tarpley does *not* view the level two "rogue network" as an ad hoc, temporary phenomenon, assembled for the sole purpose of executing the 9/11 attacks as an example merely of "neo-con" planning to use a false flag event to inject American power into the Middle East to secure the region's energy resources and to precipitate a "clash of civilizations." Rather, he points out that this "rogue network" has been a consistent feature of the American deep state since it successfully used the destruction of the battleship *USS Maine* in Havana to instigate the Spanish-American War.[27] This group, with its deep ties to the American corporate and financial world, is essentially fascist in its outlook and policies. In this respect, Tarpley might also have pointed out the corporate-planned coup attempt against the Franklin Roosevelt

---

[23] STRATCOM: Strategic Command, located at Offut Air Force Base in Omaha, Nebraska.

[24] Tarpley, op. cit., p. 320, emphasis added.

[25] Ibid., p. 321, emphasis added.

[26] Thierry Meyssan, *9/11: The Big Lie*, p. 71.

[27] Webster Griffin Tarpley, *9/11 Synthetic Terror: Made in USA*, fifth edition, p. 277.

Administration and its "New Deal" policies that involved the scions of several wealthy American corporate and financial familes, including the DuPonts, recruiting US Marine Corps general Smedley Butler to lead an armed revolt against Roosevelt. The coup failed, of course, when Butler exposed the plot to Roosevelt. Similarly, it was this same group that through its agents in the law firm of Sullivan and Cromwell, including the Dulles brothers, that sought to interfere with Roosevelt's "unconditional surrender" policy during World War Two, and which attempted to negotiate a separate peace with Nazi Germany. This same group negotiated the "deals with the Fascist devil", integrating Nazi General Reinhard Gehlen's military intelligence group *Fremde Heere Ost* (Foreign Armies East) into the postwar western intelligence structure, and which through its American IG Farben lawyer, John McCloy, postwar American High Commissioner for Germany, pardoned thousands of Nazis. This alliance between the American fascists and the European fascists will become a crucial historical point to remember in the ensuing analyses of this book.

When Tarpley considers the overwhelming amount of drills suspiciously mirroring aspects of 9/11, or stripping essential military and intelligence assets from the 9/11 operational theater, and the strategic nuclear drills being run within the time frame of the attacks, he comes to an intriguing conclusion about the implications of the drills for the structure of the "rogue network". Nothing that "the 9/11 attacks cannot be attributed to Al Qaeda, Bin Laden, the nineteen accused hijackers, Atta, nor Khaleed Sheikh Mohammed" nor could it have been coordinated from caves in Afghanistan simply due to the sheer number of drills, Tarpley concludes that it originated within the American deep state, from that long-existing "rogue network" whose current spokesmen comprise a list of well-known names: Andrew Mellon, Henry Stimson, George Marshall, John H. McCloy, McGeorge Bundy, George Schultz, and so on, with its current makeup being "arrayed as a neocon extremist faction around George Schultz and Rupert Murdoch, and a more moderate but Malthusian imperialist grouping around James Baker III and Prince Charles, which has George Soros as a pseudo-left tentacle."[28] With this in hand, Tarpley proposes the quite rational analysis of the structure of level two by following three types of people needed to plan and execute such a complex operation: (1) the patsies, being the hijackers and al-Qaeda, (2) the moles, "ensconced at key points inside the state apparatus" and whose function is to plan the operation, prevent or block normal procedures for dealing with threats

---

[28] Ibid., p. 280.

and attacks, and who conduct the cover-up after the event, and (3) the technicians who produce the effects of the operation actually observed,[29] a crucial question, as we shall discover when examining the actual mechanism of the collapse of the Twin Towers.

With this in hand, and examining the numerous drills and aspects of 9/11, he argues that "there must be some focal point where alternative dates are weighed, conflicts foreseen, and the need of maintaining a minimum distribution of assets calculated, so as not to compromise defense capabilities. Whatever office in the bowels of the Pentagon does this, it is an urgent candidate for a sweep of the presence of moles."[30] The fact that almost no air defense occurred on 9/11, even after the strike on the Pentagon, indicates for Tarpley that there was "a remarkable density of moles at high levels of the US command structure."[31]

It is precisely here that once again one is confronted with the distinct possibility of a *third* level of the 9/11 events. The standard argument is that level two of the operation represents the interests of the Anglo-American financial oligarchs and the military-industrial complex of London and Wall Street/Washington. Accordingly, level two is seen as the "neocon faction" planning and perpetrating a false flag event to project their power into the Middle East. This much *is* true about the events of that day, for there is abundant evidence to support it.

The difficulty that arises is the fact that the administration of G.W. Bush and Dick Cheney, is precisely a neo-con administration, with the prominence of neo-con figures such as Paul Wolfowitz, Donald Rumsfeld, and Cheney himself, within it. *Thus, **no coup attempt would have been necessary against it, nor would pressure need to be brought to bear against it to ensure compliance with the agenda of projecting American power into the Middle East.*** The indications that a coup was being attempted by President Bush's behavior after leaving Sarasota, Florida, and flying to Barksdale and Offut, may thus be interpreted as indicators of a *third level* that had somehow announced itself. To perceive this possibility more fully, it is now necessary to examine the "conundrum of the codes" more closely.

---

[29] Webster Girffin Tarpley, *9/11 Synthetic Terror: Made in USA*, fifth edition, p. 280.

[30] Ibid., p. 303.

[31] Ibid.

C. The Conundrum of the Codes and More Indications of a Third Level in the 9/11 Operation

In the Preface of this work, we noted that at some point during 9/11, as the events unfolded, and probably at some point *after* the World Trade Center Twin Towers had been struck, and after President Bush departed the Booker Elementary school, someone informed the American command structure that further attacks were coming, and that the President himself would be targeted. In this respect, both Jim Marrs and Webster Tarpley mention a phone call placed to the White House switch board that allegedly stated that "Angel is next," the term "angel" being a codename for Air Force One.[32]

Tarpley speculates that this call was from level two:

> The call was evidently an ultimatum to Bush from the coup faction to announce the war of civilizations by blaming the attacks on bin Laden and al Qaeda, or (else) be liquidated. Israeli, French, and Russian sources confirm that the call was made, and that it contained a series of top secret code words, suggesting that the callers were highly placed within the US military and intelligence bureaucracy. An Israeli analysis from the Debka website stresses the extent of the top-secret information controlled by the plotters, and the network that would be necessary to have gathered such information. According to Debka, the message "Air Force One is next" was received by the U.S. Secret Service ay 9 AM. Debka suggests that the code name of Air Force One is changed daily, and that "the terrorists' message threatening Air Force One was transmitted in that day's top-secret White House code words."Debka estimated that "... the terrorists had obtained the White House code and a whole set of top-secret signals. This made it possible for a hostile force to pinpoint the exact position of Air Force One, its destination and its classified procedures. In fact, the hijackers were picking up and deciphering the presidential plane's incoming and outgoing transmissions."[33]

There are two problems here, the first being that if hijackers are unlikely to have been able to plan and execute the 9/11 attacks in conjunction with concurrent drills from caves in Afghanistan, as Tarpley himself rightly observed, they are equally unlikely to have obtained the

---

[32] Jim Marrs, *Inside Job*, p. 7; Webster Griffin Tarpley, *9/11 Synthetic Terror: Made in USA*, fifth edition, pp. 324.-325

[33] Tarpley, op. cit., pp. 324-325.

codes of Air Force One. But the deeper problem is, once again, the *lack of the **necessity** of such a threat to the Bush Amdinistration if the goal was merely to provoke an American and Western armed intervention in the Middle East.*

In other words, the phone calls with the codes were not coming from level two *to force the government into a course of action it was already inclined to take,* but from an entirely different party, and the nature of the threat may have been entirely different.

To see why, one needs to look at the issue of the codes more closely. In the Preface, we cited the following quotation from Thierry Meyssan:

> And more astonishing still, *World Net Daily*, citing intelligence officers as its sources, said the attackers also had the codes of the Drug Enforcement Agency (DEA), the National Recon- naissance Office (NRO), Air Force Intelligence (AFI), Army Intelligence (AI), Naval Intelligence (NI), the Marine Corps Intelligence (MCI) and the intelligence services of the State Department and the Department of Energy. Each of these codes is known by only a very small group of officials. No one is authorized to possess several of them. Also, to accept that the attackers were in possession of them supposes either that there exists a method of cracking the codes, or that moles have infiltrated each of these intelligence bodies. Technically, *it appears to be possible to reconstitute the codes of the American agencies by means of the software, Promis, that served to create them.*[34]

Observe that the codes apparently conveyed to the American command structure involved codes from the Drug Enforcement Agency, the National Reconnaissance Office, Air Force Intelligence, Army Intelligence, Naval Intelligence, Marine Corps Intelligence, State Department Intelligence, and the Department of Energy.

In other words, the codes were not restricted simply to the military command structure. Observe also that Thierry Meyssan does not ascribe the knowledge of the codes to a collection of moles within the American command structure, as does Tarpley, but rather to possession of the notorious PROMIS software system.

Looking at the subject of code names more closely, the U.S. assigned blocks of code names to different theater commands, "such as *Market* to Europe" or "*Olympic* to the Pacific," with words being *randomly selected*

---

[34] Thierry Meyssan, *9/11: The Big Lie.*, p. 44, emphasis added.

to create code names for operations,[35] which would, of course, include drills. It goes without saying that computers and random-generation programs would be perfectly tailored for the creation of code names, and in fact, in 1975 the Pentagon did introduce a computerized system, NICKA, standing for "Code Word, Nickname, and Exercise Term System, to generate code names.[36]

Additionally, there are three *kinds* of code names:

- **Nicknames:** A combination of two separate unassociated and unclassified words (say, *Polo* and *Step*) assigned to represent a specific program, activity, exercise, or special access program.
- **Code words:** A single classified word (such as *BYEMAN*) assigned to represent a specific special access program or portion.
- **Exercise terms:** A combination of two words, normally unclassified, used exclusively to designate a test, drill, or exercise.[37]

Within each branch of government, these three types of code names are in use, and it can only be assumed that each agency has some similar computer software "code generating" program, with each agency having its own naming conventions, "used to describe organizations, projects, and sources,"[38] and in the case of the CIA and other intelligence agencies, letter combinations to designate countries or regions in which operations are conducted.

Within the intelligence community, there are three *types* of information that code names also refer to: (1) "Sensitive compartmented information" refers to anything derived from intelligence analysis methods or sources, and hence requires special clearance to access that specific type of information; (2) "Special Intelligence" designates information *within* "sensitive compartmented information" that is obtained by signals surveillance such as the NSA's well-known Project Echelon, or by satellite imagery, and so on. Each type of directed or targeted information has a code word; and finally,

---

[35] William M. Arkin, *Code Names: Deciphering U.S. Military Plans, Programs, and Operations in the 9/11 World* (Hanover, new Hampshire: Steerforth Press, 2005), p. 14.

[36] Ibid., p. 15.

[37] Ibid.

[38] Ibid., p. 16.

(3) "Collateral information," which does not fall within either of the previous two categories, but which is nonetheless classified.[39]

For our purposes, however, the most interesting category of codenames refer to "special access programs" classified above top secret; these codenames are designed

> ... to protect presidential, military, intelligence, anti-terrorism, counter-drug, special operations, and "sensitive activities," as well as classified research and development efforts where it is deemed that extraordinary secrecy is needed to protect capabilities and vulnerabilities.... The clearance and access requirements are identical to, or exceed, those required for access to sensitive compartmented information, and (special access programs) require special (and expensive) security, access, and communications measures.[40]

If one looks at this description, and compares it with Thierry Meyssan's list of codes used to communicate the depth of knowledge penetration, and threat that level three communicated to level two, represented by the Bush Administration on 9/11, it will be evident that the nature of the code names used very likely may have involved the use of *special access program* codenames, i.e., of code names above top secret, and possibly comprising not only intelligence and counter-drug codenames, *but codenames involving "classified research."*

For our purposes, it is vital to understand that such access would not have to be accomplished by a network of moles within a network of moles, but rather, by access to the programs generating the code names themselves. Meyssan has already suggested the culprit, the infamous PROMIS software stolen from the Inslaw corporation of former NSA analyst Bill Hamilton in the early years of the Reagan administration.

When one juxtaposes this observation concerning the PROMIS software, which we shall examine in chapter eight, with the observation that a coup would *not* need to threaten the Bush administration in order to guarantee American military intervention in the Middle East, given the fact that his administration was *already* deeply suffused with neocon influences and agendas, and that the threat therefore does not

---

[39] William M. Arkin, *Code Names: Deciphering U.S. Military Plans, Programs, and Operations in the 9/11 World,* p. 17. Arkin also notes that "prior to 9/11, there were roughly 300 SCI compartments within the CIA and NSA, compared with an estimated 800 in the late 1980s."(p. 17)

[40] Ibid., p. 18.

emanate from level two, but from some *other* faction, then the implication is both subtle, and profoundly disturbing.

The implication is that the third level of 9/11, the "rogue network within the rogue network" is not only of global extent, that it not only has access to trillions of dollars of funds according to Russian economist Tatyana Koryagana, but that it also has access to profoundly sophisticated software and computer capabilities able to access the very codenames of various branches of the American deep state, and therefore, of "level two."

Just how, and why, that access came about, and what it might portend for the structure and architecture—for the *composition*—of that third level, will have to await the expositions of part two.

For the moment, however, it is necessary to pause, and take stock of the argument thus far, before plunging into the twilight zone of the high financial crimes, the destructive mechanisms at work at the World Trade Center, the PROMIS software and its implications, and the occult and esoteric symbolisms and ritual, in evidence on 9/11.

*Presidential aide Andrew Card Whispering into President G.W. Bush's Ear
at Emma Booker Elementary School.
According to the official narrative, Card told Bush that America was
under attack.*

138

5
CONCLUSIONS TO PART ONE:
INDICATIONS OF A PENETRATED OPERATION

"Yet few Americans realized that these two dynasties, the Bush family and the House of Saud, had a history dating back more than twenty years. Not just business partners and personal friends, the Bushes and Saudis had pulled off elaborate covert operations and gone to war together. They had shared secrets that involved unimaginable personal wealth, spectacular military might, the richest energy resources in the world, and the most odious crimes imaginable."
Craig Unger[1]

ONE IRONIC RESULT OF 9/11 WAS THAT THE U.S.A. FOUND ITSELF waging a war on international terrorism in the name of the newly announced Bush doctrine, going to war against any nation said to harbor or support terrorism, and yet doing so without any break in the "special relationship" between the U.S.A. and Saudi Arabia, a nation clearly implicated as one such terrorism sponsor by America's own security services. This factor will eventually become signally important in determining the structure and architecture of the putative third level of the 9/11 conspiracy. Indeed, American military adventures since 9/11 have targeted nations of concern to Saudi Arabia with a consistency that can hardly be coincidental: Iraq, Syria, and Iran have all come into the Pentagon's crosshairs. Such a non-coincidental scenario, however, is a classic case of the tail wagging the dog; on its own, the brutal Saudi regime would not seem to carry enough "weight" nor possess enough leverage to make such a thing occur. Some other factor—"level three"—seems to be required in addition to it.

Thus far, the indications of that third level have been subtle, but nonetheless palpable, and before continuing our analysis of 9/11 utilizing this template, a review of the argument for the existence of this third level thus far is in order.

---

[1] Craig Unger, *House of Bush, House of Saud: The Secret Relationship between the World's Two Most Powerful Dynasties* (New York: Scribner, 2004), p. 15.

Conclusions to Part One

A. The Indications of the Existence of a Rogue Network within the U.S. National Security Structure

As we have argued in the previous chapters, this third level does not become immediately apparent unless one carefully considers the evidence for level *two*, the "rogue network" operating within American intelligence. This is evidences, as was seen, by the following factors:

1) *The evident degree of planning of the Pentagon strikes*: As noted in previous chapters, the attack on the pentagon displays few hallmarks of an actual terrorist attack, both in the maneuver allegedly executed by Flight 77, nor in the way and place the Pentagon was struck. Had the goal been simply to strike a symbol of American military power and to cause as many casualties and damage as possible, it is much more likely that the eastern side of the structure with the offices of high command authority would have been the targets. Nor would a risky and complicated maneuver—the spiraling descending turn—have been chosen to accomplish it, a maneuver most experts agree was beyond the limited ability of alleged pilot Hani Hanjour to execute. A much more simple, and less risky, "dive" into the roof of the structure would have been chosen if the goal were simple terrorism.

Instead, the Pentagon was attacked at a recently reinforced part of the structure, with low occupancy, and at the site of the Offices of Naval Investigations. Additionally, the maneuver executed by Hanjour might more easily have been done by the use of remote piloting technologies, a speculation which is buttressed by the strange movements of Frank Probst during the Pentagon attacks, movements which could have been for the purpose of coordinating the positioning and deployment of such technologies. Additionally, the failure of air defenses at the Pentagon suggest a great degree of "inside" coordination to allow the attack to proceed. As will be seen in part two, the relevance of the place of the strike—on the west side—also adds an additional argument to the existence of this level two "rogue network". It should be noted, that if one maintains that it was not an aircraft, but rather, a drone or missile that struck the Pentagon, then the strength of the argument for the existence of this rogue network, of level two, increases dramatically, for authorization for the operational use of this type of equipment would have had to come from within the American national security and military command structure.

2) *The concurrence of much of the components of the 9/11 attacks with drills and wargames mimicking aspects of the attack* means that no merely external planning of the attacks by any "terrorist network", al-Qaeda or otherwise, could have occurred without some liaison to that rogue network within the American national security and military apparatus. The concurrence of these drills and wargames with the 9/11 attacks served two functions:

a) under the cover of preparation for the drills, equipment could be procured, and unit positioning and security stripping in the theater of operations of the actual attacks could be bootlegged; and,

b) on the day of the attacks, certain aspects of these drills could be "flipped live" and the attacks could proceed under the confusion in the command and control structure caused by the drills.

3) *The concurrence of the 9/11 attacks during strategic nuclear forces exercises of the US military* also points to the fact that the planning of the 9/11 events could only have come from within the US command structure; if the goal were to create a false flag even for the projection of American military power into Central Asia and the Middle East, then a nuclear drill involving all strategic US nuclear forces would also serve as a warning and deterrent to potential hostile powers—China, Russia, Iran, Pakistan, and even potentially India—not to interfere in those efforts. As will be reviewed below, it is precisely the component of these drills which also comprises one of the indicators of a *third* level within the other two.

B. The Indications of an Interface or Nexus between Level Two and Level T hree

4) *The ease of entry of entry of some alleged hijackers into the USA and their subsequent protection and apparent "doubling"* also points to the probable existence of "national security overrides" put into place to allow the ultimate patsies of the 9/11 attacks to gain entry to the country and to travel within it uninhibited. It should be noted, however, that both level two and level three could have expedited this component, for as will be recalled (and shown below), level three revealed its existence by the use of code names *which it may have come into possession of via*

cyberattacks and penetrations of US data networks, via this access, the national security overrides could have been inserted.

C. The Indications of a Third Level and that 9/11
Was an Op within an Op within an Op

There are, finally, a number of key indicators that the rogue network itself had been penetrated by yet another network, which we have been calling level three, and which Prime Minister Blair referred to as "a global network."

5) *The statements of Dr. Tatyana Koryagana*, the Russian economist and rumored member of President Putin's then-inner circle, also testified to the existence of a global rogue network, above and beyond that of al-Qaeda, was behind the attacks, and that additionally, it had access to a financial war chest of approximately $300 trillion.

6) *The curious associations of Mohamed Atta* himself also point to his possible membership in this global network as an agent or asset of some type, for his behavior was hardly that of an Islamic fundamentalist. Additionally, he was apparently conversation-ally fluent in a variety of languages besides Arabic, including French, German, and Hebrew. It will also be recalled that Atta had a namesake who perpetrated a bomb attack in Israel against a bus, a fact which would have put the *name* Mohamed Atta and its cognates on an international watch list. Nonetheless, Atta gains easy entry into the USA from Germany, and is thus himself evidence of a "national security override" in place.

Finally, and most importantly, we discovered the potentially very significant relationship of Mohamed Atta to the *Carl Duisberg Gesellschaft*, a "philanthropic" society named for one of the principal founders of the notorious I.G. Farben cartel. This connection raises the possibility, *though does not in and of itself constitute primary evidence, of a connection between Atta and hence of the 9/11 operation to a postwar Fascist international.* This would certainly qualify as a "global network", and the presence of Rockefeller interests on the *Carl Duisberg Gesellschaft* board would tend to provide further corroboration. In and of itself, however, this is the *suggestion* of a connection, not evidence for it. That evidence will have to wait the further exposition of part two.

7) *The phone calls displaying sensitive code names, the neo-conservative nature of the Bush administration, and the strange behavior of President G.W. Bush* have been urged as an argument for the two levels of the deeper operations behind 9/11. As was seen in previous chapters, the behavior of President Bush and his security escort on the morning of 9/11 *do* suggest that they knew there was no danger of any attack against them, suggesting some degree of involvement in the second level of 9/11. However, at some point after the departure of the Presidential party from Emma Booker Elementary, the behavior become more indicative of actual anxiety and pressure. 9/11 researchers from Thierry Meyssan to Webster Tarpley have pointed out that this was because of communications being received by the US command structure that the President and Air Force One were targets, and the bona fides of this threat were communicated by a display of detailed knowledge of highly classified code names from a variety of federal agencies, implying a deep penetration of those agencies in depth and breadth, and the potential for a coup d'etat and the ability to make the nuclear drills "go live" in an actual thermonuclear war. Bush's movements and statements from this point emphasize not terrorist attacks, but a "test," and on this reading of events, he flies to Barksdale and Offut Air Force bases in order to reassert personal presidential control and prevent this possibility from happening.

As was noted in the main text, the standard interpretation of this event by the 9/11 truth community is somewhat flawed, because that interpretation of the events urges that this coup d'etat was for the purpose of threatening and forcing the Bush administration into launching the war of civilizations and invading the Middle East. However, since the Bush administration was already thoroughly neocon in its views and composition, it is unlikely that such extra persuasion would have been needed; the 9/11 attacks themselves would have constituted sufficient crisis and opportunity to do so, especially as the 9/11 patsies had all been carefully prepared to point the finger of blame to Islamic fundamentalism and Osama bin Laden.

The coup attempt, and the blackmail, was most likely therefore for some entirely *different* purpose, and that purpose has not yet ever been speculated in the 9/11 literature. We shall do so in the next part of the book. At this juncture, it is important to consider that if this coup attempt and threat originated within a third level, and if this level had "global extent" and moreover was historically entangled in Fascist networks that include the Rockefeller interests and I.G. Farben, that the "marching orders" it may have given to the Bush administration may have reflected something entirely *different* from injecting American power into the Middle East. That "something different" may have been disclosed in other aspects of the 9/11 operation, and as we shall argue in Part Two, *was* disclosed.

In other words, 9/11 was not an operation simply of two levels, of the "level one patsies" flying airplanes into buildings under the direction of their hidden level two masters within the American command structure. It was that, but much more, for at some point on the morning of 9/11, level two was in its turn surprised by a third level, issuing demands, and demonstrating it could make good on those demands by revealing its possession of highly classified code names from the breadth and depth of various federal agencies.

With this in mind, it is time to consider the deeper clues to that third level, the financial crimes, the murder weapon or weapons in evidence at the World Trade Center, the indications of deep cyber warfare and penetration of the American command structure, and the high degree of carefully planned occult symbolisms and ritual elements of 9/11.

PART TWO:
THE MYSTERIES OF THE MOTIVATION AND THE MECHANISM

"Perhaps the question of the ultimate culprit of the 9/11 terror bombings can be solved if approached through the technical means used to destroy the Twin Towers. The murder weapon classically leads to the murderer."
Laurent Guyénot,
JFK-9/11:
50 Years of Deep State, p. 188.

6

BOMBS, OR WAS THAT BONDS, IN THE BASEMENT?

"Dr. Tatyana Koryagina, a senior research fellow for the Institute of Macroeconomic Research under the Russian Ministry of Economic Development and reportedly close to President Putin's inner circle... said the 9/11 attacks were not the work of nineteen terrorists but a group of extremely powerful private persons seeking to reshape the world. This group, she added, has assets of about $300 trillion, which it will use to legitimize its power and create a new world government."
Jim Marrs[1]

IGHLY SUSPICIOUS FINANCIAL ACTIVITY WAS NOTICED almost immediately in the 9/11 event, and investigation soon demonstrated that this activity had the odor of high financial crimes and insider trading. Yet for the most part, this activity has not summoned as much detailed scrutiny and speculation in the 9/11 community as it should. Such speculation as *does* broadly exist tends to view this activity as but more confirmation of an "inside job" and hence as confirmation of "level two" and the existence of a rogue element within the American military and national security "deep state."

That said, the financial aspect of this "rogue element" reflects the more profound patterns in evidence in the American deep state, according to an article in *Le Monde Diplomatique*, and cited by the late Michael C. Ruppert. That pattern is of a deep set of interlocks between three elements: (1) governments, (2) transnational corporations, and (3) mafias, a close parallel to the three-tiered structure that we have been arguing exists within the 9/11 events.[2] Notably, the second and third levels of *Le Monde Diplomatique*'s analysis could easily be compatible with Mr. Blair's "global network," and indeed, the presence of Mohamed Atta's association with the *Carl Duisberg Gesellschaft* invokes precisely an association with a "transnational corporation" that was both partly corporation, and partly a mafia: I.G. Farben. The invocation of a mafia in the context of attacks against the major financial center of the Western world and the symbols of that financial center exemplified in the World Trade Center suggests that like all mafias, one

---

[1] Jim Marrs, *Inside Job: Unmasking the 9/11 Conspiracies* (San Rafael, California: Origin Press, 2004), p. 57.

[2] Michael C. Ruppert, *Crossing the Rubicon*, p. 77, citing Christian De Brie, "Crime—The World's Biggest Free Enterprise, Part I: Thick as Thieves," *Le Monde Diplomatique*, April, 2000, http://mondediplo.com/2000/04.

147

part of the "family" had just declared war on another part. As that war was being declared, financial activity was occurring that may have formed part of that declaration of war.

A. The Worldwide Spike in Puts and Shorts on American and United Airlines
1. The 9/11 Commission's "Warrenitis"

After the events of 9/11, the former head of Germany's intelligence service and former member of the *Bundestag,* Andreas von Bulow published a controversial book in Europe, stating that in his considered opinion, 9/11 had to have been an inside job, given the sheer amount of insider trading that accompanied the event, insider trading that he estimated to amount to approximately $15 *billion* dollars.[3] And American ABC news commentator Jonathan Winer pointed out that the trades were placed *globally,* from Europe, to America, to Japan,[4] implying, once again, that a global network of some sort existed within the operation. In addition to the sudden spike of put options generally, there was a spike of such activity concerning the two airlines whose planes would slam into the World Trade Center twin towers, with United Airlines registering a spike of activity between September 6 and September 10, 2001, *ninety* times the average for the stock, and with American Airlines put options *sixty* times the normal volume of trade the day prior to the attacks.[5]

Suffering from acute Warrenitis, that mysterious disease named after Warren Commission chairman Earl Warren, and that afflicts federal investigative commissions with the ability to go in exactly the opposite direction from where the evidence is pointing, as far as the 9/11 Commission was concerned, there was "no evidence that anyone with advance knowledge of the attacks profited through securities transactions."[6] The Commission buries an "explanatory" footnote about what this means in the back of its report:

> Some unusual trading did in fact occur, but each such trade proved to have an innocuous explanation. For example, the volume of put

[3] Paul Zarembka, "Initiation of the 9-11 Operation, with Evidence of Insider Trading," in Paul Zarembka, ed., *The Hidden History of 9-11,* 47-74, p. 64.
[4] Ibid.
[5] Ibid., p. 65.
[6] *The 9/11 Commission Report: Final report of the National Commission on Terrorist Attacks upon the United States,* Authorized Edution (New York: W.W. Norton and Company, p. 172.

options—investments that pay off only when a stock drops in price—surged in the parent companies of United Airlines on September 6 and American Airlines on September 10—highly suspicious trading on its face. Yet, further investigation has revealed that the trading had no connection with 9/11.

At this stage, the reader will have noted that there is little by way of evidence or argument to substantiate these claims. An explanation is finally offered, which raises as many questions as it purports to "answer":

> *A single U.S.-based institutional investor with no conceivable ties to al Qaeda purchased 95 percent of the UAL puts on September 6 as part of a trading strategy that also included **buying** 115,000 shares of American on September 9, which recommended these trades. These examples typify the evidence examined by the investigation.* The SEC and the FBI, aided by other agencies and the securities industry, devoted enormous resources to investigating this issue, including securing the cooperation of many foreign governments. These investigators have found that the apparently suspicious consistently proved innocuous.[7]

What the 9/11 Commission has done here is to *raise* rather than lower suspicion concerning these trades, for one is being asked to believe that all these trades were the result of *one* "U.S.-based institutional investor with no conceivable ties to al Qaeda" executed the trades, and "to take the Commission's word for it that an overall investigation led to the conclusion that the option trades were 'innocuous.'"[8]

The Commission's "explanatory" footnote, however, may be a case of telling the truth, or at least a half-truth, and may constitute an extraordinary and not-often noticed and carefully-worded admission that this institutional trading may not have had any direct connection to Al Qaeda, but rather, *to Mr. Blair's unknown "global network" to which Al Qaeda was connected*, a "'mafia' connection" that might be "part of the

---

[7] *The 9/11 Commission Report*, p. 499, n. 130. At this point, the footnote cites, in support of its statements, "Joseph Cella interview [Sept. 16, 2003; May 7, 2004; May 10-11, 2004); FBI briefing [Aug. 15, 2003]; SEC memo, Division of Enforcement to SEC Chair and Commissioners, "Pre-Eminent September 11, 2011 Trading Review," May 15, 2002; Ken Breen interview {Apr. 23, 2004); Ed G. interview [Feb. 3, 2004]."

[8] Paul Zarembka, "Initiation of the 9-11 Operation, with Evidence of Insider Trading," in Paul Zarembka, *The Hidden History of 9-11*, 47-74, p. 67.

spectrum of possibilities."⁹ In this case, the Commission's own footnote is another manifestation of the symptoms of Warrenitis, namely, telling the truth in such a way that it closes down further investigation by misdirecting it: No connection to al Qaeda here, nothing to see, move along. As Jim Marrs aptly states this point, *someone* had prior knowledge of 9/11, used it to profit, and "they were *not* members of an al Qaeda terrorist cell."¹⁰

2. The Size of the Trades

Another glaring problem with the 9/11 Commission's "investigation" of the insider trading issue is its focus solely upon United and American airlines. But in 2002, prior to the Commission's report, 9/11 researcher Nafeez Ahmed Mossadeq pointed out that the Canadian investors' trade association, the Investment Dealers Association, was asked by the United States Securities and Exchange Commission(SEC) to investigate any suspicious trading in a list of *thirty-eight* stocks between August 27th and September 11th, 2001. This the Canadian group did, and promptly published the results on the internet. Needless to say, American authorities demanded the list be removed, but unfortunately, the list was copied by various investigators before it could be wtihdrawn.¹¹

This list was, as one might imagine, a veritable who's who of American companies that would be affected by the attacks: insurance, defense, and financial and investment interests, including:

> ...the parent companies of American, Continental, Delta, Northwest, Southwest, United and U.S. Airways, as well as Carnival and Royal Caribbean cruise lines, aircraft maker Boeing and defense contractor Lockheed Martin. Several insurance companies are on the list—American International Group, Axa, Chubb, Cigna, CAN Financial, John Hancock and MetLife. Several giant companies that were former tenants in the World Trade Center were also on the list: the largest tenant, investment firms Morgan Stanley; Lehman Brothers; Bank of America; and the financial firm of Marsh & McLennan. Other major companies on the list were General Motors,

---

⁹ Paul Zarembka, "Initiation of the 9-11 Operation, with Evidence of Insider Trading," in Paul Zarembka, *The Hidden History of 9-11*, 47-74, p. 48.
¹⁰ Jim Marrs, *Inside Job*, p. 87, emphasis added.
¹¹ Nafeez Ahmed Mossadeq, *The War on Freedom*, p. 123.

Raytheon, LTV, WR Grace, Lone Star Technologies, American Express, Bank of New York, Bank One, and Bear Stearns.[12]

However, there *is* a significant problem with the insider trading theory activity of 9/11: the *profits* made by some of these trades were rather small.

The San Francisco Chronicle on September 29, 2001 reported that the investors in the United Airlines puts had yet to collect the profits from their trades, which came to an amount between $2.5 and $2.77 million dollars,[13] an amount that seems disproportionate to the tragedy, and to the idea of cynical "insiders" scheming to profit from it. After all, if one wants to profit from an event like that and has no scruples from doing so, why a few million? Why not several tens or even hundreds of millions? The problem is not restricted to United Airlines puts, for American and Merril Lynch puts profits came to about $4 and $5.5 million respectively.[14]

However, there *is* a *very* strong indicator that there was foreknowledge of the 9/11 events and that people intended to profit from it, and as we have already seen, *foreign intelligence agencies were warning the USA of impending attacks ahead of time.* This knowledge could drive trading prior to the events, and it is worth noting that U.S. Treasury note purchases were running at abnormally high volumes prior to 9/11.[15] One need look no farther than this intelligence-securities trading connection to understand that there *was* insider trading occurring prior to 9/11.

The question is, who was doing it?

The answer to *this* question once again points to the existence both of a "level two" rogue network inside the US national security apparatus, and to a "lever three" global network to some degree interfaced with it, but also acting against it.

In support of the existence of level two, investigator Jim Marrs points out a fact that is often overlooked in discussions of the 9/11 insider trading:

---

12 Nafeez Ahmed Mosaddeq, ., p. 123.

13 Ibid., p. 118.

14 Ibid., p. 119.

15 Jim Marrs, *Inside Job,* p. 88. Paul Zarembka notes that just *one* of these US Treasuries purchases amounted to no less than $5 *billion* dollars.(See Paul Zarembka, "Initiation of the 9-11 Operation, with Evidence of Insider Trading, in Paul Zarembka, *The Hidden History of 9-11*, 47-74, p. 70.

The US Government itself was holding the majority of the international and domestic "short" positions, according to commodity trading advisor Walter Burien, a former tenant of the World Trade Center. According to Burien, government money managers are the primary players within the trillion-dollar international derivative market...

... "For three months prior and going into 9/11, the government investment funds had increased their short positions to the largest *diversified* short positions ever held by them... The airline stock option transaction at issue, and that most people have heard about, is truly chump change in comparison."[16]

In other words, the issue of the airline puts and shorts is really a diversion from the fact that the US government's own pre-9/11 investments indicate a "level two" operation underway.

Once one comes to this position, it becomes easier to understand why the airline puts amounted to "chump change in comparison," for these might indeed be nothing more or less than individuals, privy to this information, placing trades through friends, intermediaries, or other cutouts. When one views the pre-9/11 trading in this way, it becomes clear that when all the small amounts of profits are added together, one might be looking at a very large network, one which, according to the International Organization of Securities Commissions in a video-conference on October 15th, 2001, "added up to several hundred million dollars, constituting the 'biggest case of insider trading ever committed.'"[17]

But where are the indications of a potential *third* level in all this activity? To answer this, one must look much more closely at:

B. The Deutsche Bank Connection
1. Alex Brown, "Buzzy" Krongard, and the CIA Connection

The *Deutsche Bank* role in the 9/11 insider trading is now a well-known theme within the 9/11 community, and yet, here again, while that community has been quick to point out all the interfaces that come together at the big German bank, some of those interfaces have remained unappreciated for what they might imply, like Atta's strange connection to the *Carl Duisberg Gesellschaft*.

The 9/11 Commission's "explanatory footnote", with its deliberately vague reference to a "U.S. based" investment firm's role, has already

---

[16] Jim Marrs, *Inside Job*, pp. 92-93, emphasis added.
[17] Thierry Meyssan, *9/11: the Big Lie*, p. 57.

been noted. What the commission's "explanatory footnote" neglects to mention, is that "The 'institutional investor' in question was Alex Brown Inc., a subsidiary of Deutsche Bank whose former CEO and Chairman A.B. 'Buzzy' Krongard (until 1998) had just become Executive Director of the CIA in March 2001."[18] This trading activity did not go unnoticed in the home country of Deutsche Bank, for the then head of Germany's central bank, the *Bundesbank,* Ernst Welteke, indicated that was also heavy trading in gold and oil futures, and that this, again, was trading activity that spanned the globe, from Europe, to North America, to Japan. None of this, Welteke observed, was coincidence nor could it have been conducted without "a certain knowledge."[19] Michael Ruppert notes that this suspicious spike in trading occurred on the markets of the "the USA, Germany, Britain, Canada, Japan (8 times above normal levels on the Osaka Exchange), Switzerland, Hong Kong, France, Italy, Spain, Belgium, Luxembourg, and Singapore."[20] Indeed, the German government-owned airline *Lufthansa* also appeared to have been involved in the activity, placing put orders on the London markets for their competitor, United and American airlines, according to suggestions made by *The New York Times.*[21]

Given the sheer scale and international extent of this trading, Ruppert observes that "No one could hope to get away with it unless they controlled all the enforcement mechanisms that would be called in afterward,"[22] And this means, of course, that if one has the power to stonewall individual national investigations, that one is dealing with a global network, a financial cabal or cabals of international extent. By deputizing members of the firms involved in investigating the insider trading, the American Securities and Exchange Commission made it illegal to disclose anything from the investigation, thus precluding any whistleblowing, and controlling the flow of information to the public.[23] This may indeed be part of the motive for such deputizations, for the existence of a "third level," one with global extent and as invisible as

---

[18] Luaren Guyénot, *JFK-9/11: 50 Years of Deep State*, p. 135. See also Nafeez Ahmed Mosaddeq, *The War on Freedom*, pp. 117, 124; Thierry Meyssan, *9/11: The Big Lie*, p. 58.

[19] Michael C. Ruppert, *Crossing the Rubicon*, p. 239.

[20] Ibid., p. 242.

[21] Ibid., p. 241.

[22] Ibid., p. 243.

[23] Ibid.

"terrorist cells," and much more powerful, would be a secret that needed to be kept.[24]

2. The Last-Second Computer Invasion and Trades through Deutsche Bank

Another indicator of a third level at work in 9/11 occurs in conjunction with one of the strangest and most suspicious incidents of insider trading on 9/11 is that of literally not last-minute, but last-*second* invasions and trades executed via Deutsche Bank's computers mere seconds before and *during* the attacks on the World Trade Center:

> More evidence appeared and had to be thoroughly ignored because it could not be explained with spin or ridicule. Convar, A German firm hired to retrieve data from damaged computer systems left in the rubble of the World Trade Center, found that there was *a deluge of electronic trading just minutes **before** the first plane struck.* Quoting a December 16 report from Reuters, write Kyle Hence (of www.911citizenwatch.org) found a compelling quotation from one of Convar's directors:
> "Peter Henschel, director of Convar... said, 'not only the volume, but the size of the transactions was far higher than usual for a day like that.' Richard Wagner, a data retrieval expert, estimated that more than $100 million in **illegal** transactions appeared to have rushed through the WTC computers before and during the disaster."
> The Reuters story was partially confirmed for me when I was contacted by a Deutsche Bank employee who had survived the attacks by fleeing the WTC after the first plane hit. *According to the employee, about five minutes before the attack the entire Deutsche Bank computer system had been taken over by something external that no one in the office recognized and every file was downloaded at lightning speed to an unknown location.* The employee, afraid for his life, lost many of his friends on September 11, and he was well aware of the role that the Deutsche Bank subsidiary Alex Brown had played in insider trading. He also volunteered something that was being increasingly recognized around the world. *Mohamed Atta and many of the 9/11 hijackers who had lived and planned for*

---

[24] Mark H. Gaffney states that the deputizations by the SEC resembles "a surgeon who opens a patient on the operating room table to remove a tumor only to sew him back up again after finding that the cancer has metastasized throughout the body." (*Black 9/11: Money, Motive, and Technology*, p. 45) In other words, many in the financial sector knew ahead of time.

months with al Qaeda leaders in Frankfurt, Germany had kept accounts with Deutsche Bank.[25]

The question that inevitably occurs is why a German firm was hired to conduct data retrieval on the surviving computers from the World Trade Center. But more importantly, the German connections of Mohamed Atta must not be expanded to include not only the *Carl Duisberg Gesellschaft* but now also one of Germany's, and the world's largest banks, Deutsche Bank.

3. The Promise of PROMIS

Why Deutsche Bank? Because the bank, oddly enough, has long been "a favorite of the bin Laden family," and additionally, was involved with banks in Bahrain and Kuwait "that had served George W. Bush when he was engaging in his own illegal insider trading of the shares of his company Harken Energy just prior to the first Iraqi war."[26] With this in hand, Ruppert asks a significant question, noting first that "international wire transfers of terrorist groups had been blocked and bank accounts monitored. *So why couldn't it be done with the put options?*"[27] His answer is that U.S. intelligence made use of the now infamous PROMIS software system to infiltrate the Deutsche Bank computers and to place the international put options trading.[28] The PROMIS software was developed in the 1980s and stolen from its corporate developer, former NSA analyst William Hamilton's Inslaw Corporation, by the Reagan Justice Department under then Attorney General Ed Meese. While the PROMIS story will be reviewed in a subsequent chapter, for our present purposes we note that after the software was stolen, it was purportedly modified with "back doors," prior to being sold to a variety of nations, allowing the American national security establishment to access foreign nations' and corporations' computer networks. The PROMIS software, it is to be noted, allegedly was sophisticated enough that it was able to

---

[25] Michael C. Ruppert, *Crossing the Rubicon*, pp. 243-244, italicized emphasis added, boldface emphasis original.

[26] Michael C. Ruppert, *Crossing the Rubicon*, p. 250. See also Nafeez Ahmed Mossaddeq, *The War on Freedom*, p. 211. Ruppert makes the observation that "Intelligence agencies can't be loyal to the national interest when their national governments have been quietly replaced by multinational corporations and/or organized crime syndicates." (p. 248.)

[27] Ibid., p. 249, emphasis added.

[28] Ibid.

read databases written in a variety of computer coding languages and to integrate them into one database.[29]

This insight, however, also carries with it an implicit admission that one was dealing with a problem for the hypothesis that 9/11 involved only two levels, that of the "terrorist-hijacker" patsies, and that of a rogue network existing merely within the American national security "deep state," for as the *New York Times* itself noted, a terrorist group would be unlikely to signal its intentions by engaging in such high trading volume prior to its intended attacks,[30] but a global group could, and more importantly, the existence of such a global network *would* account for "the veil of secrecy that has fallen over the issue."[31]

Clearly, the Deutsche Bank computers in lower Manhattan were "invaded" by someone utilizing power cyber penetration software, and this, as Ruppert rightly suggests, implicates a capability such as that alleged for the now infamous software. So how might this suggest a *third level* or player? Here we can only speculate briefly: in the process of providing the software with a covert "back door" allowing American intelligence to access foreign computer networks, the possibility arises that, like all "doors," it was potentially and theoretically permissive of two way traffic, provided programmers could find a way to exploit that back door *in reverse*. We shall consider the potentials of this scenario in slightly greater detail in a subsequent chapter. For the moment, it forms the assumptive context by which to view 9/11 from an entirely different point of view, that of E.P. Heidner, for whom it was principally a financial crime.

---

[29] Michael C. Ruppert, *Crossing the Rubicon.*, p. 152. Ahmed also notes that this, wedded with AI programs, gave the program a powerful predictive capability to foresee market moves and, on that basis, "to detect trades that are anomalous, as a result of those projections." (Nafeez Mosaddeq Ahmed, *The War on Freedom*, p. 121.) I have made similar observations in my previous book, *Covert Wars and Breakaway Civilizations* (Kempton, Illinois: Adventures Unlimited Press, 2012), pp. 119-125.

[30] Michael C. Ruppert, *Crossing the Rubicon*, p. 253.

[31] Ibid., Ruppert also observes that "All the insanity and depravity suggested by 9/11 insider trading was made clear when the Pentagon announced, and then immediately scrapped, plans for a futures market on terrorist attacks called the Policy analysis Market. This official program constituted a frank admission that people with advance knowledge of terror attacks would always seek to capitalize on that knowledge." (p. 253.)

C. The Heidner Hypothesis: 9/11 as a Crime of High Finance
1. The Bonds in the Basement

One of the most provocative pieces of investigation to come from the 9/11 truth community is E.P. Heidner's "Collateral Damage: U.S. Covert Operations and the Terrorist Attacks on September 11, 2001," a lengthy document circulated on the internet. A review of this work with some additional information was also published in book form by Mark H. Gaffney, in *Black 9/11: Money, Motive, and Technology*.[32] The significance of these analyses, however, has largely gone unnoticed by that community, for again, when close attention is paid to the details, it becomes clear that 9/11 was, at its second level, a penetrated operation. But to make this clear, one has to review their data carefully and thoroughly.

Heidner begins his treatise with an intriguing and arresting thesis:

On September 11, 2001, three hijacked airliners hit three separate buildings with such precision and skill that many observers believe those flights were controlled by something other than the poorly trained hijackers in the cockpits. This report contends that not only were the buildings targets, *but that specific offices within each building were the designated targets*. These offices unknowingly held information which if exposed, subsequently would expose a national security secret of unimaginable magnitude. *Protecting that secret was the motivation for the September 11th attacks*. This report is about that national security secret, its origins and impact.[33]

Expanding on this, Heidner indicates that the motivation for the 9/11 attacks was simply to cover up a financial crime, albeit, one of extraordinary magnitude:

The hypothesis of this report is: the attacks of September 11th were intended to cover-up the clearing of $240 billion dollars in securities covertly created in September 1991 to fund a covert economic war against the Soviet Union, during which 'unknown' western investors bought up much of the Soviet industry, with a focus on oil and gas./ *The attacks of September 11th also served to derail multiple Federal investigations away from crimes associated with the 1991 covert operation*. In doing so, the attacks were

---

[32] Mark H. Gaffney, *Black 9/11: Money, Motive, and Technology* (Walterville, Oregon: Trine Day, 2012),
[33] E.P. Heidner, "Collateral Damage," p. 1.

justified under the cardinal rule of intelligence: "protect your resources" and consistent with a *modus operandi* of sacrificing lives for a greater cause.[34]

With this in hand, Heidner states that there were vaults in the World Trade center which, on the morning of 9/11, contained less than a billion dollars in gold bullion, but billions of dollars in these covert securities that "had to be destroyed." Heidner argues that this rationalizes the eyewitness accounts of bombs going off inside buildings 1, 6, and 7 of the World Trade center as well as the eyewitness statements of hearing bombs in the basements of the Twin Towers. Additionally, "a critical mass of brokers from the major government security brokerages in the Twin Towers had to be eliminated to create chaos in the government securities market" in order to quietly clear that $240 billion dollars in covert securities.[35] To understand all of this, Heidner also argues that it is necessary to understand the history of what this author has called the "hidden system of finance" that has been the subject of two of my previous books.[36] The operations of 9/11, and the deaths of the people caused on that day, were viewed by the perpetrators controlling this hidden system of finance as merely necessary collateral damage in order to protect and perpetuate its existence.[37]

2. Axis Loot, the Hidden System of Finance, and the Origins of "the Rogue Network"

Not surprisingly, this hidden system owes its origins to the same underlying causes as I and others have argued: to the secret off-the-books recovery and use of Axis loot, including the huge cache of riches that was part of Imperial Japan's Operation Golden Lily. This cache of riches, as I have argued, could only have been recovered and exploited by deep and secret collaboration with the very Axis elites that had plundered it initially, and with the cooperation of major western financial and intelligence institutions. Thus, in Heidner's account of this hidden system of finance, one encounters the now familiar names of the "American fascists," John J. McCloy, former American counsel for I.G. Farben prior to World War Two, postwar American high commissioner

---

[34] E.P. Heidner, "Collateral Damage," p. 1.

[35] Ibid. This clearing was done in part, Heidner alleges, by replacing the original illegal bonds with U.S. Treasury notes. (p. 5.)

[36] See my *Covert Wars and Breakaway Civilizations* and *Covert Wars and Clash of Civilizations*.

[37] E.P. Heidner, op. cit., p. 6.

for occupied Germany and pardoner of thousands of Nazis, and member of the Warren Commission, General Bill Donovan, head of America's wartime intelligence and covert operations service, the OSS, Henry L. Stimson, Bill Casey, Reagan's CIA director and close associate of Prescott Bush, Allen Dulles (predictably enough), and various other men, connected to the banks Heidner and others including this author believe to be or to have been involved in this international hidden system of finance: The Import-Export Bank, the Bank of New York, the former CIA fronts Nugan Hand International Bank, and the notorious Bank of Credit and Commerce International, and so on.[38] In Heidner's recounting of this story, the hidden system of finance is called the Black Eagle Trust, which "takes its name from the Nazi Black Eagle stamped on the gold bars of the Third Reich."[39]

Significantly, Heidner also provides a crucial detail on how this hidden system of finance was interfaced with the international criminal underworld, with the Mafia. According to Heidner, it was General Ed Lansdale, who first learned of the vast amount of Japanese loot cached in the Philippines and who brought it to General MacArthur's and ultimately President Truman's attention,[40] that also deepened the postwar ties between American intelligence and such Mafia bosses as Carlos Marcello, Santos Trafficante, and Meyer Lansky.[41] This network expanded when former Philippine president Ferdinand Marcos began his own independent recovery of the Japanese loot on the Philippines. Barrick Gold was founded and quickly became associated with this recovery, and in turn, became a principal investment focus for gold bullion banks. "These banks would loan gold to Barrick, which would then sell the borrowed gold as derivatives, which the promise of replacing the borrowed gold with their gold mining operation. The records of many of those transactions disappeared when Enron collapsed and the trading operation and all its records were taken over by (United Bank of Switzerland), another major recipient of Marcos gold."[42]

It is important to pause and note what Heidner, and what I and others who have investigated this hidden system of finance, are suggesting: *virtually every financial scandal of the postwar world and virtually every large financial story—such as Germany's recent demands to repatriate its gold—may and probably does have some connection to*

---

[38] E.P. Heidner, "Collateral Damage pp. 7-8.

[39] Ibid., p. 9.

[40] Joseph P. Farrell, *Cover Wars and Breakaway Civilizations*, pp. 133-143.

[41] E.P. Heidner, op. cit., p. 10.

[42] Ibid., p. 11.

this hidden system of finance and its hidden intelligence and underworld criminal masters.

Given these deep connections, Heidner states that

> By the end of the 1980s, the banks that had their agents in the OSS intelligence operations at the end of World War II were the banks that would be the dominant global players by 2001:
> - Morgan Guaranty Trust
> - Chase Manhattan
> - Citibank
> - Jardine Matheson
> - UBS (United Bank of Switzerland)
> - Deutschebank (sic)
> - HSBC (Hong Kong and Shanghai Banking Corporation)[43]

Heidner then follows this up with a crucial observation about the historical origins of what the 9/11 truth community calls "the rogue network", and what we have been calling "level two":

> The covert operations funded by the Black Eagle Trust in the 1960s and 1970s became visible stains on the global image of the U.S. despite all efforts to keep them under cover. In an effort to clean house, President Jimmy Carter would order the retirement of over 800 covert operatives. Many of these operatives would move into private consulting and security firms and be employed as subcontractors for covert operations. Thus began a loose association of private operatives that would be referred to as "the Enterprise" in the years to come.[44]

In other words, what was created was a *private* and largely *informal, polycentric* network existing within and behind the various corporations and agencies of the federal government which, with its operatives carefully positioned, could conceivably plan an event like 9/11, and which additionally *might* have been able to collect a comprehensive list of codenames and code words.

3. Destabilizing the Russian Ruble

As I have argued in previous books and in presentations to various conferences, this hidden system of finance ran into the trillions of

---

43 E.P. Heidner, "Collateral Damage," p. 12.
44 Ibid.

dollars over the decades. This is an important point, for most people examining it have argued that its purpose was *solely* as a slush fund for various American covert operations. However, the sheer scale of the finances involved suggested to me that it could and probably did have an entirely different principal purpose, and that is simply that it was used to fund covert and highly secret black technologies research projects.

The third possibility, mentioned by Heidner, is that it was finally used for the biggest covert operation of them all: direct covert economic warfare on the Soviet Union, to bring about its collapse and an economic "buy out" of Russia's resources. This proceeded in several phases:

1) In the first phase, American and corrupt Russian officials, largely in the KGB, created a "complex international network of banks and holding companies that would be used to take over the Soviet economy."[45]

2) In the next phase, President George H.W. Bush allegedly authorized various people to destabilize the Russian ruble on international currency markets, forcing Russia to sell off vast amounts of its bullion reserves, which at the time amounted to about $35 billion dollars. [46] This was done by creating the $240 billion dollars in false securities, managed by a CIA covert operative, Colonel Russell Hermann, via the "secretive Durham Trust." These bonds were backed by secretly recovered Marcos gold.[47] Since this gold was secret, it could be used to flood both paper and actual physical bullion trading, suppress the value of gold, at the same time that the assaults on the ruble were under way.

3) Once these mechanisms were in place, the coup against Mikhail Gorbachev was launched by KGB Generals Vladimir Kruchkov, and Viktor Cherbrikov, both men business partners with British financier Robert Maxwell.[48]

4) Once the coup had succeeded, the buyout of Russia proceeded under the Russian oligarchs, whose financial and money laundering connections included various western banks, including the Bank of New York.[49]

---

[45] E.P. Heidner, "Collateral Damage," p 18.
[46] Ibid.
[47] Ibid.
[48] Ibid., p. 19. The tangled and suspicious death of Maxwell is reviewed on p. 19.
[49] Ibid., p. 20.

With this in hand, Heidner reviews the individual perpetrators, and how all this was accomplished:

> 1. There has been a body of investigative reporting that suggests that between 1991 and 1992, the ruble was under a massive attack, with an unknown source of funding. The capital flight from the Soviet Union in U.S. dollars was estimated by Fidel Castro at $500 billion, and by Gorbachev at one trillion dollars. Somebody had to put up the lion's share of funding for those dollars. The most authoritative source on the subject, Claire Sterling, writes that unknown intelligence operations were behind the attack.
>
> "The fact that scarcely anyone outside Russia has heard of the Great Ruble Scam may be explained partly by its seemingly unbelievable details, but partly, too, by Western reluctance to touch exquisitely sensitive political nerves. Western governments rejoicing in the collapse of the evil empire wanted to assume, and to all appearance did assume, that all the evils in an emerging democracy emanated from politicians identified with the fallen communist state. No one was prepared to acknowledge indelicate evidence to the contrary. *The ability of three or four characters to mount such a planet wide operation, their extraordinary impact on what was still a world superpower, and their singular immunity from beginning to end suggest the guiding hand of not just one, but several intelligence agencies.*"[50]

Before continuing, it is worth noting that the "guiding hand of not just one, but of several intelligence agencies" suggests once again a global network, i.e., that *all* of those intelligence agencies are penetrated by something deeper, and international in extent.

4. The Dreadful Bush Family Once Again

Heidner then mentions yet another alleged Bush connection to all these activities, one whose significance will become evident at the end of this chapter:

> Mrs. V.K. Durhan, wife of Russell Herman(sic), who was a fund controller for the CIA's covert fund, has contended in sworn testimony that George H.W. Bush, Oliver North, and Alan Greenspan forced her husband into relinquishing the funding for the bonds... They later forged Hermann's signature on related

---

[50] E.P. Heidner, "Collateral Damage," p. 26, citing Claire Sterling, "Thieves World,"(No further information given), emphasis added by me.

financial transactions. She also claims they were responsible for his death three years later because Hermann believed these funds were the property of the U.S. citizens rather than the private slush fund of the Bush circle, and protested the manner in which they were being used.[51]

The private personal use of the existence of such a hidden system of finance is, to a certain extent, the inevitable consequence of President Truman's decision establishing it in 1947, and placing it under the direction of the President's National Security Council. A secret system could indeed be converted to personal use, *or to that of a secret and international network*, for a temporary period of time, and any "borrowed funds" returned prior to any internal audits such a system might have put into place to control funds. It is a practice similar to the well-known practice of banks, which use the period before trades are cleared to use the funds for their own private trading before posting the funds to the account(s) involved in the transaction. This, essentially, is Heidner's argument.

5. The Federal Investigations and the 9/11 Attacks

It is at this juncture that the hidden system of finance, and its use by an international group for which it was not intended, came to the attention of Federal intelligence agencies, one of them being the Office of Naval Investigation (!) which

> ...released over 100 pages of bank transactions detailing transactions in the range of 100s of billions of dollars. These are the same files released also by Derek(sic) Vreeland from a Canadian prison, from which he warned his guards about the forthcoming attack on the World Trade Center. Vreeland contended he was an ONI operative. The files cover three periods of transactions which correspond to this covert war on the Soviet Union; while the transactions do not directly show securities going to the Soviet Union, they do support the theory that the Bush Vulcans were spending massive amounts of cash in a manner inconsistent with US Federal budget spending caps in effect at the time, and moving massive funding into covert accounts at key trust funds—most notably Pilgrim Investments, to the account of "Jorge" Bush.[52]

---

[51] E.P. Heidner, "Collateral Damage," p. 26.
[52] E.P. Heidner, "Collateral Damage," p. 26.

These transactions documents three periods of financial activity coordinated with the phases of economic warfare on the Soviet Union, including a second phase that saw the stripping of bullion and hard currency assets of the Soviet Treasury and Communist Party.[53]

As a number of federal investigations were under way concerning the use (and misuse) of public funds, Heidner argues that the 9/11 attacks were for the purpose of killing (quite literally) those investigations,[54] and that this is why the Pentagon was attacked where it was, that is, *at the Office of Naval Investigations.*[55] Similarly, when the north tower of the twin towers was struck, it was struck at the 95th and 96th stories, where the offices of Marsh and McLennan, one of the world's largest insurance companies, had its headquarters. Marsch and McLennan also had close ties to the private intelligence and security firm Kroll Associates, which was the holder of the World Trade Center's security services contract.[56] A strike against these targets would thus conceivably wipe out any suspicious financial records as well as any records indicating the potential preparation of the towers for demolitions.[57]

On the day of the attacks, one of the most significant events occurred, one tending to confirm the analysis of Heidner, when the Securities and Exchange Commission suspended Ruls 15c3-3, which prohibits a seller from substituting one set of securities set to clear, with another, without a buyer agreeing to allow a seller to substitute other securities. Other provisions suspended on that day to allow various securities to be cleared were a relaxation of "blind broker" provisions

---

[53] Ibid., p. 27. While the story is too lengthy to be reviewed here, the role of U.S. ambassador Leo Wanta has always figured in the reviews of the suspicious financial aspects of 9/11. In this respect, Wanta maintained that the bonds created to fund this economic warfare were also used "to fund an undesignated 'join venture' with Russia."(Heidner, op. cit., p. 27.) $240 billion dollars of funding buys a lot of "joint venture" and this might be something related to secret technologies, or hidden infrastructures, including those associated with space. The bonds also provided the cash funneled to Russia... through (you guessed it) Deutsche bank.

[54] E.P. Heidner, "Collateral Damage," p. 29.

[55] Ibid., p. 3.

[56] Mark H. Gaffney, *Black 9/11*, p. 31. Gaffney provides a table of the companies involved in suspicious trading activity prior to 9.11 on p. 39, and notes that the American defense contractor Raytheon's call options trading had surged to six times its normal volume of call option trading (p. 38).

[57] Laurent Guyénot also observes that Bryan C. Jack, a Pentagon worker responsible for various aspects of accounting the American defense budget, was on board Flight 77(Guyénot, *JFK -9/11: 50 Years of Deep State*, p. 145.)

which allowed clearing houses to clean up their accounts reconciliations. In other words, on 9/11, "the Federal Reserve and its (Government Securities Clearing Corporation) had created a settlement environment totally void of controls and reporting—where it could substitute valid, new government securities for the mature, illegal securities, and not have to record where the bad securities came from, or where the new securities went, all because the paper for the primary brokers for US securities had been eliminated."[58] Additionally, even with this rather carefree securities clearing environment, there was a dramatic rise in "fails" on and immediately after 9/11, as clearing failed to occur in a number of cases.

While the Federal Reserve attempted to portray these clearing failures as more or less dispersed across the financial sector, closer examination revealed them to be concentrated in one bank: the Bank of New York, even while J.P. Morgan and Deutsche Bank, both banks using the same trading hubs in lower Manhattan, reported no serious trading disruptions for the day. Indeed, Deutsche Bank's offices were in the World Trade Center complex, while Bank of New York's offices were not structurally damaged. Thus, neither the Government Securities Clearing Corporation nor any of its associated dealers could verify "what came into and what left their custodial accounts at (the Bank of New York); they could not advise (the Bank of New York) of securities they expected to receive and they could not give (the Bank of New York) instructions for delivering securities. Additionally (the Government Securities Clearing Corporation) was unable to verify the movement of funds into and out of its account at (the Bank of New York)."[59] This in turn would have allowed off-balance sheet liabilities to be moved "to the balance sheet and claim the offsetting claims are in the rubble of the World Trade Center,"[60] or in other words, many of the liabilities of the hidden system of finance could be moved into the public sector, as assets of the public sector were moved to that of the hidden system of finance and the global network it represented.[61]

---

[58] E.P. Heidner, "Collateral Damage," p. 29.

[59] Ibid., citing The Government Securities Clearing Corporation, Important Notice GSCC 068.01.

[60] Ibid., p.33.

[61] Heidner notes that "According to leaked documents from an intelligence file obtained through a military source in the Office of Naval Intelligence (ONI), on or about September 12, 1991, non-performing and unauthorized gold-backed debt instruments were used to purchase ten-year "Brady" bonds. The bonds in turn were illegally employed as collateral to borrow $240 billion—120 in Japanese Yen and 120 in Deutsch Marks—exchanged for U.S. currency under false pretenses; or counterfeit and unlawful conversion of collateral against which an unlimited

6. The Erle Cocke Deposition:
Back to the Gold-Backed Bearer Bonds?

A crucial confirmation of the existence of this hidden system of finance, and to the global network behind it, was provided by Erle Cocke, who recorded testimony in New York District Court in April 2000, just ten days prior to his death from pancreatic cancer. When asked about the size of the funds available for the covert operations against the Soviet Union, Cocke stated that is was "$223, 104, 000, 008.03" or $223 billion. This, he stressed, was during the period of November-December 1991, and represented not the size of the hidden system itself, but merely of the profits it had generated and which were being used to fund the operation.[62] This was used to create an asset base "as collateral for sales of large numbers of leveraged derivatives or banking instruments that were then marketed at a discount," or which were also then treated as collateral![63]

And this is where the off-ledger accounts and gold-backed derivatives and securities, which "though heavily leverages, were still gold-backed, and hence more secure than the US dollar and more desirable from a trading standpoint"[64] comes in, for one can hide trade—no matter how large, even in the trillions of dollars—in these off ledger accounts simply by structuring trades in such a fashion that all traces cancel out at the end of the day, when off ledger accounts are reconciled. This implies possession of large scale computing databse systems like PROMIS. By balancing and structuring these trades, the off ledger balance "would remain unchanged" and "the total amount of business conducted that day would be off the record, hence, invisible, even if the trading was in the trillions."[65]

But what does this mean for the thesis of a third level, a global network with trillions of dollars of assets, to recall the observation of Dr. Tatyana Koryagina? Very simply, it means that *globally*, there is a hidden system which trades in gold-backed highly leveraged *physical* securities on a hidden market, recalling all the bearer bonds scandals that followed 9/11, while the public tier of finance has effectively a

---

amount of money could be created in derivatives and debt instruments." (p. 48, citing "Cash Payoffs, bonds and murder linked to White House 9/11 finance, tomflocco.com). Heidner also notes that the Dulles brothers helped found the Bank of New York.

[62] Mark H. Gaffney, *Black 9/11*, p. 110.
[63] Ibid.
[64] Ibid., p. 113.
[65] Ibid., p. 112.

different kind of currency, the national currencies of the various nations, which function rather like Hjalmar Schacht's scheme of the *Rentenmark*, as a currency good only in the country of issue. In short, 9/11 was a key event in the history of that hidden system of finance and of the global financial system, as liabilities began to be deliberately shifted to the public sector, and assets to the private and hidden global network.

And this brings Heidner to a consideration of the most bizarre financial and historical connections of them all.

D. Nazis... Again:
The Nazi Banker to the Bin Laden Group

Like other 9/11 researchers, Heidner is aware of the bizarre and suggestive association of hijacker ring-leader Mohamed Atta with the *Carl Duisberg Gesellschaft*, but here he departs from the norm by digging deeper:

> Mohammad Atta (sic), as can best be determined, received funding from three foreign intelligence agencies aligned with the US: Pakistan, Syria (!) and Germany. His father contended he actually worked for a fourth—the Mossad![66]

Having made this declaration, Heidner continues by noting a fact often mentioned by other 9/11 researchers, namely, that the head of Pakistan's ISI intelligence agency, Lt. General Mahmud Ahmad was meeting with Bob Graham, Porter Goss, and Richard Armitage in the USA on the morning of 9/11, and that he was responsible "for having transferred $100,000 to Mohammed Atta."[67] But then he continues:

> While in Germany, Atta worked as an employee of Tatex trading which was owned primarily by Mohamad Majed Said, a former head of Syria's General Intelligence Directorate.

Then comes the bombshell:

> In coming to Germany, Atta was funded with a scholarship and employed as a tutor by an organization known as (the) Carl Duisberg Gesellschaft.

---

[66] E.P. Heidner, "Collateral Damage", p. 39.
[67] Ibid.

Subsequent Internet reports linked the Carl Duisberg Society to administration by the U.S. Information Agency, but this had not been verified by any government documentation. *There are Internet reports that the scholarship was jointly funded by US AID. The more interesting aspect of Carl Duisberg Geseelschaft is that it's (sic) Managing Director is Bernd Schlich, the same individual who is Managing Director of InWEnt (Internationale Welterbildung und Entwicklung). If one investigates the activities and research of InWEnt, it appears to be a commercial intelligence operation that does studies on such matters as money-laundering, weapons trades, drug smuggling, and anthrax control in such places as South America, Central Asia and Africa.* Carl Duisberg Gesellschaft has a fellowship funded by Alpha Group, the Russian Bank represented in the U.S. by former G.H.W. Bush administrators Ed Rogers and Lanny Griffith.[68]

Unlike many 9/11 researchers, Heidner notes that the *Carl Duisberg Gesellschaft* was named for one of the founders of the notorious multinational I.G. Farben cartel,[69] but does not pursue this any further for any possible significance it might have.

So the question that hovered over this detail in chapter one, confronts us once again: is there any significance to this detail? And if so, what is it?

There is, and the answer once again lies in Saudi Arabia, with the Bin Laden group, and with the historical connections between Nazism and radical Islamic groups. As already has been seen, the giant Saudi construction and financial group, the Saudi Bin Laden Group, prefers to bank with Deutsche Bank. The question is, why? And the answer is, that

> Up until 1996, the setting up of the (Saudi Bin Laden Group's) subsidiaries were prepared in Lausanne by its councilor, the Nazi banker François Genoud, executor of Dr. Goebbels's will and a donor of funds to the terrorist Carlos.[70]

But that's not all there is to say about François Genoud, not by a long shot.

According to the article in *Wikipedia* on Monsieur Genoud, he journeyed in 1934 to Palestine, and met the notorious Grand Mufti of Jerusalem, Al-Husseini, establishing a life-long friendship with him,

---

[68] E.P. Heidner, "Collateral Damage," p. 39, emphasis added.

[69] Ibid., p. 58.

[70] Thierry Meyssan, *9/11: The Big Lie*, p. 98.

maintaining this relationship with him when the latter came to Berlin in order to coordinate the establishment of Muslim units of the Waffen SS. Genoud became the Grand Mufti's banker of choice.[71] A member of ODESSA (*Organization der Ehemalige SS Angehörigen*), Genoud was also instrumental in coordinating the Nazi ratlines out of Europe after the war, and their financing.[72]

This was not all. Genoud was also the financial executor of the affairs for Nazi Propaganda Minister Dr. Josef Goebbels, for Adolf Hitler himself, and most importantly, for Martin Bormann, and as such was also the principal manager for Nazi assets in Swiss banks after the war. In the context of the Nazi International theme I have developed in previous books, it may be said that Genoud was the principal financial officer for the post-war Nazi International.[73]

More importantly, Genoud was a principal financier and arms supplier for a variety of Palestinian causes, which received support from from "the Lausanne-based New European Order organization" which met in Barcelona, Spain, in 1969, with Palestinian groups—Yasser Arrafat's PLO among them—received financial support from Genoud, who "placed them in contact with former Nazis who would assist their military training."[74] Additionally, he even provided financial support to the Ayatollah Khomeini during his exile in France![75] This Nazi-Swiss connection is important, for recall that one of Atta's most odious companions was from Switzerland.

As if to emphasize his signal importance, Katharine Kanter, a researcher for Lyndon LaRouche's *Executive Intelligence Review* also noted that Genoud seemed to have been protected both both "certain influential Zionists" *and* by the faction of the American deep state and high finance represented by the Dulles brothers.[76] Indeed, according to Kanter, it was Genoud who helped found the Malmö group, the "formal" founding of the Nazi International, which for the LaRouche network constitutes "the 'successor phase' in Anglo-American deployment of fascist networks," and which had as a goal the co-opting of emerging

---

[71] "François Genoud," *Wikipedia.* En.wikipedia.org/wiki/Fran%C3% A7ois_Genoud.

[72] Ibid.

[73] Ibid., see especially the section in the *Wikipedia* article titled "Post-War."

[74] Ibid., see the section titled "Palestine."

[75] Ibid, see the section "Notable Aid Recipients and Associations."

[76] Katharine Kanter, "François Genoud: 60 Years as an Anglo-Swiss Spook," in *EIR Books,* July 5, 1996, p. 46.

movements and groups dedicated to Arab and Muslim nationalism.[77] As a component of his "Nazi International" activities, Genoud also maintained a close working relationship with Interpol, including with its post-World War two head, Paul Dickopf, who was a former official of Nazi counter-intelligence under the *Abwehr* of admiral Wilhelm Canaris.[78] It was also Genoud who arranged the initial contact between Allen Dulles and SS General Karl Wolff.[79]

Needless to say, Genoud's role as "chief financial officer" for this post-war Nazi International also put him into direct and sustained contact with the former Reichsbank president, Hjalmar Horace Greeley Schacht, who became involved with Genoud's Banque Commerciale Arabe, a bank established during the crisis between France in its then Algerian colony.[80] In this role, Genoud was also a close associate, and presumably chief financial officer, of Werner Naumann,[81] who of course was the principal player in the 1953 "Naumann plot," an ostensible Nazi coup attempt to overthrow the government of postwar West German Chancellor Dr. Konrad Adenauer.[82]

When one considers these revelations, it becomes apparent that Mohamed Atta's connections to the *Carl Duisberg Gesellschaft* are not happenstance nor insignificant, but rather exemplary of a pattern of postwar fascist support of terrorist groups and operations, and that this postwar "global network" may have a fascist international component that showed its hand on 9/11.

In this respect, it is important to recall the argument advanced in part one, that the 9/11 operations simply could *not* have been planned and executed by the alleged terrorists and hijackers acting on their own, nor even by Osama bin Laden, for all his family's wealth, power, and connections. The concurrence of mirroring drills on that day, planned by the American national security apparatus, indicates rather that a rogue element within that apparatus had to have been involved.

---

[77] Katharine Kanter, "François Genoud: 60 Years as an Anglo-Swiss Spook," in *EIR Books*, July 5, 1996, p. 47.

[78] Ibid., p. 47.

[79] Ibid.

[80] Ibid., p. 48. Kanter also notes that Schacht, in turn, helped set up the Harriman International Company with Allen Dulles' brother, and later Secretary of State under Eisenhower, John Foster Dulles. The purpose of the Harriman International Company was to coordinate all exports from the Third Reich into the United States. (see p. 48).

[81] Ibid., p. 49.

[82] For the Naumann coup, see my *The Third Way: The Nazi International, European Union, and Corporate Fascism*, pp. 65-67.

This conclusion is now buttressed by the revelations that high financial crimes were involved in, and covered up by, the 9/11 operation, and these again, could only have originated within that deep state and more importantly, by people with access to and knowledge of that vast postwar hidden system of finance. While originally an American system, designed to be a covert slush fund and black projects research fund totally free from any oversight, that hidden system, by 9/11, had become a truly *global* system in its own right, a "breakaway civilization" able to remake the global financial system and redraw borders according to its designs.

Yet...

...something happened, as we have seen, that signaled all was not going according to plan, for the President himself—whose family historically had deep ties to this fascist component via the family patriarch, Prescott Bush, and his Union bank dealings with Hitler financier Fritz Thyssen on the one hand, and via his close association with Averill Harriman on the other—had to fly to Barksdale and Offut to head off what was an apparent coup attempt.

And this means that level two was being challenged by level three, or that factional cracks had appeared in that global network of which the Bush dynasty was very much a part.

This problem may be considered from another angle of approach, for if the goals of the 9/11 operation were (1) to create a false flag event to project American power into the Middle East in order to secure its energy reserves, and (2) to wipe out evidence of financial crimes and its own involvement in them, then the mere *attacks* would have sufficed. The records of the crime could have been destroyed in fires, and the devastation of the attacks would still have required an American "response". The *"overkill"* in evidence on that day, with the destruction of the Twin Towers, might therefore possibly indicate the service of divorce papers between the two groups. In this connection, it will be recalled that the third level communicated its bona fides by indicating knowledge of a breadth and depth of highly classified American code names.

This might have indicated the deep penetration of level two by several moles, or a cyber-hacking ability—an exploited "backdoor" in the system—or both.

And it might, equally, have announced its presence by a clear demonstration of mechanisms of destruction not accessible to level two. It is therefore to a consideration of these two capabilities, the mechanism of the destruction of the Twin Towers, and the possible cyber-hacking abilities, that we must now turn in the next two chapters.

171

François Genoud, 1915-1996

7
THE MYSTERY OF THE MECHANISM

*"You see the underground work is one of the most expensive parts of the tower. In this system that I have invented it is necessary for the **machine to get a grip of the earth, otherwise it cannot shake the earth. It has to have a grip on the earth so that the whole of this globe can quiver,** and to do that it is necessary to carry out a very expensive construction."*
Nikola Tesla[1]

MURDER WEAPONS TYPICALLY CONSTITUTE A PRINCIPAL, if not *the* principal means of connecting the criminal to the crime, and of identifying the criminal himself. The difficulty with 9/11 is that other than videos of airplanes flying into the Twin Towers, there is no clear murder weapon or mechanism. As was noted in the Preface, even the *obvious* murder weapons are disputed: there were airplanes piloted by men with poor piloting skills, the aircraft were taken over and flown by remote control, the aircraft carried missiles, and finally, there were no aircraft at all.

In the case of the Twin Towers, however, it matters little whether there were airplanes or no airplanes, for the mechanism of their collapse has formed the center of ongoing controversy ever since that day, and for a very simple reason: the government's official narrative that the Towers collapsed because burning airplane fuel weakened the structures, and the floors "pancaked" down, makes no sense from any number of points of view, including the video records of their destruction. In the wake of this failure to explain, and thereby to state a clear case for what the murder weapon was, four basic theories have been proposed, all of them variations on the idea that *some* form of controlled demolitions was used. These four theories are:

1) The towers were destroyed by conventional controlled demolitions explosives;
2) The towers were destroyed by the use of nanothermite explosives;

---

[1] Testimony of Nikola Tesla, New York State Supreme Court, Appellate Division, Second Department: Clover Boldt Miles and George C. Boldt, Jr. as Executors of the Last Will and Testament of George C. Boldt, Deceased, Plaintiffs-Respondents, versus Nikola Tesla, Thomas G. Shearman, et al. as Defendants-Appellants, 521-537, pp, 174-179, cited in my book *Babylon's Banksters: The Alchemy of Deep Physics, High Finance and Ancient Religion* (Port Townsend, Washington: Feral House, 2010), p. 149, emphasis added.

    3) The towers were destroyed by small, portable nuclear weapons, or "mininukes"; and finally,

    4) The towers were destroyed by some form of exotic or directed energy weapon.[2]

Unfortunately, the advocates of these positions have defended their own positions and attacked advocates of others so vociferously and with such vitriol, a detached examination of the evidence for and against each point of view has become all but impossible. Advocates of the mininuke theory, for example, attack those who argue for the exotic, or directed, energy weapons hypothesis, as being "gatekeepers," "shills", "government disinformation agents", and as lacking any proposal for a model of how such a weapon might have worked, while conveniently providing no models for how mininukes might work: what is their critical mass? What is their fuel? Were these predominantly small fusion weapons? Boosted fission weapons? Neutron bombs? Viewed objectively, the attacks from advocates of mininukes on advocates of energy weapons reveal as much weakness in their own positions as they do in that which they oppose. Accordingly and to the extent possible, our method here will avoid using or referring to the names of people that have been engaged in this type of vitriolic, *ad hominem* attacks and arguments from authority in order to avoid becoming involved in disputes about personalities.

    The four theories highlight yet another methodological difficulty, namely, the advocates of each position have tended to view their hypothesis as an *exclusive* one, i.e., as the *sole* mechanism used. It is precisely at this juncture that the idea of *more than one deeper level* to the 9/11 conspiracy finds its utility in the complex relationship between

---

[2] Again, I am using the terms "directed energy" and "exotic energy" as implying two distinct categories. For the sake of simplicity, "directed energy" weapons would refer to a category of weapons using electromagnetic beams of some sort, either coherent or non-coherent, in a "point and shoot" mode of use, while "exotic weapons" I am using as a term of art to refer to weapons utilizing the local structured potential of the quantum vacuum in some fashion. These are *targetable* weapons, but are not "directed" in the "point and shoot" sense. The distinction will, I hope, become clearer when this topic is examined in more detail subsequently. While I do personally favor the exotic energy weapons hypothesis, I do not view this as an exclusive hypothesis. However, since the other three theories have received the most attention, I shall spend more time with the exotic energy weapons hypothesis, in order to outline a method and model of how it might have occurred. I *do not* view this model as entirely satisfactory, nor without its own deep problems. I propose it simply for the sake of argued speculation.

the murder weapon or weapons, and the people wielding them. In this respect, it will be observed that the higher one goes in the various theories, the narrower the circle becomes of people who would have access to the mechanism in view, and who would be able to deploy and use them with technical competency. Conventional controlled demolitions methods would be the most widely accessible and deployable, while "mininukes" and exotic energy weapons would be restricted to a narrow base of people with the access and technical competence to deploy them. Additionally, if one presupposes there was more than one level or layer to the deeper layers of the conspiracy behind the first level of poorly trained hijackers piloting aircraft into buildings, then it becomes possible to admit that *more than one mechanism* might have been in play on 9/11, and hence, more than one level of deeper players and plotters.

To put all of this very differently and succinctly, the World Trade Center attacks are "the center of the tragedy"[3] and thus the vital *crux interpretum* of the event.

Such a methodology might seem a violation of the principle of parsimony, or "Ockham's razor" as it is more popularly known, and discussions and invocations of this principle often occur in the acrimonious debates that have surrounded the "mystery of the mechanism" of the destruction of the Twin Towers. While a philosophical discussion of this principle itself is long overdue, the constraints of our presentation preclude such a discussion here. We merely point out two things: 1) the "razor" itself was a principle that arose in *mediaeval scholastic theology, and not science,* and hence the possibility arises that science has misunderstood and misappropriated the principle, and 2) if the principle of parsimony is favored by nature, as its scientific users typically understand it, then if one pursues the principle to its logical reductio, no diversity in nature would exist at all, It is therefore an inappropriate basis on which to reject an hypothesis on the basis of its "complexity" or "simplicity"; these are purely *qualitative* evaluations, and more often than not simply serve as a device for closing down considerations of opposing points of view. They do not, as such, constitute argument.

---

[3] Webster Griffin Tarpley, *9/11 Synethtic Terror: Made in USA,* fifth edition, p. 221.

The Mystery of the Mechanism

A. The Beginning of the Pancake Theory:
A Clear Case of Data Obfuscation
1. Planting the Meme of the Pancake Theory
a. Mark Walsh's Statement

Before the date of September 11th, 2001 was a bitter and sad memory, the hypothesis that the Twin Towers had "collapsed" because the burning airplane fuel had weakened the structures, causing the floors to collapse and "pancake" on top of one another, had already gained traction. This became the official government narrative of the National Institute for Standards and Technology's *Final Report on the Collapse of the World Trade Center Towers* when it was published four years after the attacks, in September 2005. Many observers, however, on the day of the events, were already skeptical of the pancake theory even before it had been endorsed by the National Institute of Standards and Technology, a group which should have known that what they were saying was nonsense, for many observers watching the Towers "collapse" collapse on TV observed that they had fallen at nearly freefall speed. Under the "pancake" theory, this would have been physically impossible. These observers also pointed out that if the pancake theory were true, there should have been considerably more rubble in the footprints of the buildings than was actually observed. The pancake theory, in other words, began to die almost before it was born.

However, long before the National Institute of Standards and Technology endorsed the pancake theory, that hypothesis was already being carefully "seeded" into the public mind, and this is a strong indicator of the presence of the level two or "rogue network" player. Anyone who recalls the news commentary of that day will recall the talking heads almost immediately raising the possibility that the burning fires in the twin towers might cause a structural collapse. Then there was the case of Mark Walsh, noted by Laurent Guyénot:

> Mark Walsh was interviewed by Fox News (for which he works as a freelancer) in the hour following the disintegration of the towers, providing the ideal eyewitness testimony.
> "I saw this plane come out of nowhere and just ream right into the side of the Twin Tower exploding through to the other side, and then I witnessed both towers collapse, the first, and then the second, *mostly due to structural failure because the fire was just too intense.*"
> Conflating the observation and the technical explanation, in the very terms destined to become official, serves to cover the explanation which naturally comes to the mind of a neutral

176

witness, such as a journalist Don Dahler commenting on ABC News: "The entire building has just collapsed, as if a demolition team set off..."[4]

The statements of Walsh resemble someone "delivering lines" rather than simply stating what they saw, for he is offering *an explanation* of what he saw, one that is moreover couched in technical terms, whereas Don Dahler is offering *an analogy* for what he saw that others might be able to identify with in their experience. Like the Kennedy assassination and the focus on Lee Harvey Oswald, a scenario, complete with murder weapon, is being offered to divert attention away from the deeper layer of players and the *actual* murder weapon. During periods of shock, it is essential for authority to plant an interpretation of an event into the memory when the rational faculties are most vulnerable.[5]

b. Osama Bin Laden Obliges the Pancake Theory

Within three months of 9/11, the pancake theory was under such fire from the growing 9/11 truth community, and with it, the official narrative that al-Qaeda, and al-Qaeda alone, pulled off the attacks without any deeper players. On December 9th, 2001, *The Washington Post* carried a front page article stating that a video from Osama Bin Laden had surfaced which obligingly advocated the physically impossible pancake theory. The video was allegedly recorded on 9/11 itself by a close associate of Osama,[6] and its utility to the official narrative was quickly pointed out by Deputy Secretary of Defense Paul Wolfowitz during an interview on ABC News' *This Week*:

> It's repugnant. I mean here is a man who takes pride and pleasure from killing thousands of innocent human beings. This confirms what we already know about him. There's nothing new or surprising in there. It's only a confirmation. And I hope it will finally put a stop to these insane conspiracy theories according to which in some way the United States or somebody else are the guilty parties.[7]

---

[4] Laurent Guyénot, *JFK-9/11: 50 Years of Deep State*, p. 129, citing You Tube, "Fox News—Rick Leventhal interviews 9/11 WTC witness, Mark Walsh": www.youtube.com/watch?v=07hJhmiWZSY.
[5] Laurent Guyénot, *JFK-9/11: 50 Years of Deep State*, p. 129.
[6] Thierry Meyssan, *9/11: The Big Lie*, pp. 103-104.
[7] Ibid., p. 104.

Needless to say, Assistant Secretary Wolfowitz neglected to mention that the official narrative was being questioned precisely because it made no scientific sense. Apparently, to do so was "insane."

The actual video tape of (the alleged) Bin Laden was released by the Pentagon on December 13th, 2001. In it,

> Osama bin laden delivers "confessions" on the tape *that correspond on every point with the official version* that we know is far from the truth.
>
> "I was thinking that the fire from the gas in the plane would melt the iron structure of the (WTC) building and collapse the area where the plane had hit and all the floors above it only."[8]

If a son of one of the world's most wealthy families and prestigious construction and engineering groups thought that, then indeed terrorism took a gigantic step backwards when it made him its criminal mastermind, as we shall see below. Given the difficulties of the pancake theory, it seems more likely that this video was simply more planted "evidence" to buttress a quickly failing official narrative.

2. The Problem of Damage in All the Wrong Places

As the events and investigations unfolded, however, the airplane fuel-pancake theory began to exhibit severe problems. For example, on the day of 9/11, the CNN network ran a video showing smoke coming from the *street* level of building 6 of the World Trade Center. Building 6 was never struck by any aircraft, and, as we shall see subsequently, was severely damaged in a most unusual manner, leading researcher Jim Marrs to ask "Did the billowing smoke come from a premature detonation?"[9]

The "building 6 problem" is not the only difficulty for the pancake-airplane fuel theory. There is also the "twenty-seventh floor problem" of the South Tower:

> Many have wondered about the witnesses who claimed to have heard multiple explosions within the buildings. One such witness was the head of WTC security, John O'Neill, who stated shortly before he himself became a victim that he had helped dig out survivors on the 27th floor before the building collapsed. Since the

---

[8] Thierry Meyssan, *9/11: The Big Lie*, p. 104.
[9] Jim Marrs, *Inside Job*, p. 36.

aircraft crashed into the 80th floor, what heavily damaged the 27th floor?[10]

Damage to areas of the South Tower, and to building six which were not even hit by any aircraft, bring us directly to the consideration of the first hypothesis of the destruction of the Twin Towers, the theory of standard controlled demolitions.

B. The Controlled Demolition Theory

One of the most thorough and early examinations of the video and photographic records of the destruction of the World Trade Center was Eric Hufschmid's study, *Painful Questions: An Analysis of the September 11th Attack,* published in 2002. This work, while often referred to in the 9/11 truth community, is difficult to come by, and yet it is the essential work for the controlled demolitions theory. In a certain sense, it is also the core and essential book for the *other* theories, since in many cases they are based on reconsiderations of Hufschimdt's data and interpretations, or add new data to it. We shall therefore follow Hufschmidt's presentation of the basic case for the controlled demolitions theory closely here, referring to other 9/11 researches for comment and expansion when necessary.

Eric Hufschmidt's "Painful Questions" Book Cover

---

[10] Ibid., p. 33.

First, it is essential to have an understanding of the general plan of the World Trade Center Complex, as viewed from space:

The World Trade Center Complex from Space. North is to the top of the picture. Buildings 1 and 2 are the North and South Towers of the Twin Towers, Buildings 4, 5, and 6 are to the east of the Twin Towers, and building 7 is to the north of buildings 1 and 6.[11]

---

[11] Eric Hufschmid, *Painful Questions: An Analysis of the September 11th Attack* (Goleta, California: Endpoint Software, 2002), p. 21, citing spaceimaging.com.

Early in his presentation, Hufschmidt zeros in on the question and problems already hinted at, namely, that there was evidence of damage to *other* buildings in the World Trade Center Complex that were *not* struck by airplanes during the attacks, and which show clear signs of deliberate demolitions. Reproducing this picture taken shortly after the north tower has been struck,

View of North Tower, note the arrow pointing to a plume or cloud of smoke, appearing to originate from the area of Building 6, closer to the ground.[12]

Hufschmidt then notes that this is an indicator that some *other* mechanism must be in play besides airplanes and burning jet fuel to produce this cloud of smoke.

Zeroing in on this problem, he then reproduces the following aerial photograph taken of building six after the attacks:

---

[12] Eric Hufschmid, *Painful Questions*, p. 13, citing an unknown source for the picture. Careful examination of the picture in Hufschmid's book, which is in color, seems to indicate that it may be a frame from a television broadcast, as the appearance of the word "earlier" in the top left of the frame would indicate.

Building Six of the World Trade Center. Note the arrow on the right, pointing to debris from the cladding of one of the Twin Towers. But note the arrows to the left, pointing to holes in building six.[13]

The question is, what produced these holes? Since the first frame cited above shows a plume of smoke rising from the approximate area of build six shortly after the North Tower has been struck, and *thus prior to the destruction of either of the Twin Towers*, this cannot be due to damage from the debris of their collapse. Additionally, no airplane debris has ever been mentioned in connection with this damage. And in the case of the strikes against the Twin Towers, rough silhouettes of the aircraft were evident after the strikes. Here, no such silhouette is visible. Thus, something *else* must have made the holes in evidence.

In support of the idea that buildings six and five were damaged by some other means, Hufschmid reproduces this photograph of fires within building six (which, he points out, did *not* collapse simply because it was on fire):

---

[13] Eric Hufschmidt, *Painful Questions*, p. 14, citing James R. Tourtelotte. I have added the three arrows to clarify Hufschmid's argument.

Building Six on Fire on 9/11[14]

In short, it is the probable presence of damage to buildings five and six without any visible airplane attack that already calls into question the "pancake theory," and raises the possibility for controlled demolitions.

1. Evidence for the Theory
a. Drills and "Upgrades" Prior to 9/11

In any controlled demolitions scenario, be it that of conventional explosives, nanothermite, or micro-nukes, and with the sole possible exception of exotic or directed energies technologies, the buildings scheduled for demolition must be prepared: explosives have to be placed near crucial load bearing junctions, the detonators have to be rigged for a carefully timed and controlled sequencing of the explosions, and so on. Is there any evidence confirming this activity in the Twin Towers, or any activity that would confirm a *context* for such building preparation for demolitions, prior to 9/11?

Here the indicators of at least the *opportunity* for building preparation are quite strong. Marvin P. Bush, younger brother to then-president George W. Bush, owned a portion of the Securacom Company,

---

[14] Eric Hufschmid, *Painful Questions*, p. 68, photograph source unknown.

which in turn was a provider of security for the World Trade Center, being "a principal in this company from 1993 to 2000."[15] It was Securacom that provided security for the World Trade Center from 1996 until the attacks of 9/11, and needless to say, the Bush Administration never publicized this connection of the president's brother to the security company.[16] Moreover, five days prior to the 9/11 attacks, a security alert which *had* been in place at the World Trade Center was *lifted*, and bomb-sniffing dogs were removed from the center. As David Ray Griffin notes, "This fact is possibly significant because, if the wiring for controlled demolition had been installed earlier, the explosives could perhaps have been affixed during that period."[17]

However, there was a much more significant indicator of potential opportunity for building preparation than this, and it came in a personal letter from Scott Forbes, an employee for Fiduciary Trust, with offices in the WTC, to Griffin:

> In 2001 we occupied floors 90 and 94-97 of the South Tower and lost 87 employees plus many contractors.
> On the weekend of September 8-9, 2001, there was a "power down" condition in the WTC tower 2, the south tower. This power down condition meant *there was no electrical supply for approximately 36 hours from floor 50 up.* I am aware of this situation since I... had to work with many others that weekend to ensure that all systems were cleanly shutdown beforehand... and then brought back up afterwards. *The reason given by the WTC for the power down was that* **cabling in the tower was being upgraded...** *Of course without power there were no security cameras, no security locks on doors (while) many, many "engineers" (were) coming in and out of the tower.* [18]

This is a crucial observation, for such cable upgrades could be viewed as preparation work for each of the four types of controlled demolitions theory being advanced in the 9/11 community, including an "exotic energy" hypothesis, as we shall see subsequently in this chapter. Such wiring's role in the first types of controlled demolitions are obvious, but not so in the fourth case, unless the building was being wired for some

---

[15] David Ray Griffin, *The New Pearl Harbor*, p. 180.
[16] Ibid.
[17] Ibid.
[18] Ibid., pp. 180-181, all emphases added.

sort of *power broadcasting or transmission*.[19] In any case, this event should be born in mind as we proceed to consider the various theories of controlled demolitions.

Corroborating the fact that the World Trade Center towers were the subject of curious activity prior to 9/11 is the testimony of Ben Fountain. Fountain was employed by the Fireman's Fund as a financial analyst, and worked in the South Tower. In the weeks prior to 9/11, Fountain stated that the twin towers were "evacuated 'a number of times' which, he said, was 'unusual.'"[20] Additionally, Mark H. Gaffney, observes that there were yet *other* types of "upgrading activity" under way at the World Trade Center prior to 9/11, as the Twin Towers were being upgraded with "thermal insulation, to guard against building fires."(!)[21] Notably, in the case of the North Tower, this upgrade extended from floor 92 and upward, and in the case of the South Tower, from floor 77 and upward. In each case, the buildings were struck by flights 11 and 175 *above* the points where these renovations had taken place.[22] Webster Griffin Tarpley also reports that a businessman told him "in an interview three years after the fact that he had visited a client in one of the towers numerous times during the months before the attack, and had always found that certain elevators were out of service."[23]

b. Indicators of Controlled Demolitions:
Ejecta, Low Oxygen Fires, and Eyewitness Testimonies

William Rodriguez was a janitor working in the basement of the North Tower of the World Trade Center on 9/11, and like many witnesses, heard several powerful explosions emanating from the lower portion of the structure on that day.[24] Such statements dovetail perfectly with the clear evidence for demolitions explosions in the Twin Towers. New York City auxiliary fireman, Lt. Paul Isaac Jr. of Engine Company 10, gave an interview to Internet reporter Randy Lavello in

---

[19] This point also points to those who argue that the aircraft, or whatever may have struck the Twin Towers, may have been guided to their targets by homing beacons transmitted from inside the Towers.

[20] David Ray Griffin, *The New Pearl Harbor*, p. 181.

[21] Mark H. Gaffney, *Black 9/11*, p. 1.

[22] Ibid.

[23] Webster Griffin Tarpley, *9/11 Synthetic Terror: Made in USA,* fifth edition, p. 230.

[24] Laurent Guyénot, *JFK-9/11: 50 Years of Deep State*, pp. 114.

which he stated that the firemen knew that bombs were in the buildings.[25]

Teresa Veliz was a software company manager working on the 47th floor of the North Tower when it was hit. Her statements are yet another clear indicator of explosions:

> "I got off (the elevator), turned the corner and opened the door to the ladies' room. I said good morning to a lady sitting at a mirror when the whole building shook. I thought it was an earthquake. Then I heard those banging noises on the other side of the wall. It sounded like someone had cut the elevator cables. It just fell and fell and fell."

> Veliz reached ground level with a coworker when the South Tower collapsed, knocking them down. In near total darkness, she and the coworker followed someone with a flashlight. "The flashlight led us into Borders bookstore, up an escalator and out to Church Street. There were explosions going off everywhere. I was convinced there were bombs planted all over the place and someone was sitting at a control panel pushing detonator buttons. I was afraid to go down Church Street toward Broadway, but I had to do it. I ended up on Vesey Street. There was another explosion. And another. I didn't know which way to run."[26]

Veliz was not alone in hearing explosions.

Webster Griffin Tarpley references two witnesses who clearly not only heard explosions, but felt their effects:

> Kim White, 32, who worked on the 80th floor of the South Tower, was another eyewitness who reported hearing an explosion. "All of a sudden the building shook, then it started to sway. We didn't know what was going on," she told *People* magazine. "We got all our people on the floor into the stairwell... at that time we all thought it was a fire... We got down as far as the 74th floor... then there was another explosion."

> A black office worker wearing a business suit that was covered with dust and ashes told the Danish television network DR-TV1: "On the eighth floor we were thrown back by a huge explosion."[27]

---

[25] Webster Griffin Tarpley, *9/11 Synthetic Terror: Made in USA,* fifth edition, p. 221.

[26] Jim Marrs, *Inside Job*, p. 34.

[27] Webster Griffin Tarpley, *9/11 Synthetic Terror: Made in USA*, fifth edition, p. 224, citing *American Free Press,* December 2, 2001.

Tarpley also cites witnesses that hear things that could be indicative of *other* types of demolitions technologies in play than standard explosives:

> Another European documentary showed a man with glasses recovering in a hospital bed who recalled "All of a sudden it went bang, bang, bang, like shorts and **then** *three unbelievable explosions.*"
>
> An eyewitness who worked in an office near the WTC described his experiences to a reporter for the *American Free Press*. He was standing in a crown on Church Street, about two and a half blocks from the South Tower. Just before the South Tower collapsed, he saw "a number of brief light sources being emitted from inside the building between floors 10 and 15." He saw about six of these flashes and at the same time *heard 'a crackling sound' just before the Tower collapsed."*[28]

These statements could be interpreted in two basically different ways, firstly, as the type of confusion of memory that is normal under such stressful circumstances. In this instance, they simply become more confirmation of the theory of controlled demolitions utilizing conventional explosives. But secondly, the "cracking sound" and the sequence of "bangs" before "explosions" could also be signatures of high electrostatic properties in evidence on that day, or, for that matter, of the sounds that nanothermite might make, in the case of the crackling sounds, and of a two-stage explosive device such as a thermobaric, or "fuel-air", bomb, in the case of the bangs followed by explosions.

Given these difficulties, it is now time to turn attention to the actual problems of the pancake theory, not the least of these being the assertion that burning airplane fuel weakened the steel load-bearing columns sufficiently to bring about a collapse. The principal problem, as most 9/11 truth community researchers have pointed out, is that fires have never collapsed a high-rise structure. As Eric Hufschmid puts the problem, the important questions that need to be born in mind are "How much *heat* was generated?" and "how long a period of time was the heat in contact with the steel?"[29] There is a fundamental problem here:

---

[28] Webster Griffin Tarpley, *9/11 Synthetic Terror: Made in USA*, fifth edition, p. 224, emphases added.

[29] Eric Hufschmid, *Painful Questions*, p. 33.

A lot of jet fuel was mixed with air when the planes crashed into the towers, and an enormous amount of heat was generated when it burned. However, that jet fuel burned so rapidly that it was just a momentary blast of hot air. The blast would have set fire to flammable objects, killed people, and broken windows, but it could not have raised the temperature of a massive steel structure by a significant amount. A fire will not affect steel unless the steel is exposed to it for a long enough period of time for the heat to penetrate. The more massive the steel beams are, the more time that is needed.[30]

This jet fuel, in both cases, was burned off fairly quickly, as the fireballs attest. Moreover, as most researchers have pointed out, after the initial strikes on the Twin Towers, and the burning off of the jet fuel in the fireballs from each, the fires from both towers were relatively *black* in the smoke they gave off, indicating an oxygen-poor environment, and a *cool* fire.

Then, there is the problem of the manner of the destruction of the South Tower, for just prior to its "collapse," the top of the tower had begun to *tilt*:

South Tower's Top "Tilt and Twist"[31]

---

[30] Eric Hufschmid, *Painful Questions*, p. 33.
[31] Ibid., p. 44, citing AP/Wide World Photo.

One need look no further than this photo to see that this is *not* evidence of the official narrative's "pancake" theory, for the top of the south tower is self-evidently *not* "pancaking" into the floors beneath it.[32]

The problem is exacerbated if one believes that this tilt was caused by the severing of the outer load-bearing steel cladding of the building, for in that case, how does one explain the pulverizing of the concrete?[33] More importantly, Hufschmid points out a problem that will become a core argument in all versions of the controlled demolitions theory, namely, that in picture of the rubble from the 9/11 attacks, "All we can see is dust and pieces of steel. Also, no section of the rubble resembles a stack of pancakes. Obviously, when these towers collapsed, the tower and every object inside was shredded, pulverized, and/or burned to ash."[34] But they most assuredly were not "pancaked."[35]

Other evidence from the photos themselves, Hufschmid argues, point clearly to controlled demolitions, including the ejecta from the buildings, and plumes of smoke and dust being flung horizontally from the buildings.

South Tower Collapse. Note the arrow pointing to horizontal plumes.[36]

---

32 Eric Hufschmid, *Painful Questions*, p. 47.

33 Ibid.

34 Ibid., p. 51.

35 There is yet another problem that Hufschmid points out, namely, what happened to the section of the top of the South Tower that had begun to twist and topple over? There is little evidence that it crashed into building four underneath it, even though it had begun to lean more than twenty degrees over the footprint of the tower itself. See his discussion from pp. 48-51.

36 Eric Hufschmid, *Painful Questions*, p. 53, citing a Reuters photo. I have cropped this photo and added the arrow.

North Tower Collapse. Note the arrow indicating horizontal ejecta.[37]

Hufschmid then elaborates the standard controlled demolition scenario, with particular focus on the problems posed by the South Tower, as follows:

---

[37] Eric Hufschmid, *Painful Questions*, p. 60, citing an unknown photograph source.

Since the airplane hit the South Tower on one side, the collapse was initiated by detonating explosives near the crash zone. This caused the tower to tilt toward the crash zone, creating the illusion that the columns in the crash zone had become weak from the fire and the airplane crash.

Within milliseconds other explosives along the crash zone were detonated to break all the columns along the crash zone. This instantly disconnected the top section without altering its position or orientation....

Once the top section was severed, it began to fall downward at the rate which all objects fall due to the force of gravity. It also continued to tilt towards the crash zone as it fell.

Photographs show ribbons of dust coming out of both towers as they collapse. Two suspicious aspects of these ribbons are:

1) The dust comes from a floor while that area of the tower stull appears structurally intact, rather than forming at the location where the tower is in the process of crumbling....

2) The dust comes out very precisely. Specifically, almost the same quantity of dust comes out of each window, and only along one floor at a time, as opposed to appearing haphazardly in different windows along different floors...[38]

As for what happened to the steel beams in the severed section of the South Tower, Hufschmid believes these were hidden by the clouds of dust as this section fell.[39]

2. Contraindicating Evidence for the Theory: High Temperatures Long After the Event

However, it is when one considers these ejecta of plumes and debris that one is confronted with yet a new problem, for these are not the signatures of standard controlled demolitions, where the goal is typically to collapse a building by *imploding* them into their footprint, rather than *exploding* them and literally pulverizing as much of them as possible. Indeed, building 7 of the World Trade Center, which was demolished via controlled demolition, shows little of the signs of the "explosion" and pulverization signatures of the Twin Towers:

---

[38] Eric Hufschmid, *Painful Questions*, p. 75.
[39] Ibid., p. 76.

Building Seven about halfway into its collapse. Note the absence of ejecta, as the building falls more or less straight down into its footprint, a signature of standard types of controlled demolitions.[40]

There were additional problems for the theory of standard controlled demolitions, and it was again Hufschmid who was one of the first to point out one of the most significant problems, a problem that would give rise to the two next theories to be proposed for the mechanism that brought down the Twin Towers: nanothermite, and micro-nukes. Noting that the U.S. Geological Survey had compiled a report from NASA satellite infrared imaging of the World Trade Center

---

[40] Eric Hufschmid, *Painful Questions*, p. 65, citing Roberto Rabanne.

complex after 9/11, highly anomalous temperatures were recorded at eight locations around the complex. These eight hot spots registered the following temperatures fully five days after 9/11:

1) *Building 7:*
    a) Location A: 1341°F, 727°C
    b) Location B: 1034°F, 557°C
2) *The North Tower:*
    a) Location C: 1161°F, 627°C
    b) Location D: 963°F, 517°C
3) *The South Tower:*
    a) Location F: 801°F, 427°C
    b) Location G: 1377°F, 747°C
4) *In the Vicinity of the Towers:*
    a) Location E: 819°F, 437°C
    b) Location H: 1017°F, 547°C[41]

He reproduces the following diagram of the locations of these measurements:

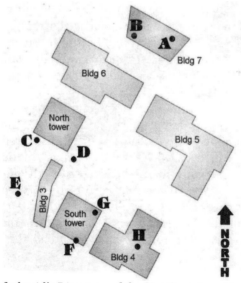

Hufschmid's Diagram of the Hot Spot Locations[42]

---

[41] Eric Hufschmid, *Painful Questions*, p. 70.
[42] Ibid.

C. The Nano-Thermite Theory
1. Evidence for the Theory

Such temperatures, so long after an event like 9/11, are not consonant with standard controlled demolitions and the use of standard explosives. This fact, and other evidence, gave rise to the *next* theory that quickly emerged in the 9/11 community, the nanothermite theory. While this theory generated something of a firestorm when it first appeared, it quickly faded from popularity in certain quarters due to a number of corollary problems with it. Consequently, our review will be comparatively briefer than will be our examination of the two remaining competing theories, mininukes and exotic and/or directed energy weapons.

The nanothermite theory was first advanced in a paper by Dr. Stephen Jones in the technical journal *The Open Chemical Physics Journal*, in a paper titled "Active Thermitic Material Discovered in Dust from the 9-11 World Trade Center Catastrophe."[43] This detailed and scholarly review noted the presence of nanothermite particles in the dust of the WTC. Essentially an incendiary "micro-explosive," nanothermite is capable of burning at high enough temperatures to burn through steel. And thus was "solved" the primary difficulty not only with the "pancake" theory, but with the standard explosives controlled demolitions theory, for such materials could just possibly account for the lingering presence of high heat in the rubble of the attacks, long after 9/11.

The presence of nanothermite meant something else as well, for this "stunning piece of information" meant nothing other than "the collapse of the Al-Qaeda theory. Nanothermite is a sophisticated explosive that only a high-tech industry is capable of producing."[44] What nanothermite signified was the not only the presence of a viable mechanism of the destruction of the Twin Towers, but also of the presence of a deeper level and player in the 9/11 attacks, one that, moreover, most likely originated within the "rogue network" inside the American military-national security complex, for it would have had the access to such technologies.

---

[43] Laurent Guyénot, *JFK-9/11: 50 Years of Deep State*, p. 188.
[44] Ibid.

2. Contraindicating Evidence for the Theory

While this theory did answer certain technical problems, it did not, however, account for others, and these were quickly seized upon by critics of the theory. These criticisms very quickly raised the prospects of the *third* theory of the mechanism, micro-nukes.

The first problem of the nanothermite theory was simply the difficulty of prepping the Twin Towers for destruction by this method, for this would have mostly likely have required "hundreds of people, months of work, and a lot of highly visible masonry work to reach the steel column."[45] More importantly, the *amount* of nanothermite that would have been required not only to melt or sever steel columns but to pulverize the vast amounts of concrete power and dust in evidence in photographs and videos of the destruction of the Twin Towers would have been prohibitive:

> Professor Neils Harrit has actually estimated the amount of nanothermite needed to blow the Twin Towers (to be) between 29,00 and 144,00 metric tons. Just to unload the lowest estimate would have needed 1,500 tractor trailer loads with a crew working 24 hours a day for 300 days non-stop. That seems inconceivable for a foreign power. In fact, it is inconceivable altogether.[46]

As has been stated previously, there *were* indications of opportunities to prepare the buildings for demolitions in the various evacuations and upgrades conducted on the Twin Towers. However, none of these were of sufficient duration and scale to accommodate the preparation for the buildings for destruction by this means.

Why, then, were nanothermite particles even found in the dust of the World Trade Center? Here, where evidence fails, one must speculate, and one speculation springs immediately to mind: perhaps it was a deliberate salting of evidence, perhaps done even during some of those "upgrades and renovations," to misdirect and obfuscate the investigations of the 9/11 events even further. And given our thesis of a potential *third* layer of the operation that may have announced its presence at some point to the "rogue network" that planned and executed the attacks, perhaps this was also done after the event in some fashion to distract attention from the presence of that third level. One will never know for certain.

---

[45] Laurent Guyénot, *JFK-9/11: 50 Years of Deep State*, p. 190.
[46] Ibid.

Yet another difficulty for the nanothermite theory was its inability to explain the *ejecta* of plumes and debris several tens of yards beyond the footprint of the towers themselves. While nanothermite could supply sufficient *heat* to melt steel, it could not supply sufficient kinetic energy to propel the debris ejecta in evidence in photographs of the destruction of the towers. Additionally, nanothermite does not account for some the approximately 1100 victims whose bodies were never recovered.[47]

The final problem with the nanothermite theory concerns those lingering "hot spots" long after 9/11. In fact, the temperatures recorded at the World Trade Center site lingered long after the event, and some sources reported even hotter measurements than those mentioned by Hufschmid. These temperatures ranged from 600 to 1600° F for almost *six* months after 9/11. These temperatures, plus other effects, pointed to the next theory that emerged: mininukes.

D. The Micro-Nukes Theory
1. Evidence for the Theory

It was not just the anomalous high temperatures that pointed to the existence of the "mininuke" theory. It was also the long-term after effects and residual chemical evidence that provoked consideration of this hypothesis. As Laurent Guyénot observes, the nanothermite theory does not explain:

> ... the high percentage of some residuals of nuclear fusion/fission reactions in the rubble(barium, strontium, thorium, uranium, lithium, lanthanum, yttrium, chromium, tritium), and neither does thermite explain the high rate of rare cancers (thyroid cancer, leukemia, and multiple myeloma) among Ground Zero workers, typical of radiation exposure. For these reasons and more, a growing number of scientists are now rejecting the nanothermite thesis and believe that mini-neutron bombs (perhaps no bigger than apples) had been planted in the core columns of the buildings.[48]

Advocates of this hypothesis point to the anomalies of the October 2003 Bali bombing as corroboration of the existence and use of this technology:

---

[47] Laurent Guyénot, *JFK-9/11: 50 Years of Deep State*, p. 189.
[48] Ibid.

196

On October 12, 2003, an extremely powerful explosive device destroyed an Australian nightclub in Bali, Indonesia, blamed on Islamists, stopping a movement of protest in Australia against the Iraq war. The device was planted in a monsoon drain approximately five feet under the road nearby. According to Australian investigator Joe Vialls, the force of the blast, which set some 27 buildings in the neighborhood on fire, is indicative of a micronuclear device. So is the fact that 30 people were totally vaporized by the explosion, while many around the blast received severe flash burns of a kind which Australian surgeons declared having "never seen before." Vialls concludes to the use of a plutonium fission bomb, which leaves behind only alpha radiation "invisible" to a standard Geiger counter.[49]

A small fission bomb of very high reaction efficiency, or perhaps even a neutron bomb, would account for the ejecta seen in evidence from the Twin Towers on 9/11, and would also account for the pulverization of much of the concrete and steel, since both spit out a high number of thermal neutrons which would act like an "atomic shotgun," literally shooting billions of tiny neutron-sized holes in matter in their vicinity, be it organic matter such as human bodies, non-linear materials such as concrete, or linear materials such as steel, conceivably pulverizing it.

It is also worth noting that The Project for a New American Century, the group that noted that a "new Pearl Harbor" would be required for the projection of American military force into the Middle East and Central Asia in order to dominate the region's energy resources, also called for "the development of 'a new family of nuclear weapons' designed to address new sets of military requirements.'"[50] Micro-nukes would certainly fit the label of "a new kind of nuclear weapon."

2. Implications of the Micro-nuke Theory for the Assumptions of Levels Two and Three of the 9/11 Operation

Before considering the contraindications of the mininukes theory, it is worth pausing to consider its implications for the suppositions of the second and third levels of the 9/11 operation. While the advocates of this theory are quick to criticize advocates of exotic or directed energy weapons of "not providing a model" for the hypothesis, the same difficulty might be leveled as well against it: what is the critical mass of a "micro-" or "mini-nuke"? What is the fuel? What is its purity? What is

---

[49] Laurent Guyénot, *JFK-9/11: 50 Years of Deep State*, p. 190.
[50] Ibid., p. 101.

the yield? Such questions are crucial to the exposition of a model, and hence to the hypothesis.

We shall assume here *that* such a weapon exists, without providing a model complete with calculations of neutron flux, purity of fuel, reaction efficiency, yield, and so on. The question then becomes "Is there evidence for such a small nuclear weapon?" Indeed there is, and it is directly related to the questions of who might comprise levels two and three.

In my book *The SS Brotherhood of the Bell: The Nazis' Incredible Secret Technology*, I pointed out that there were indications that the Nazis may have tested such a device in March, 1945, at the troop parade ground in Ohrdruf, Germany. While much about this claim remains problematical, it is the first occurrence in the historical record that I am aware of for the existence of a class of "micronukes," and for this reason, it is worth pausing to consider this story briefly once again.[51] The Ohrduf test supposedly involved a nuclear device which, according to German researchers, weighed a mere 100 grams! This was *well* below then contemporary estimates for a critical mass of uranium or plutonium for a functioning atomic bomb by several times an order of magnitude.[52] If this test did indeed take place and if it was indeed of a nuclear device, then I argued that it would likely have had to employ two things in order to make it work: (1) plutonium 239 of *extremely* high purity, and (2) the boosted fission concept, utilizing deuterium or (more unlikely) tritium to "boost" the yield of the device.[53] Most histories of the Nazi atom bomb project dispute the idea that the Germans ever synthesized plutonium, even though the possibility was known to them. The reason is simply because, according to the postwar standard narrative, they never successfully developed a nuclear reactor, which is necessary to synthesize plutonium via neutron bombardment.

But even assuming they were successful in synthesizing the element, the problem of producing the extremely high purity necessary for such a small critical mass remains. The only real viable technology to do so is via laser isotope enrichment.[54]

---

[51] I discuss this problem in the wider context of an examination of the "red mercury" legend, and the development of the neutron bomb in the USA by its inventor, Sam Cohen. See my *SS Brotherhood of the Bell*, pp. 278-283.

[52] Ibid., pp. 297-298.

[53] Ibid., p. 300.

[54] I present the case that the Nazis may actually have *had* a prototypical and crude chemical laser isotope enrichment technology in *The Philosophers' Stone: Alchemy and the Secret Research for Exotic Matter* (Port Townsend, Washington: Feral House, 2009), pp. 206-230.

This brings us back to the micronuke theory, for in order for such putative devices to work, any fusion reactions they might employ must be initiated by a *fission* device in order to reach the thermal and pressure gradients of radioactive pressure to initiate fusion. In short, they would require a small atomic bomb, unless other, unknown principles of nuclear explosives are employed, and this remains problematic, for self-evident reasons.[55] This bomb in turn would require plutonium of extraordinarily high purity, *and the technology—laser isotope enrichment—to enrich it.*

Consequently, in so far as micronukes may have been used on 9/11, this technology would restrict the level two and level three players to a very small and select group of powers with the technology to do this— the United States, Russia, France, United Kingdom, Germany, Italy, China, India, and so on. Even second-tier nuclear powers such as Pakistan or Iran would have difficulty mastering and deploying such technology in a scale large enough to produce several of these putative weapons. And that means the principal actors of 9/11, whoever they were, if the micronukes theory is true, is restricted to the Great Powers themselves, and no others. Notice that as we consider each theory of the mechanism of the destruction of the Twin Towers, the circle of potential perpetrators narrows as the technological demands of the mechanism increase.

There is one final important thing to note about this enrichment technology and its relationship to the micronukes theory. While the installations for this technology are appropriately complex to engineer, *the labor needed to run them, as opposed to more conventional enrichment technologies such as centrifuges or mass spectrographs, is much less intensive.*[56] Thus, conceivably, this would be the technology of choice for an extra-territorial group or cabal interested in producing micronukes. All that would be needed is a source for the feedstock of plutonium to be enriched.[57]

3. Contraindicating Evidence for the Theory

The micronukes hypothesis is not, however, without its own problems or contraindications. One of these is simply that even the National Institute of Standards and Technology itself admitted that none

---

[55] For this possibility, see my *SS Brotherhood of the Bell*, pp. 278-282, 288-296.

[56] See my *The Philosophers' Stone*, pp., 218-225.

[57] In this respect, it should also be noted that firefighters were fighting fires at Ground Zero for approximately three *months* after 9/11, and that nuclear waste removal protocols were apparently in evidence in the clean up.

of the steel in the Twin Towers appeared to have been exposed to temperatures over 600° for "as long as fifteen minutes."[58]Of course, this is a weak argument, since the use of micronukes would have vaporized any steel in their close proximity.

A much more difficult set of problems emerges when one considers some of the data already presented in previous chapters. We have pointed out, for example, that the German firm Convar was hired to recover data on the computer hard drives from the WTC. This is problematic for the very fundamental reason that any nuclear explosion, no matter its yield, produces two things that fry electronic devices in their vicinity: electromagnetic pulse, and thermal neutrons, both of which would erase computer hard drives. Here the problem of the micronukes theory breaks upon the same rocks that its advocates criticize the exotic and directed energy weapons hypothesis, for in the absence of clear knowledge of how these would work, a number of them used in a controlled, synchronized set of explosions, should conceivably have rendered electronic devices unusable. To argue that they might *not* have done so is an appeal to "unknown principles", and hence, invalid.

A similar difficulty arises when one considers the vast amount of surviving *papers* from the World Trade Center. It has already been noted that in the Bali explosion, a case of a suspected micronuke, fires were started from the heat effects of the blast on nearby buildings, i.e., on any flammable materials in proximity to the devices. In the case of the Twin Towers, the use of a number of micronukes would seem to require that flammable materials would have caught fire from proximate effects; one should have seen burning papers wafting through the air. The volume of surviving paper would thus appear to be a contraindication of the hypothesis.

E. The Directed and Exotic Weapons Theory
1. Contraindicating Evidence and Arguments

The hypothesis of directed and/or exotic energy weapons is beyond any doubt the most vilified hypothesis in the 9/11 research community, and accordingly, we shall spend the most time with it. While this hypothesis is usually associated with the name of Dr. Judy Wood,[59] others have held it at one time or another:

---

[58] Laurent Guyénot, *JFK-9/11: 50 Years of Deep State*, p. 113.
[59] See Judy Wood, B.S.,M.S., Ph.D., *Where Did the Towers Go? Evidence of Directed Free-Energy Technology on 9/11* (Printed in China: 2010). ISBN 978-0-615-41256-6.

Jim Hoffman... is a leading expert on the collapse of the World Trade Center, co-author of *Waking Up from Our Nightmare* and author of the website wtc7.net. Hoffman calculates that the energy necessary to create the mushroom clouds, expand them to the extraordinary dimensions actually observed, pulverize virtually all the concrete in the towers, and to chop the steel into segments, is on an order of magnitude greater than the gravitational energy represented by the buildings.

Hoffman points out that the Twin Towers were demolished "in a decidedly different manner from the conventional demolitions to make it (appear) consistent with the story that the towers collapsed as a result of the jet impacts and fires. Explosions started at the impact zone and proceeded down the intact portion of the tower and up the overhanging portion, instead of starting at ground level.... Much more powerful explosives were used than in a conventional demolition... The Twin Towers exploded rather than Imploded." In a classic demolition from ground level, like the implosion of (World Trade Center building 7), gravity brings the mass of the building down; but in the twin towers, much of it was pulverized and ejected outwards as dust. Hoffman further notes a number of features of the Twin Towers' collapse which suggest that they may have been *"demolished through some entirely different process, perhaps involving some form of directed energy weapon,"* in addition to explosives. For a possible explanation of what kind of energy source could have been at work, we must turn our attention to the realm of new physical principles, and thus to the class of directed-energy weapons which are probably most familiar to the general public in connection with President Reagan's so-called Star Wars speech of March 23, 1983.

High energy microwave interferometry using coaxial beams for constructive and destructive interference might be a possibility. However, engineer Ken Jenkins has pointed out that this would require so much energy that, if it had to be delivered as a conventional electric current, it would necessitate a cable about half a meter in diameter- and there is no evidence of this. So the problem remains intractable, and will require more time and research.[60]

While Hoffman himself has now apparently abandoned this theory, it is worth noting that Hoffman himself clarified what he maintained:

---

[60] Webster Griffin Tarpley, *9/11 Synthetic Terror: Made in USA*, fifth edition, pp. 246-248, emphases added.

In an interview I gave in January of 2004 I entertained a hypothesis that interferometry of coaxial electromagnetic beams generated by powerful masers[61] *in the Twin Towers' basements* might have been used to produce the descending wave of destruction that consumed the Towers. After reviewing the hypothesis, *I rejected it* and posted a note on the Edited Transcript of the interview to explain my reasons for rejecting it...[62]

In rejecting his own theory, Hoffman elaborated on the primary difficulties of any such exotic or directed energy weapons theory, namely, the enormous energy requirements needed to pulverize two steel and concrete buildings each weighing several tens of thousands of tons, and over one thousand feet high. Additionally, as noted in the previous section, there were residual amounts of trace elements typical of nuclear explosions, and no model exists of microwave interferometry producing such nuclear reaction by-products from steel and concrete.

Other criticisms of the directed and exotic energy weapons theories have been advanced, from the simplistic one of the lack of evidence for the existence of such weapons, to more complex and convincing arguments, most being variations on the twin and related problems of the enormous amounts of energy required, and the mechanism for directing it:

> There are at least three serious problems with any theory that (electromagnetic) weapons were used to destroy the Twin Towers.
> 1. The electromagnetic energy beam would have to have emanated from some source. What was the source, and how did it escape notice?
> 2. The weapon would have needed to possess an extremely high-powered energy supply. What was that supply, and how did it escape notice?
> 3. The weapon would have needed to direct energy into the regions within the Towers and move that locus down to produce the descending pattern of destruction observed in each Tower. How could such a weapon deliver energy to such zones without producing visible disturbances to objects in the beam's path?

---

[61] Masers are simply laser-like devices that operate in the microwave, rather than the optically visible, wavelengths of the spectrum.
[62] Jim Hoffman, "Repudiations," March 1, 2007, 911research.wtc7.net/about/repudiations.html.

The coaxial beam microwave interferometry theory postulates that the energy source was some ultra-high-powered maser or antenna in the foundation of each Tower, that the energy supply was electricity piped in via fat copper or superconducting cable from a distant location, and that the energy was delivered to a limited and time-varied zone of each Tower through interferometry. Leaving aside the matter of how so much electrical energy could be stored and/or transported to the site, and how a maser of antenna could be engineered to produce such high-energy multiple directed microwave beams, we see a number of problems with the idea that the energy could have been delivered to the zone of destruction through interferometry.

- Each floor slab of the Towers consisted of concrete poured into corrugated steel pans. Steel is electrically conductive, and therefore affects the propagation of electromagnetic waves— the "Faraday cage effect." It is difficult to imagine that (electro-magnetic) beams with the wavelengths required by this theory to produce controlled zones of constructive and destructive interference (radio or microwave) could have passed through so many floor pans without being blocked or severely attenuated.
- The production of a slow-moving zone of constructive interference depends on the individual beams being standing waves. But it is difficult to imagine how an antenna or maser could be modified to produce standing waves, rather than waves propagating at the speed of light.[63]

It is to be noted that the assumption throughout both the theory and throughout these criticisms is that the electromagnetic energy and its interferometry is producing the effects seen. We shall see that this may not necessarily be the case later in this chapter, and that conventional electromagnetic analysis may not be the best model for approaching the subject of interferometry on non-linear materials such as concrete.

---

[63] No Author, "EM Weapons: Theories that Directed Electromagnetic Energy Weapons Destroyed the Twin Towers." 911researchwtc7.net/ wtc/analysis/theories/energybeam.html. While no author for this paper is given, it should be noted that it originates on Jim Hoffman's website.

The Mystery of the Mechanism

*a. Revisiting Jim Hoffman's Theory as First Articulated on Bonnie
Faulkner's "Guns and Butter" Radio Show*

Since it was Hoffman who first proposed the most detailed model
for a directed energy hypothesis for the mechanism of the Twin Towers'
destruction, it is necessary to revisit it in detail, as he first articulated in
in an interview given in January, 2004, on the *Guns and Butter* radio
show with hostess Bonnie Faulkner, titled "Your Eyes Don't Lie;
Common Sense, Physics, and the World Trade Center Collapses." We
shall refer to the transcript of this interview.[64]

Faulkner begins the interview by noting that Hoffman had his work
in the discovery of embedded minimal surfaces reviewed in various
scientific journals, such as *Science News, Scientific American, Science
Digest* and the prestigious journal, *Nature.*[65] After welcoming him to her
show, she then begins the interview with a question of how Hoffman
came to examine the World Trade Center towers' collapse:

> **BF:** What was your first impression, on September 11, 2001, when
> the Twin Towers collapsed?
>
> **JH:** ... when I looked at the images of the Twin Towers blowing up
> into these huge clouds of dust, suddenly it didn't fit the
> explanations of these buildings falling down. It became
> incredibly obvious that these buildings were demolished. And
> yet, when I watched some of the same footage on September
> 11, 2001, I don't remember even seeing all that dust. I
> remember seeing the towers disappear. The building is there,
> and the next moment it's gone. Shocking. But I don't remember
> seeing the dust. And the dust is one of the most damning pieces
> of evidence for the official story. Because how were these
> buildings pulverized in mid-air? They turned to dust in mid-air.
> Clearly, it makes no sense according to the official story.[66]

Expanding on this theme of the pulverization of the Twin Towers in his
later book co-authored with Don Paul, Hoffman wrote:

---

[64] Jim Hoffman and Bonnie Faulkner, "Your Eyes Don't Lie: Common Sense,
Physics, and the World Trade Center Collapses, An Interview of Jim Hoffman by
Bonnie Faulkner. *Guns and Butter.* (Radio show.)
Transcript. www.911researchwtc7.net/ interviews/ radio/ youreyesdontlie/ index.
tml. Rather than repeat this entire link in future footnotes, I shall simply refer to the
title and page number.
[65] Hoffman and Faulkner, "Your Eyes Don't Lie," p. 2.
[66] Ibid.

Most of the non-metallic components and contents of the Towers were converted to fine dust *in mid-air*. Photographs and accounts from Ground Zero confirm that what was left of the Towers consisted of the shredded remains of the Towers' steel skeletons, other metallic remnants, paper, and fine dust. There is a striking absence of evidence of macroscopic pieces of concrete from the approximately 90,000 tons of concrete that constituted the four-inch-thick floor slabs of each Tower. Analysis of powder samples shows that the concrete, glass, gypsum, and fiberglass insulation were converted to a homogeneous mixture of dust, mostly consisting of sub-100-micron particles.[67]

Then follows a lengthy discussion of the demolition of Building 7, followed by a review of various "catastrophic failure" theories.[68]

(1) Pulverization (Dust) and Calculations

Eventually, their conversation returns to the subject of the dust and the clouds of pyroclastic flow generated from the Towers' destruction:

BF: Well, Jim, that brings me to an article that you wrote called "The North Tower's dust Cloud: Analysis of energy requirements for the expansion of the dust cloud following the collapse of One World Trade Center." You have written that it would require a lot of energy to bring the building down *and* form the gray dust clouds, that it does form, I believe you refer to them as pyroclastic clouds.

JH: ... Now this dense cloud of dust that these buildings were being converted into in mid-air—it started very early in these events—we often talk about as a pyroclastic cloud. That's a term from volcanology that describes a dense suspension of solids in air or some fluid that behaves almost as a separate fluid. It expands and doesn't mix very much with the surrounding air. It's not like smoke could such as the smoke clouds rising from the towers. These pyroclastic clouds that had all this pulverized material were traveling down; they

---

[67] Don Paul and Jim Hoffman, *Waking Up from Our Nightmare: The 9/11/01 Crimes in New York City* (San Francisco, California: Irresistable/Revolutionary [I/R], 2004), p. 32, citing Paul J. Lioy, et. Al., "Characterization of the Dust/Smoke Aerosol that Settled East of the World Trade Center (WTC) in Lower Manhattan after the Collapse of the WTC 11 September 2001, *EHP Online*, ehp.niehs.nih.gov/members/2002/110p703-714lioy/lioy-full.html.

[68] Ibid., pp. 11-12,

were pulled by gravity... There is a photograph that's in the FEMA report that's taken from about thirty seconds after the initiation of the North Tower collapse in which I was able to estimate the volume of the cloud by measuring numerous sample points on the frontier of the dust cloud. I made a conservative estimate of the volume of the cloud. It is about five times the volume of the original building. Now, even in controlled demolition the amount of explosive charges isn't so great and you tend to get a lot of dust with a controlled demolition, but it's usually not much larger than the size of the original building. Because—think about it—where did all this material come from? It was gases and solids inside the original building. In a typical demolition the resulting dust cloud is just a little bit larger than the intact building, since there is some mixing with the ambient air. So, in my paper I first make this estimate of a fivefold expansion, and then I reduce it to account for mixing. I assume there is probably some mixing with the surrounding air even though I don't think very much because as I said this pyroclastic cloud is behaving as its own fluid and it's so much denser than the surrounding air that it doesn't mix—at least in the early part of this event—it takes several minutes before it gets more diffuse. So, given an allowance for mixing, I reduce my expansion estimate to 3.5 times the original volume. And to achieve that level of expansion there are, if you discount the notion of explosives, two ways you could achieve that expansion.... I see really only two ways to achieve the expansion:

The first way is through thermodynamic expansion of the gases, such as air, that makes up the cloud...

The other cause of the expansion is the conversion of water from liquid to steam. There are a number of sources of water in the buildings, like in the plumbing system, maybe in cisterns, various things. When water is vaporized, and that only requires raising it to the boiling point of water, a lot of energy is required but it expands it greatly, because the expansion ratio of liquid water to steam is 1 to 1800.

Now, based on which of those two factors is dominant, I get different estimates of the total amount of energy to achieve the expansion. But in both cases *it's far greater (than) the available energy from the elevated mass of the building—the gravitational potential energy, which is on the order of 111,000 kilowatt-hours.* The estimate that I get by ignoring water vaporization and only looking at the thermodynamic expansion of the gases is about 400,000 kilowatt-hours, already *four times the gravitational energy budget.* But then if you factor in the fact that you would also have to heat up all of the suspended materials in the cloud because the heat would exchange between the gases and the suspended solids, and depending on what your estimate is of the amount of solids at that thirty-second mark, *it could be as great as eleven million kilowatt-hours* of energy. Okay, so that's one calculation. The other calculation is just looking at water vaporization and assuming that it is not supply-limited, that there is enough water to soak up all the heat that's there to produce the amount of expansion. Using that estimate I get 1.4 million kilowatt-hours, which is more than ten times as great as the gravitational energy.

So there is huge imbalance between the amount of energy required to drive the heat sink of the dust cloud expansion, and the gravitational energy available in the elevated mass of the building—supposedly the source that was driving all this destruction.[69]

Lest the significance of this be missed, recall that Faulkner and Hoffman first discussed the controlled demolition of Building 7, which produced a much smaller dust cloud from the conventional explosives in the building. In other words, what Hoffman is *really* saying is that the energy requirements for the pyroclastic cloud far exceed the capabilities of conventional explosives, and, as we saw earlier, nanothermite cannot account for this either.

Thus, the first two theories—conventional explosives and nanothermite—must be rejected.

(2) The Strange Evidence of the Surviving Steel

The discussion then proceeds to a discussion of the molten steel that continued to be evident in the rubble of Ground Zero long after 9/11, but here, Hoffman diverts the discussion into the strange properties of the steel itself:

BF: I have read that molten steel was observed in pits below the Twin Towers up to a month or more after the collapse. And also I believe, you had mentioned to me that some of the steel was melted to the point where it draped over the ruins.

---

[69] Jim Hoffman and Bonnie Faulkner, "Your Eyes Don't Lie," pp. 17-19.

JH: ... (If) you look at some of the pictures of Ground Zero, you see it looks like the steel had been melted as it was falling, or softened as it was falling, because you see large pieces of steel draped over World Trade Center Three, one of the buildings that was largely crushed by the fallout from the North and South Towers, and they looked like wet noodles covering these buildings. Also photographs from World Trade Center Six— large parts of it were crushed by falling debris... it's very striking the way steel beams looked like, kind of like wet noodles. Moreover, some of the studies, even that appeared in the FEMA Report, interestingly, one of the appendices talk about some limited studies of the steel that show some very peculiar features like *intra-granular melting, and like rapid oxidation where entire pieces of steel a few inches thick were oxidized away so that they become like thin scrolls. Other reports describe some of this steel as looking like Swiss cheese.* All of this makes no sense in terms of the official story. I mean hydrocarbon fires would never do that to steel. *It's something very energetic that's going on here.* Also residues of sulfur were discovered in the steel and where did that come from?[70]

At this point, one notes that while such effects might be attributable to micronukes, this effect, when combined with the pulverization, presents that theory with added difficulties. Indeed, "intragranular melting" seems to describe a process where the molecules of steel themselves were exploding internally.

(3) The Problem with **Any** Explosives Model

The hostess of *Guns and Butter,* Bonnie Faulkner, then asks a crucial and very insightful question of Hoffman, one that brings him to the crux of his argument for a directed energy hypothesis. Faulkner asks a question about explosives, but Hofman's response indicates that there is a fundamental problem with *any* kind of explosive, including that of micronukes:

BF: But what I want to ask you about that now... Van Romero, the demolition expert, from Albuquerque, New Mexico—didn't he

---

[70] Jim Hoffman and Bonnie Faulkner, "Your Eyes Don't Lie," pp. 20-21, emphases added.

say in the article that it wouldn't have taken that many of explosives? (sic)

JH: ...There are a number of factors, which make me skeptical of that, *such as the lack of evidence of high overpressures in the first second or two of the collapses. You don't see walls blowing out right away. You see them kind of sloughing down into themselves.* Also the thoroughness of the pulverization of the concrete makes me wonder about conventional demolition, because with explosive charges the destructive power of the charge falls off with the square of the distance[71] from the charge. So if you even have a chunk of concrete forty feet away from the nearest charge, you would need a pretty strong charge to make sure that that gets pulverized; and it just doesn't seem plausible to me because the analysis of the dust reveals that most of the dust was probably less than one hundred microns in diameter. That's thinner than a human hair. And this is just so thorough so consistently throughout the building.[72]

Hoffman's argument here might be considered to be weak, since photographs and videos *do* show ejecta being blown out of the Twin Towers during their destruction, clear signs of overpressure. However, his argument cannot be dismissed too casually, for his reasoning here is a bit more subtle than it first appears.

To understand why, consider its second foundation: the more or less uniform and consistent pulverization of concrete, glass, gypsum and other materials in the Twin Towers to particles less than the size of a human hair. If this were to have been accomplished via conventional explosives, in order to keep the pulverization *uniform*, explosives would have had to have been planted throughout the building and on the floor pans to achieve this, via interferometry of the pressure waves, crushing material. Similarly, the use of the number of "micronukes" would have to be distributed in such a fashion to achieve this, or their individual yields increased. In either case, however, this may have resulted in more overpressure signatures, such as "walls blowing out right away." As was seen, there *were* opportunities that would have allowed the Towers to have been prepared. But the *extent* of the preparation needed seems to exceed the opportunities to do it.

---

[71] Hoffman appears to make a mistake here.
[72] Jim Hoffman and Bonnie Faulkner, "Your Eyes Don't Lie," pp. 22-23.

The Mystery of the Mechanism

(4) Hoffman's Theory as He Articulated It

This becomes a problem with Hoffman's own hypothesis, which he now elaborates in response to the following question from *Guns and Butter* hostess, Bonnie Faulkner, who zeros in:

> **BF:** You have your own theory in terms of what may have caused the Twin Towers to collapse. A theory about what could have generated the amount of energy that in your opinion that was required to collapse the Twin Towers.
>
> **JH:** It's sort of a working theory. It's somewhat speculative but I think it's physically possible, *and it's not really a theory of where the energy came from but of how the energy was delivered to where it was required to produce the observed destruction.* Note that the gross features of the collapses, such as the top-down destruction, can be explained by the conventional or distributed explosives theories I just described, just by controlling the order in which the charges are detonated in order to stimulate a "progressive collapse." But, there are a number of more subtle features in the collapses that I don't think are adequately explained by a conventional explosives theory. There are things like the lack of overpressures that are observed in the first about two seconds of each collapse, in which you don't see the walls just blowing out as I'd expect you'd see if there were high explosives in there. Rather, you see the whole thing just telescope into itself. The North Tower just neatly telescopes into itself and then it starts to puff out with all of this pulverized concrete. Another feature is the fineness of the pulverization of particularly the floor slabs in which there is hardly any evidence of even like gravel-size pieces...

Observe that Hoffman has now articulated the argument I summarized above, though again under the pressures of ad libitum talk during a talk show, the argument he is making may not be entirely clear. Also observe the interesting fact that Hoffman's description of the Towers "telescoping" into themselves resembles, in some respects, the Pentagon witnesses who describe the aircraft (or whatever hit the Pentagon) as "melting" into the building. He now comes to the most detailed exposition of this theory:

> **(JH):** So this rather Sci-Fi theory that I have can be described as a kind of microwave interferometry, but it's a particular

configuration of microwave beams that could have been driven by some kind of device *that was, say, tucked into the basement of the towers.* Now, there were subterranean roads and things in this deep sub-basement of the towers, so there is a way that you can drive a truck into there, and you could have a maser, say, which is *pumped by some source of energy,* and I don't know how you pipe energy in. Based on my analysis of the North Tower dust cloud I'm thinking that *energy in the neighborhood of 1.5 gigawatt-hours* were required to produce this destruction and that energy would have had to have been delivered in about fifteen seconds because that's how long it took this wave of demolition to travel from the crash zone down to the ground. However it seems... and that's a huge amount of energy and it kind of stretches the imagination to wonder how they would have piped that much energy into this device that created those microwave beams, but I calculated that it would take something like a copper cable of maybe a foot thick or maybe a little less, to deliver that much energy. Furthermore, *since Building Seven straddled a ConEd electrical substation that might have had something to do with the delivery of energy, or maybe even the storage of the energy— perhaps they had banks of super capacitors or something—to provide the energy,* to deliver it when the towers were actually destroyed.[73]

While Hoffman's statements are clear enough, it is crucial to understand what his process of reason thus far is, and what his speculative conclusions are:

1) The principal problem with destroying the Twin Towers via directed microwave interferometry energy weapons *is not the process itself, which is theoretically possible,* the problem is the very practical one of *where does one get the energy to do so?* With this practical problem comes another:
2) Given the enormous energy requirements for such a system, how would one conceal it and avoid detection?

Hoffman points to the existence of two possibilities as a power source: the electrical substation beneath building 7, and "super-capacitors", huge banks of batteries, whose sheer physical size would easily attract

---

[73] Jim Hoffman and Bonnie Faulkner, "Your Eyes Don't Lie," pp. 23-24, emphases added.

attention. Hoffman also points out that the cabling for such vast amounts of power would itself be enormous, and in various presentations of the idea, has given figures of cables from eight inches to one yard in diameter.

There is another problem, and we have already mentioned it, namely, that the steel floor pans would effectively prevent the broadcast of the microwave via the "Farraday cage" effect. However, this invites my own speculation: if the pans and core columns of the buildings themselves could somehow be rigged to *be secondary transmitters via resonance,* then the interferometry scheme might work. In this case, the outer steel cladding of the Towers themselves would act as a sort of Farraday cage of their own, like the grating on a microwave oven, keeping the energy locked in the Towers.[74]

The problem with all these schemes remains, however, the enormous energies required.

Hoffman now explains how all this might have worked:

(JH): Now about the specifics of how these microwave beams would have worked. My theory is that they had coaxial microwave beams that were sort of conical. In other words, they originated from a point source down in the basement and formed a narrow cone that kind of grows as (it) extends up, thereby encompassing almost all the tower except for the lower part of the perimeter walls, which I mentioned were the only parts of the buildings that survived above the rubble pile. And if you have microwave radiation in the region of say the centimeter wavelength— microwave radiation is another form of electromagnetic radiation just like radio waves and light—visible light and x-rays and that kind of thing—but microwaves are invisible to solid materials. So you can project microwaves right through solid material but the material, depending on the type of material will pick it up or not pick it up....

So you'd have these multiple superimposed beams that are being projected up through the buildings, and phase shifts and *wavelengths of the individual components are being precisely controlled so as to generate a zone of constructive interference*—a very precise zone of constructive interference that delivers the energy to wherever they want to, so they start at the crash zone

---

[74] With respect to the idea of a secondary transmitter effect, it is to be noted that radar, which most people popularly perceive as a "bounce", is really a secondary transmitter effect, as the incident radio waves on an object stimulate an electrical current via resonance effects, which in turn stimulates its own "broadcast" of electrical energy which is picked up by a radar's receiver and amplifier.

where the planes hit and that starts to break up the buildings at those points, and then they vary the wavelengths to march this zone of constructive interference down the building, causing thorough destruction of the building... [75]

This, in effect, is Hoffman's theory. It is worth pointing out that Hoffman disregards the idea of a space-based platform, since there would be a problem with beam scattering through the atmosphere.[76]

(5) A Reconsideration of Hoffman's Theory:
(a) The Particulate Remains as a Resonance Effect,
the World War Two Nazi Radar Stealth Experiments, Phase Conjugation,
and the Energy Supply Problem

Before simply abandoning Hoffman's theory simply because of the impracticalities of its enormous energy requirements, it is worth looking at its other features that are indicative that it might, in fact, be true. One of these is the pulverized dust of the pyroclastic flows itself. Needless to say, here I am speculating beyond what Hoffman himself did, but the dust, as he avers, is itself a clue to the mechanism, though for a very different reason than he mentions.

This reason may be simply stated as follows: *the size of the particulate matter of the dust of the World Trade Center Towers is a resonance response to the microwave environment which created it.* Thus, *the size of the particles is in resonance to the wavelengths of the beams.* A simple analogy may explain what is meant here. Imagine you have a piece of wood, with a small hole in it. The hole represents the wavelength of the microwave field. Now imagine you have a large lump of modeling clay, which represents all the matter in the Towers. In order to push the clay through the hole, the clay has to assume the size of the hole itself.

The question is, is there anything in the historical record that might indicate that such an idea as Hoffman's may have been utilized and perhaps even weaponized?

Indeed there is.

In my book *The SS Brotherhood of the Bell*, I recounted late war German radar experiments on their stealth materials. This material itself *was a mixture of linear and non-linear materials*, being composed of small metal balls of various diameters, each *in resonance with known*

---

[75] Jim Hoffman and Bonnie Faulkner, "Your Eyes Don't Lie," pp. 24-25, emphasis added.

[76] Ibid., p. 26.

frequencies of Allied radar detection systems. These balls—the linear material—were impressed in random fashion into a sheet of rubber which is, of course, a non-linear material. Here is what Lt. Col. Tom Bearden wrote about these experiments:

> In WWII the Germans invented radar absorbing materials, to coat their submarine snorkels and prevent Allied antisubmarine warfare bombers from tracking the snorkels and destroying the subs. A wide variety of highly nonlinear, doped materials were investigated. In addition to single beam radar cross section, the Germans also examined the materials in multi-beam illumination circumstances.

Lest it be missed, "multi-beam illumination circumstances" is simply another way of saying "interferometry." Continuing:

> It appears that, in some multibeam experiments with some materials, conditions were just right so that the multi-illuminated absorbing material *acted as a pumped phase conjugate mirror(PCM), and wave-to-wave interactions emerged.* This meant that the absorber material PCM would suddenly gather up all the energy in the pumping beams, use one of the other beams as a signal input beam, wrecking the equipment and creating havoc in surrounding equipment.
>
> When the German radar team went to Russia, their knowledge of these anomalies went with them. In the desperate Russian scientific climate to find *just such anomalies*, this startling and anomalous phenomenon would have been exhaustingly examined and studied, once the German radar engineers got to Russia to their new laboratories.
>
> In short, it appears that the Russians quickly came up with what today is called "nonlinear phase conjugate optics," but first in the radar band rather than optics.[77]

Radio waves are, of course, in the same basic range of the spectrum as microwaves, and this allows us to speculate further.

It is to be noted that this type of experimentation in an effect that could easily be weaponized began in wartime Nazi Germany, and would not have required anything more expensive than powerful radar sets

---

[77] Joseph P. Farrell, *The SS Brotherhood of the Bell*, pp. 225-226, citing Tom Bearden, *Fer De Lance*, pp. 68-69. For a complete discussion of these wartime German radar interferometry experiments on nonlinear materials, see *SS Brotherhood of the Bell*, pp. 222-226.

and access to materials that were both linear and non-linear, like the German radar absorbing materials, to continue experimentation. Experiment on varieties of materials—such as steel, concrete, gypsum, glass, and so on—would have given experimental knowledge of how to use such effects on a variety of targets...

... like buildings.

Such experimentation additionally could have been conducted by any group with the means and money to purchase the equipment to develop and weaponize the phenomenon. Such installations would have been relatively easier to equip and conceal than, say, a nuclear isotope enrichment plant, and would have paid bigger dividends, and a similar "bang for the buck" than more conventional nuclear weapons and the enormous facilities required to manufacture them.

And finally, there is the obvious thing: we have already noted the strange lingering Nazi connection hovering over Mohamed Atta and his connection to the *Carl Duisberg Gesellschaft*, and now a Nazi experiment in technologies that might have made Hoffman's scenario plausible.

But how precisely does this make Hoffman's scenario plausible? Recall what Bearden has said: under certain conditions of interferometry in the radar-microwave range on a target of mixed linear and non-linear materials, the target acts as *a phase conjugate mirror*, energy is stored, and then one of the incident beams becomes a carrier beam for the discharge of that energy. This phase conjugate effect is sometimes called a *time reversed wave* for the simple reason that these waves *do not obey the inverse square law*, and hence, energy is not *dispersed* on a target, but *collected upon it*. With this, the energy problem, while still enormous, might not prove to be so intractable.

In this case, we indulge in more "high octane speculation," for if one recalls Nikola Tesla's experiment in beaming "wireless power" from his Wardenclyffe tower, it will be recalled that he insisted that the steel and iron supports for this tower had to "Get a grip on the earth":

> You see the underground work is one of the most expensive parts of the tower. In this system that I have invented it is necessary for the **machine to get a grip of the earth, otherwise it cannot shake the earth. It has to have a grip on the earth so that the whole of this globe can quiver,** and to do that it is necessary to carry out a very expensive construction.[78]

---

[78] Testimony of Nikola Tesla, New York State Supreme Court, Appellate Division, Second Department: Clover Boldt Miles and George C. Boldt, Jr. as Executors of the Last Will and Testament of George C. Boldt, Deceased, Plaintiffs-Respondents, versus Nikola Tesla, Thomas G. Shearman, et al. as Defendants-

Why was it necessary to make the globe quiver? Because in the view of some electrical theorists, what Tesla was doing with his Wardenclyffe tower wireless broadcasting of power system, was *inverting* the roles of antenna and ground in the broadcast circuit, using the Earth itself as the antenna, and the tower as the receiver to close the circuit, making the Earth, to some extent, the power source in the system. As we have seen, Hoffman comes close to this view with his suggestion that equipment might have been in the basement of the towers. We propose the simple modification that the core columns *and the attached steel floor pans* of the Towers themselves were used as a secondary transmitter in a Tesla-like system. In this respect, recall the "upgrades" that included the installations of new *cabling* in the towers prior to 9/11. In such a system, a large power source could be located anywhere on Earth, and its broadcast through the globe would be configured to be resonant to the Towers themselves.[79] Calculation of the resonance would be a (relatively!) simple matter of calculation of the height of the towers and the steel columns, their mass, and approximate resonances of the materials in them, which would have been gained by prior experimentation on such materials. In this instance, masers would not necessarily have had to draw on vast amounts of power(the buildings themselves are doing that), but simply would have provided the necessary "kick" from the interferometry they provided. Additionally, they could have been stationed anywhere: neighboring buildings, or even in space.

(b) Interferometry, Phase Conjugation, and Space-Based Platforms

It has been noted that Hoffman opined that a space-based system was *not* feasible for the simple reason that beams disperse not only due to the inverse square law, but also because of the random conditions of the atmosphere and its conditions through which they are passing.

Appellants, 521-537, pp, 174-179, cited in my book *Babylon's Banksters: The Alchemy of Deep Physics, High Finance and Ancient Religion* (Port Townsend, Washington: Feral House, 2010), p. 149, emphasis added.

[79] While it is difficult to conceive how it might work within such a scheme, it should be noted that Hoffman's figure of 1.5 gigawatt-hours of power brings to mind the power output of the HAAARP array in Gakona, Alaska at full broadcast power. Space-based microwave systems, however, have been discussed by the US military, and presumably were under consideration by the militaries of other powers, as early as the early 1960s. See my *Covert Wars and Breakaway Civilizations: The Secret Space Program, Celestial Psyops, and Hidden Conflicts*, p. 244.

Phase conjugate mirrors, however, solve this dilemma in effect by taking a "picture" of such conditions, and then configuring a beam exactly out of phase with them, and then beaming this wave through the conditions, which then reverse the effects, allowing the beam to be *in phase and coherent* on the receiving end, *minimizing the effects of atmospheric distortions*. It is thus possible that *with the use of sophisticated phase conjugation in the microwave range of the spectrum*, that a space based system would be possible, assuming, of course, that phase conjugate mirrors of great sophistication could be constructed and then placed into space.

One other factor is worth mentioning in this regard, and that is that international treaty strictly prohibits the weaponization of space, and a phase conjugate system of this type would easily be conceived to be a weapons system, or the space based components of an Earth-based system. Such treaties, however, do not seem to prohibit *the private and corporate* world from placing such systems into space, and given that we have all along been dealing with the possibility of a "global network" that is not a recognized "state actor or agency" under international law, this possibility should not be ignored.

There is a final factor that must now be briefly entertained, a factor that most will find incredible, and unbelievable. Certainly from any standard scientific model, that is exactly what it is. But imagine, for a moment, that every specific atom of matter of any known element is but a collection of *interfered waves* in the medium. Through interferometry, then, it might be possible to *change* the composition of materials, literally break them down, and recombine them, to produce effects that otherwise could only be produced by adding neutrons and splitting, or fusing, atoms. The use of *this* kind of "interferometry in the medium" thus functions as a kind of quantum potential, allowing one to change the actual composition of things, or produce effects, as it were, from a template of interferometry. Such a process, then, *might* account for the presence of nuclear residues—strontium, tritium, and so on—where no conventional nuclear or thermonuclear process occurred. This is, of course, the stuff of science fiction. But it is worth noting that it is also in a sense the stuff of cold fusion, and its uses of various types of systems that might—to oversimplify—be qualified as electrical or even electrolytic.

2. Miscellaneous and Circumstantial Data in Loose Confirmation of the Theory

There are miscellaneous and circumstantial data that loosely tend to confirm this theory. Most people are familiar with the pictures of people hanging out of the Twin Towers prior to their destruction, and even, tragically, of people deliberately jumping out of them. The standard explanations have simply been that this is because they were trying to escape the heat and smoke from the fires, and indeed, this is a plausible explanation. However, if microwaves were being used on that day, if they were being "tuned" prior to their use in the destruction of the Towers, then these unfortunate people were also trying to escape what had essentially become a microwave oven. At full power, of course, this would have become an unspeakable horror; most people know what happens to live animals inside of microwave ovens on full power.

But this bit of data is ambiguous, it can support *any* of the mechanisms advanced for the Towers' destruction, since the most likely explanation is simply that being they were trying to escape the heat and smoke from the fires. There is more suggestive data from some of the statements of eyewitnesses that, while not at all conclusive, is suggestive of strong electrostatic forces, such as might be encountered in an intensely localized microwave environment (and, for that matter, in a nuclear environment).

David Handschuh was a photographer for the *New York Daily News* and was in lower Manhattan on the day of 9/11.[80] In addition to describing the jumpers and seeing "body parts" of victims around Ground Zero,[81] Handschuh also states that he was picked up by the roiling pyroclastic cloud of debris and flung a full city block. As this was happening, he reports hearing a locomotive sound and "cracking and creaking,"[82] sounds that can be associated with strong electrostatic fields—like intense microwaves—and their effects on the atmosphere. Witness Christine Haughney describes seeing a firefighter covered in a thick silvery-gray debris that clung to his arm hairs "like cotton", yet another possible indicator that the debris "dust"[83] had electrostatic properties. Nick Spangler, a journalism student, was at the World Trade Center within minutes of the North Tower being struck, and described

---

[80] Chris Bull and Sam Erman, eds. *At Ground Zero: 25 Stories from Young Reporters Who Were There* (New York: Thunder's Mouth Press, 2002), p. 1.
[81] Ibid., p. 5.
[82] Ibid., p. 6.
[83] Ibid., p. 15.

meeting Alan Mean, a man who worked in the South Tower and who took an elevator down *after* the tower was struck. The elevator crashed and, when Spangler met him, was being attended by an emergency medical technician, whom he told that his leg was tingling.[84] Such sensations are common after injuries. But such sensations are also common in strong electrostatic fields.

There were other phenomena that also support the idea that strong electrical fields of *some* sort may have been in play on 9/11, including exploding electrical transformers[85] and, as we have seen, a witness mentioned by Webster Tarpley who described hearing crackling sounds just prior to the collapse of the South Tower.[86]

---

[84] Chris Bull and Sam Erman, eds. *At Ground Zero: 25 Stories from Young Reporters Who Were There* (New York: Thunder's Mouth Press, 2002), p. 43.

[85] Webster Griffin Tarpley, *9/11 Synthetic Terror: Made in USA*, p. 223.

[86] Ibid., p. 224. It is intriguing to note that a famous incident involving Nikola Tesla was reported by the *New York World-Telegram* on July 11, 1935. Tesla had been testing his "mechanical oscillator" on his laboratory building. The oscillator operated on the mechanical-acoustical resonance properties of materials(in this case, the building!), and unbeknownst to Tesla, was producing minor earthquakes in lower Manhattan. Tesla described this incident in the article as follows: "I was experimenting with vibrations. I had one of my machines going and I wanted to see if I could get it in tune with the vibration of the building. I put it up notch after notch. *There was a peculiar cracking sound.*

"I asked my assistants where did the sound come from. They did not know. I put the machine up a few more notches. *There was a louder cracking sound.* I knew I was approaching the vibration of the steel building. I pushed the machine a little higher.

"Suddenly all the heavy machinery in the place was flying around. I grabbed a hammer and broke the machine. The building would have been about our ears in another few minutes. Outside in the street there was pandemonium. The police and ambulances arrived. I told my assistants to say nothing. We told the police it must have been an earthquake. That's all they ever knew about it."(Dale Pond and Walter Baumgartner, *Nikola Tesla's Earthquake Machine* [Santa Fe, New Mexico: The Message Company, 1997], pp. 5-6)

The Mystery of the Mechanism

F. The Theories of Mechanism of the Destruction of the Twin Towers, and the Second and Third Operational Levels of 9/11:
A Scenario

Careful attention to each of the previous theories about the mechanisms of collapse will reveal that they all have their individual strengths, and their individual problems. In terms of the scenario being advanced here, however, they each signify ever-narrowing circles of people that would have had access to them. While a "rogue network" orchestrating the events of 9/11 might have been able to salt the Towers (or their rubble pile) with controlled demolitions or even nanothermite or "evidence" thereof, when one comes to the question of micronukes (as inevitably one must, if one takes the evidence of nuclear reaction products at Ground Zero seriously), or to the question of exotic or directed energy weapons (as again, one must, if one considers the *consistency* of the pulverization as a resonance effect), then one is left with two hypotheses where access to the technologies narrows considerably, particularly in the last case, that of energy weapons. While the last two hypotheses seem the most unlikely, there is a further possible reason that they must be taken seriously.

As we have argued in previous chapters, at some point, the perpetrators of 9/11, the *level two* "rogue network" realized that its carefully planned operation *itself* had been turned against it, just as the concurrent drills had been "turned live." A coup was possibly under way, and it had announced itself by the possession of highly classified code names. Additionally, as we have argued, there may have been high financial crimes that the perpetrators were attempting to cover up with the specifically targeted areas of the Twin Towers and the Pentagon that were struck, crimes which, if revealed, might have exposed the very existence of that group. Thus, they would have contrived an operation to destroy the evidence, and combine it with the objective to create a false flag operation implicating Muslim terrorists to project their power into the Middle East.

Controlled demolitions and even nanothermite would have suited this objective well. All that was necessary for the projection of power was to create significant damage and loss of life, while destroying evidence. But the third level, in order to signal its bona fides, might have used more than just codes to do so; it might have used an exotic technology in a display of power to bring the towers down. In other words, one possible signal that the coup was very serious may have been an event completely unprepared for by the plotters and planners of level two: the destruction of the Twin Towers. I am not alone in this

220

possible reading of the events of 9/11, for Jean Baudrillard advanced the idea first: "It is even probable that the terrorists (like the experts!) did not anticipate the collapse of the Twin Towers, which was, far more than (the attack of) the Pentagon, the deepest symbolic shock. The symbolic collapse of a whole system is due to an unforeseen complicity, as if, by collapsing (themselves), by suiciding, the towers had entered the game to complete the event.."[87] Once they had collapsed, the level two plotters were pinned: they not only had to continue with their plan, but they also had to obfuscate the data, conceal the existence of a third level, with whom they were now really at war. This third level had revealed its possession of sophisticated technology, and willingness to use it under certain circumstances.

It is perhaps germane to this highly speculative scenario that Secretary of Defense Donald Rumsfeld stated in May of 2001 that Bin Laden—who must now be understood as a foil or symbol of that "global network" of Prime Minister Blair—was on the verge of acquiring atomic weapons and adding them to an arsenal of already existing biological and chemical weapons, and was also preparing to launch a satellite.[88]

More significantly, in January of 2001, Rumsfeld chaired a commission which recommended the creation of a new branch of the military, a "space force" which, among other things, recommended that this space force:

1) be directly under presidential authority;
2) that *all national intelligence agencies be coordinated and subordinated to the space force* on the President's National Security Council;
3) that the Space Force itself be both an armed force *and* an intelligence agency;
4) that the Space Force be superior to all other U.S. armed forces in the chain of command and thus be able to call upon their assets and capabilities; and that,
5) "Very important budgetary means should be released for the space military program."[89]

Concluding its recommendations, the Rumsfeld Commission stated that

---

[87] David MacGregor, "September 11 as 'Machiavellian State Terror,'" in Paul Zarembka, ed. *The Hidden History of 9-11*, p. 183.

[88] Thierry Meyssan, *9/11: The Big Lie*, p. 101.

[89] Ibid., pp. 150-151. The quotation here is that of Meyssan, not the Rumsfeld Commission.

History is replete with instances in which warning signs were ignored and change resisted *until an external, "improbable" event* forced resistant bureaucracies to take action. The question is whether the U.S. will be wise enough to act responsibly and soon enough to reduce U.S. space vulnerability. Or whether, as in the past, a disabling attack against the country and its people—*a "Space Pearl Harbor"*—will be the only event able to galvanize the nation and cause the U.S. Government to act."[90]

In the wake of 9/11, the U.S. expanded its space-based capabilities, even as the Bush administration was calling the events of that day a "new Pearl Harbor," and in the light of the foregoing speculations, perhaps they knew that the "external, improbable event" had in fact taken place that day as someone attacked the U.S.A. with exotic and possibly space-based components and capabilities. If one is combating an extra-territorial global network with big pockets and exotic capabilities, space capabilities would be essential.

There is a weakness to this argument and speculation, and that is, if that network *indeed exists* (as I most definitely believe it does) *then why does it not simply use those capabilities again and impose its will?* There are two possible answers here. One is that while it may possess such capabilities, its possession is limited to a few select, and therefore, highly vulnerable platforms and locations. Overuse would expose them to potential interdiction and destruction. The other is that American intervention in the Middle East may have had as hidden objectives the removal precisely of some of those platforms or research projects. Even the Baghdad Museum looting may have formed a small episode in this larger struggle. "Could the rush to war with Iraq," Jim Marrs asks, "and the 'inside job' at the Baghdad museum have something to do with gaining control over recently discovered knowledge, and perhaps even technology, which might undo modern monopolies in religion and science?"[91] I suspect that it does, for we all know what *other* nation has had a long archaeological interest in the region, and which was assisting Saddam Hussein in uncovering the ancient Iraqi sites.[92]

For now, we must turn to the other indicator of a third level in 9/11, and examine once again the "promise of PROMIS."

---

[90] Thierry Meyssan, *9/11: The Big Lie*, pp. 151-152, emphasis added.

[91] Jim Marrs, *The Terror Conspiracy*, p. 217.

[92] I have written of my own suspicions regarding the Baghdad museum looting in various books and in "The Baghdad Museum Looting: Some More Thoughts, August 20, 2008. www.gizadeathstar.com/the-baghdad-museum-looting-some-more-thoughts/

8

THE CONUNDRUM OF THE CODES
AND THE PROMISE OF PROMIS

*"...Bill Hamilton, the founder of Inslaw, had told her that one version of
PROMIS has been modified by the National Security Agency specifically in
a 'bank surveillance version' to monitor proceeds from drug sales. In
other words, the technology was intimately tied to the financial
community, **and** to the vast underground economy of the international
drug cartels and criminal syndicates. The software was, so to speak, the
gatekeeper of the interface between the 'overworld', the visible system of
finance, and the hidden system, a system that used drugs as an
international currency, and referred to them as gold."*
The author[1]

C ONSIDER THE FOLLOWING PICTURE OF TWO GENIAL-LOOKING elderly men,
sitting outside on patio furniture somewhere, engaged in private
conversation, and apparently having a chuckle, perhaps at some
"inside joke."

---

[1] Joseph P. Farrell, *Covert Wars and Breakaway Civilizations: The Secret Space
Program, Celestial Psyops and Hidden Conflicts*, pp. 123-124.

The elderly genial men in question are, of course, the newly-elected socialist President of France, François Mitterrand, and the President of the United States, Ronald Reagan, also recently elected. The picture was taken during one of the annual summits of the leaders of the top ten economic powers, where they smile and wave and pretend to render great decisions of state and international diplomacy, which decisions have already been prepared for them. In this case, the picture was taken during the summit in Ottawa, Ontario, Canada, in July 1981, as the two leaders shared a moment of private conversation, requested by the new French President.

The question remains, what were they smiling and chuckling about?

Any theories that Mr. Reagan had shared his inside information about the French leader's alleged past with the pro-Nazi Vichy French regime of *Marechal* Petain would be very wide of the mark, as would any theories that Monsieur Mitterrand had responded in kind by sharing his inside information about the deep role of the various "national fronts" and "émigré societies" that were deep backers of the Republican Party, and which were in turn connected to Nazi General Reinhardt Gehlen's wartime German military intelligence organization, *Fremde Heere Ost.*

What they were probably laughing about what was that M. Mitterrand had disclosed to Mr. Reagan one of the French government's most highly classified secrets: the French DST, the equivalent of the USA's FBI, had a mole inside the KGB. And not just any mole, but a mole *deeply* inside the branch of the KGB responsible for technological intelligence and theft, and that this mole had provided the French government with the KGB's complete "shopping list," an inventory of items it was desperate to procure from the West. This too, M. Mitterrand had shared with his American counterpart, sometime during the Ottawa summit. One can only imagine what Mr. Reagan's tickled response must have been, but it very likely might have included a hearty "Vive la France!", as any lingering doubts about the firmness of France's new socialist leader's commitment to the West were dispelled, and the two men maintained a cordial and friendly relationship from that point.

The mole in question was Soviet KGB Lt. Colonel Vladimir Ippolitovich Vetrov, to whom the French DST had assigned the codename "Farewell," and it is under this name that France ran what was probably the most deeply-embedded mole in a foreign intelligence service in the twentieth century, a mole who may have single-handedly so damaged and weakened the Soviet Union that its ultimate collapse— a Reagan Administration covert objective—was inevitable. Vetrov, by providing French intelligence with a steady flow of documents from the

KGB's technical branch, had literally given Mitterrand, and now Reagan, a clear picture of the "scope, structure, and operations of technological espionage as practiced by the USSR,"[2] revealing a key strategic weakness in Soviet technology: computer hardware, and software, and these in turn indicated that with careful coordination, the Soviet Union could be choked and strangled economically.

Lt. Col. Vladimir Ippolitovich Vetrov,
Official KGB Identification Photograph

The "Farewell" case file was turned over to Gus Weiss, a senior Reagan Administration National Security Council advisor, who conceived of an idea to use the information Vetrov had provided in a way that would not only cripple the Soviet Union economically, but riddle the country's computer networks with bugs, viruses, implanted "clipper chips", and, as an added bonus, paralyze the Soviet apparatchiks and nomenklatura with paranoia and suspicion about the

---

[2] Sergei Kostin and Eric Raynaud, *Farewell: The Greatest Spy Story of the Twentieth Century*, trans. from the French by Catherine Cauvin-Higgins (Las Vegas: Amazon Crossing, 2011), p. vii.

vulnerability of their most sensitive computer networks and equipment.[3]

A. Ka-boom:
Gas Explosions and Reagan's Strategic Defense Initiative

It is precisely here that a likely connection to 9/11, and to a festering left-over scandal from the Reagan era begins, for Weiss had come up with a plan, using the KGB's "shopping list":

> The VPK, the organization centralizing technology requests from the military-industrial complex, compiled in what was informally called the Red Book a detailed "shopping list" for each Soviet ministry.
>
> In January 1982, Weiss proposed to William Casey, director of the CIA and personal friend of Ronald Reagan, to put in place a vast plan for sabotaging the Soviet economy by transferring false information to the KGB Line X spies. Reagan approved the plan immediately and enthusiastically.
>
> Weiss focused his attention more specifically on the oil and gas industry which, as mentioned earlier, was a sector of the Soviet economy Washington had decided to handle in a special way.
>
> A gas pipeline between Siberia and Western Europe had been in the design phase for many years. It was supposed to be commissioned soon. Implementing European technology, this gas pipeline was the source of tensions between the (European Economic Community) countries and the United States. Europe's a need for energy independence through diversification was in direct conflict with the economic war the Americans had launched against the Soviet Union. Mitterrand and Reagan, just after their honeymoon over the Farewell case, had a serious confrontation on the issue.
>
> Weiss's plan allowed everybody to agree. *He arranged to have software delivered to Line X through a Canadian company. This software was meant to control gas pipeline valves and turbines, and it was delivered with viruses embedded in the code by one of the contractors. The viruses were designed to have a delayed effect;* at first the software seemed to work as per the contract specifications.
>
> *The sudden activation of the viruses in December 1983 led to a huge three kiloton gas explosion in the Urengoi gas field, precisely in Siberia...*

---

[3] Sergei Kostin and Eric Raynaud, *Farewell*, pp. 284-285.

226

Observed from space by satellite, the explosion was allegedly so powerful that it alarmed NATO analysts, who later described it as the most powerful non-nuclear (man-made) explosion of all times.[4]

This event occurred after Reagan's famous "Star Wars" speech of March 1983, in which he announced the U.S. effort to create a missile defense system, knowing full well that the Soviet Union lagged far behind Western capabilities in computer technology and software development, two key components in making any such missile defense system work.[5] The point was underscored with the December 1983 gas explosion, and the Soviet leaders could not have missed the message.

1. Wild Speculations

The Farewell case is the first use that we know of in the public record where infected computer software—and presumably hardware—was used to significantly sabotage a nation's infrastructure, and it is worthwhile to speculate that perhaps other significant events may have been cases of similar activity: the Chernobyl nuclear reactor meltdown, and even the difficulties encountered by the coup against Gorbachev that ultimately led to the demise of the Soviet Union. There are rumors and arguments that the Fukushima meltdown was a deliberate act of sabotage via infected computer programs, and that Iran's nuclear program has been delayed by the same means. All of this activity suggests *that there is a common platform* allowing saboteurs to "ride in" and accomplish their objectives.

---

[4] Sergei Kostin and Eric Raynaud, *Farewell*, pp. 283-284, emphasis added. Kostin and Raynaud also maintain that the "red mercury" scare of the early 1990s was in fact an elaborate disinformation scheme cooked up by the western intelligence services. (See pp. 286-287) As if to reinforce any paranoia the Soviet regime might have had over its virus-ridden software and computer systems, a novel was published in France at approximately this same time period, and later translated into English, by Thierry Breton and Denis Beneich, *Softwar* (New York: Holt Rinehart and Winston, 1985). The theme of this book precisely mirrored the actual events: virus-ridden computer software was sold to, and "allowed: to be stolen by, the Soviet Union. These viruses were then later activated to take down key areas of Soviet ministries and economies.

[5] Ibid, p. 285.

*2. The Route of the Infected Software from the West to the Soviet Union
and the Timing of the Urengoi Gas Explosion*

But *was* there a common platform that could have allowed such global cyber-sabotage?

Recall from the Farewell case and the explosion of the Urengoi gas field that

1) The program was initiated by and with the express approval of American President Ronald Reagan;
2) A computer program infected with viruses and a "backdoor" was allowed to make its way to Russia, via *Canada*; and fnally,
3) The explosion occurred in December 1983, meaning the action of the transference of the software had to have occurred sometime between July 1981, when Mr. Reagan first learns of the French mole from French President Mitterrand, and the 1983 explosion.

These three facts, and particularly the *timing* an *route* of the software, connect the Farewell case directly and ineluctably to a scandal from the Reagan era that continues to this day.

B. The Inslaw Scandal and PROMIS Software Once Again
1. The Capabilities of PROMIS

The PROMIS software system was a development of the Inslaw Corporation, a corporation founded by former National Security Agency insider, William Hamilton, and his wife. The plan and implementation behind the software was simple, for by the early 1980s, each department of the American federal government had its own computer systems and databases, each using their own computer languages, and hence, were incapable of quick coordination.

PROMIS, standing for Prosecutor's Management Information System, was a software whose architecture allowed it to search and compile information from any database, regardless of what computer language it used. It was a "multilingual" computer database management system,[6] and as such, a revolution in software design and architecture for the day. Initially the program was designed for the Department of Justice, to allow federal prosecutors to track individuals through the court system, either by case, by their attorneys, sitting judges, prior arrest records, and so on. In other words, in addition to

---

[6] Michael C. Ruppert, *Crossing the Rubicon*, p. 153.

being a multilingual program, it was also extremely flexible, and with modifications, could track money flows,[7] stock transactions, drug trading, utility usage, and even, as we shall discover, nuclear weapons and their platforms.

2. The Theft by the Reagan Department of Justice

By 1982-1983, however, the U.S. Justice Department had stolen the software from Hamilton and his Inslaw Corporation, and rumor began to reach him that the Justice Department and other federal agencies were modifying it. Additionally, the Department of Justice refused to pay Hamilton's company for the software, and various attempts were made to drive his company out of business. By 1986, Hamilton sued, and thus began a controversy that continues to this day.

3. The Modifications

Since its theft, the program filtered through a number of federal agencies, each one, apparently, adding backdoors and other methods of secret access. The Inslaw scandal created such a ruckus, that Congressman Jack Brooks (D-Texas), then chairman of the House Judiciary Committee, decided he would hold hearings and investigate. What the committee uncovered was astonishing:

> The Hamiltons have alleged that after the Enhanced PROMIS software was stolen, it was illegally disseminated with the Department of Justice, *to other Federal Government agencies and to governments abroad.* This dissemination included the distribution of PROMIS to U.S. intelligence agencies, *the FBI and DEA.* The Hamiltons have also claimed that the PROMIS software was *sold to foreign governments for use by their inteliigence and law enforcement agencies.* The Hamiltons have strongly asserted that *prior to PROMIS being distributed, it was modified by individuals connected with covert U.S. intelligence operations. These modifications possibly allowed for the creation of a "back door" into the system which would allow the U.S. intelligence agencies to break into the systems of these foreign governments whenever they wished.*[8]

---

[7] Michael C. Ruppert, *Crossing the Rubicon*, p. 156.

[8] House Judiciary Committee, 102nd Congress, 2nd Session, *The Inslaw Affair: Investigative Report by the Committee on the Judiciary together with Dissenting and Separate Views*, p. 42, emphasis added.

Note that this is *exactly* the pattern in evidence in the Farewell affair, and note also that this activity was *extended throughout the Federal government and its agencies, and to as yet unnamed "foreign governments."* And in all these versions, there was a "back door" allowing the U.S. government access to the sensitive intelligence of foreign governments whose agencies were using the software.

Recall from the preface that at some point during 9/11, the "level three" players revealed their knowledge of highly classified codes from *a variety of federal agencies,* including the FBI and DEA. As we shall discover, these are two of the agencies implicated in the PROMIS software theft and modifications.

4. The Countries known to Have Acquired Versions

Originally Inslaw's corporate plan was not only to develop the software for use by the American Federal Government, but by foreign countries and individual American states and local governments as well, and to this end Inslaw International, a subsidiary of the Inslaw Corporation, "licensed PROMIS in Ireland, Scotland, Australia, Holland, and Italy."[9] Under the Department of Justice's "pilot program," the software was extended to Pennsylvania and Massachusetts.[10]

One of the most explosive—literally—revelations disclosed during the Judiciary Committee hearings came from two Israelis, Ari Ben-Menashe and Juval Aviv:

> Additional allegations of unauthorized distribution of INSLAW's Enhanced PROMIS software have been hbrought to the committee. Such allegations have been made by Charles Hayes (a surplus computer dealer), Ari Ben-Menashe and Juval Aviv (former Israeli intelligence officers) and Lester Coleman (self-professed writer and security consultant). These sources have stated that PROMIS has been illegally provided or sold to foreign governments including *Canada, Israel, Singapore, Iraq, Egypt, and Jordan.*[11]

Recall that the infected software that was allowed to be "stolen" by the Soviet Union in the Farewell case came via a Canadian route. And recall also that *warnings about 9/11 came from Egypt, Israel, and Jordan,* three of the recipients of PROMIS.

---

[9] House Judiciary Committee, 102nd Congress, 2nd Session, *The Inslaw Affair*, p. 43.
[10] Ibid., p. 44.
[11] Ibid., p. 50, emphasis added.

a. The Affidavit of Michael J. Riconosciuto

Yet another witness in the Inslaw affair, Michael Riconosciuto,[12] claimed to have made backdoor modifications on the PROMIS software for the Wackenhut Corporation on the Cabazon Indian Reservation in California. In testimonies to various congressional committees, Riconosciuto maintained that PROMIS, in its modified "back door" forms, was sold to Canada, *Libya, Iran, Iraq, and South Korea*.[13]

Riconosciuto also provided an affidavit to the Inslaw Corporation's bankruptcy trial, and it contains a number of revelations about the context in which the PROMIS modifications were made. I include the entire affidavit below:

UNITED STATES BANKRUPTCY COURT
FOR THE DISTRICT OF COLUMBIA

IN RE: INSLAW, INC., Debtor,	Case No. 85-00070 (Chapter 11)

INSLAW, INC.,
    Plaintiff,
v.
UNITED STATES OF AMERICA,
And the UNITED STATES
DEPARTMENT OF JUSTICE,
    Defendants.
	Adversary Proceeding
	No. 86-0069

AFFIDAVIT OF MICHAEL J. RICONOSCIUTO

State of Washington) ss:

---

[12] Riconosciuto is a name well known in the alternative research community, for he is connected directly not only to the Inslaw affair, but, as a one-time celebrated "child genius," appears to have worked on a number of black projects. Additionally, he claims to have worked on the development of the fuel air/thermobaric bomb development, as detailed in the following affidavit in the main text.

[13] Rodney Stich, *Defrauding America: Dirty Secrets of the CIA and Other Government Operations,* Second Edition (Reno, Nevada: Diablo Western Press, Inc., 1994), p. 377.

The Conundrum of the Codes and the Promise of PROMIS

I, MICHAEL J. RICONOSCIUTO, being duly sworn, do hereby state as follows:

1. During the early 1980's, I served as the Director of Research for a joint venture between the Wackenhut Corporation of Coral Gables, Florida, and the Cabazon Bank of Indians of Indio, California. The joint venture was located on the Cabazon Reservation.

2. *The Wackenhut–Cabazon joint venture sought to develop and/or manufacture certain materials that are used in military and national security operations, including night vision goggles, machine guns, fuel-air explosives, and biological and chemical warfare weapons.*

3. *The Cabazon Band of Indians are a sovereign nation. The sovereign immunity that is accorded the Cabazons as a consequence of this fact made it feasible to pursue on the reservation the development and/or manufacture of materials whose development or manufacture would be subject to stringent controls off the reservation.* As a minority group, the Cabazon Indians also provided the Wackenhut Corporation with and enhanced ability to obtain federal contracts through the 8A Set Aside Program, and in connection with government-owned contractor-operated (GOCO) facilities.

4. The Wackenhut-Cabazon joint venture was intended to support the needs of a number of foreign governments and forces, including forces and governments in Central America and the Middle East. The Contras in Nicaragua represented one of the most important priorities for the joint venture.

5. The Wackenhut-Cabazon joint venture maintained closed liaison with certain elements of the United States government, including representatives of intelligence, military and law enforcement agencies.

6. Among the frequent visitors to the Wackenhut-Cabazon joint venture were Peter Videnieks of the U.S. Department of Justice in Washington, D.C., and a close associate of Videnieks by the name of Earl W. Brian. Brian is a private businessman who lives in Maryland and who has maintained close business ties with the U.S. intelligence community for many years.[14]

7. *In connection with my work for Wackenhut, I engaged in some software development and modification work in 1983 and 1984 on the proprietary PROMIS computer software product. The copy of PROMIS on which I worked came from the U.S. Department of Justice.* Earl W. Brian made it available to me through Wackenhut after acquiring it from peter Videnieks, who was then a Department of Justice

---

[14] The circle closes, for it is also worth noting that Brian was a close friend and associate of the Reagan Administration's U.S. Attorney General, Ed Meese, whose Justice Department stole the PROMIS software.

contracting official with responsibility for the PROMIS software. I performed the modifications to PROMIS in Indio, California; Silver Springs, Maryland; and Miami, Florida.

8. *The purpose of the PROMIS software modifications that I made in 1983 and 1984 was to support a plan for the implantation of PROMIS in law enforcement and intelligence agencies worldwide. Earl W. Brian was spearheading the plan for this worldwide use of the PROMIS computer software.*

9. *Some of the modifications that I made were specifically designed to facilitate the implementation of PROMIS within two agencies of the government of Canada; the Royal Canadian Mounted Politic (RCMP) and the Canadian Security and Intelligence Service (CSIS). Earl W. Brian would check with me from time to time to make certain that the work would be completed in time to satisfy the schedule of the RCMP and CISIS implementations of PROMIS.*

10. The proprietary version of PROMIS, as modified by me, was, in fact, implemented in both the RCMP and the CSIS in Canada. It was my understanding that Earl W. Brian had sold this version of PROMIS to the government of Canada.

11. In February 1991, I had a telephone conversation with Peter Videnieks, then still employed by the U.S. Department of Justice. Videnieks attempted during this telephone conversation to persuade me not to cooperate with an independent investigation of the government's piracy of INSLAW's proprietary PROMIS software being conducted by the Committee on the Judiciary of the U.S. House of Representatives.

12. Videnieks stated that I would be rewarded for a decision not to cooperate with the House Judiciary Committee investigation. Videnieks forecasted an immediate and favorable resolution of a protracted child custody dispute being prosecuted against my wife by her former husband, if I were to decide not to cooperate with the House Judiciary Committee investigation.

13. Videnieks also outlined specific punishments that I could expect to receive from the U.S. Department of Justice if I cooperate with the House Judiciary Committee's investigation.

14. One punishment that Videnieks outlined was the future inclusion of me and my father in a criminal prosecution of certain business associates of mine in orange County, California, in connection with the operation of a savings and loan institution in Orange County. By way of underscoring his power to influence such decisions at the U.S. Department of Justice, Videnieks informed me of the indictment of these business associates prior to the time when that indictment was unsealed and made public.

15. Another punishment that Videnieks threatened against me if I cooperated with the House Judiciary Committee is prosecution by the U.S. Department of Justice for perjury. Videnieks warned me that credible witnesses would come forward to contradict any damaging claims that I made in testimony before the House Judiciary Committee, and that I would subsequently be prosecuted for perjury by the U.S. Department of Justice for my testimony before the House Judiciary Committee.

FURTHER AFFIANT SAYETH NOT.
Michael J. Riconosciuto[15]

The pattern that emerges here is intriguing, and one quite in keeping with a covert operation, for the PROMIS modifications were made on an Indian reservation, which, in U.S. law, is sovereign territory, in conjunction with a corporation. This was used, according to Riconosciuto, not only to modify PROMIS, but to produce fuel-air bombs![16] More importantly, Riconosciuto combines the modifications made to PROMIS with a clear program to disseminate the software on a worldwide basis. Finally, he again emphasizes the Canadian connection.

b. The Affidavit of Richard H. Babayan

Richard H. Babayan was another witness for the Inslaw Corporation, as it was seeking to recover monies owed to it by the Department of Justice, and with his affidavit, more countries, and characters, are added to the PROMIS saga:

UNITED STATES BANKRUPTCY COURT
FOR THE DISTRICT OF COLUMBIA

IN RE:	Case No. 85-00070
INSLAW, INC.,	(Chapter 11)
Debtor,	
INSLAW, INC.,	Adversary Proceeding
Plaintiff,	No. 86-0069

---

[15] Rodney Stich, *Defrauding America*, pp. 389-391, emphasis added.

[16] While not directly related to the subject of 9/11 or to the hypothesis of a possible third layer involved in it, it is worth noting the disturbing implications of Riconosciuto's affidavit, for it means that very small sovereignties, in conjunction with corporations, could gain access to non-nuclear technologies of weapons of mass destruction.

v.

UNITED STATES OF AMERICA,
And the UNITED STATES
DEPARTMENT OF JUSTICE,
Defendants.

AFFIDAVIT OF RICHARD H. BABAYAN

State of Florida SS:
Palm Beach County

I, Richard H. Babayan, being duly sworn, do hereby state as follows:

1. During the past several years, I have acted as a broker of sales of materials and equipment used by foreign governments in their armed forces, intelligence and security organizations.

2. In the capacity described in paragraph #1, I attended a meeting in Baghdad, Iraq, in October or November, 1987, with Mr. Abu Mohammed of Entezamat, an intelligence and security organ of the government of Iraq. Mr. Abu Mohammed is a senior ranking official of Entezamat and a person with whom I had extensive dealings over the previous three years.

3. During the aforementioned meeting with Mr. Abu Mohammed, I was informed that Dr. Earl W. Brian of the United States had recently completed a sale presentation to the government of Iraq regarding the PROMIS computer software. Furthermore, it is my understanding that others present at Dr. Brian's PROMIS sales presentation were General Richard Secord, of the United State, and Mr. Abu Mohammed.

4. In early to mid-1988, in the course of subsequent visits to Baghdad, Iraq, I was informed that Dr. Earl W. Brian had, in fact, provided the PROMIS computer software to the government of Iraq through a transaction that took place under the umbrella of Mr. Sarkis Saghanollan, an individual who has had extensive business dealings with the government of Iraq since the late 1970/s in the fields of military hardware and software. *I was also informed that the government of Iraq acquired the PROMIS software for use primarily in intelligence services, and secondarily in police and law enforcement agencies.*

5. During the course of the visits described in paragraph #4, *I also learned from Mr. Abu Mohammed that the government of Libya had acquired the PROMIS computer software prior to its acquisition by the government of Iraq; that the government of Libya had by then made extensive use of PROMIS;* and that the government of Libya was highly recommending the PROMIS software to other countries.

235

I was informed that the high quality of the reference for the PROMIS software from the government of Libya was one of the principal reasons for the decision of the government of Iraq to acquire PROMIS.

6. In the capacity described in paragraph #1, I attended a meeting in early 1988 in Singapore with Mr. Y.H. Nam of the Korea Development Corporation.

7. The Korea Development Corporation is known to be a cutout for the Korean Central Intelligence Agency (KCIA).

8. *I learned from Mr. Y.H. Nam during the meeting described in paragraph 36 that the KCIA had acquired the PROMIS computer software, and that Dr. Earl W. Brian of the United States had been instrumental in the acquisition and implementation of PROMIS by the KCIA.*

9. In the capacity described in paragraph #1, I attended a meeting in Santiago, Chile, in December, 1988, with Mr. Carlos Carduen of Carduen Industries. During this meeting, I was informed by Mr. Carduen that Dr. Earl W. Brian of the United States *and Mr. Robert Gates,* a senior American Intelligence and national security official, had just completed a meeting in Santiago, Chile, with Mr. Carlos Carduen.

10. I hereby certify that the facts set forth in this Affidavit are true and correct to the best of my knowledge.

FURTHER AFFIANT SAYETH NOT.
Richard A. Babayan[17]

One may now add further confirmation that Iraq's security services acquired PROMIS, and that Libya did as well, an odd circumstance, since both Iraq and Libya suffered subsequent American invasions and bombings, and the regimes which acquired the software—Saddam Hussein's and Moammar Qaddafi's—are now long gone. Notably, Mr. Robert Gates was present at a meeting in Santiago, Chile, presumably for the purpose of Chile's acquisition of the software. Gates would go on to become secretary of Defense, and it would be Robert Gates who

---

[17] Rodney Stich, *Defrauding America*, pp. 392-393, emphasis added. Stich also notes that Iraq acquired its chemical weapons from the Cardeon Corporation of *Chile* (p. 386), but this raises the question of where Cardeon in turn acquired them. Peter Levenda notes, however, that the notorious Nazi compound in Chile, *Cologna Dignidad*, was producing Sarin gas and other deadly chemical weapons. (See Peter Levenda, *The Hitler Legacy: The Nazi Cult in Diaspora: How it was Funded, and Why it Remains a Threat to Global Security in the Age of Terrorism* [Lake Worth, Florida: Ibis Press, 2014], p. 172, citing the documentary by Jose Maldavsky, *Colonia Dignidad: A Nazi Sect in the Land of Pinochet*, www.youtube.com/watch?v=5oObdFq78_s).

issued a stern warning to the Government of Japan not to insist on closure of the US military base on Okinawa or there would be dire consequences. Fukushima, of course, occurred after this warning, and some maintain it was caused by a virus in computer software.

The notorious Russian mole inside the FBI, Robert Hanssen, also provided a copy of the software to the Russian mafia, which in turn apparently sold a copy to Osama Bin Laden.[18] This implies that Saudi Arabia itself, and the Bin Laden group, might also have had the software, and been covertly monitored by the U.S. intelligence services. More importantly, Hanssen was also apparently involved in repairing and upgrading versions of the PROMIS program used by the United Kingdom and Germany,[19] until both countries discontinued its use after 9/11,[20] a clear indicator that those countries knew that there was a deep connection between PROMIS and the events of that day.

c. The U.S. Agencies and Corporations Using PROMIS, the Nuclear Connection, and a Summary

The software also made deep and extensive penetrations throughout the military-industrial complex, the "deep state" of the U.S.A. itself:

> The paper tracking of the refinements in Promis after the legal dispute erupted between INSLAW and the Reagan administration, verifies that at least one version of Promis was given to Martin Marietta, now Lockheed-Martin, which is now the nation's second largest defense contractor. Until late 2000, Lynne Cheney, the wife of Vice President Dick Cheney sat on Lockheed's board of directors. Research conducted by many investigative journalists has indicated that Promis has spread widely throughout the defense contractor network. (I) received multiple reports of Promis use by companies and institutions like *DynCorp, Raytheon,. Boeing, SAIC and the Harvard Endowment* as well as by government agencies

---

[18] Michael C. Ruppert, "Promis Software—Bin Laden's Magic Carpet," www.rense.com/general17/maf.htm. Ruppert cites both Fox News, and a June 15, 2001 story by the *Washington Times* reported Jerry Seper. The House Judiciary also corroborates the sale of PROMIS to the Soviet Union, although in its *public* version. (Q.v. House Committee on the Judiciary, *The Inslaw Affair*, p. 57).

[19] Ibid.

[20] Ibid.

such as the *Financial Criminal Enforcement Network(FINCEN) and the U.S. Treasury.*[21]

Additionally, there is a direct connection to the international drug trade, for the United States Drug Enforcement Agency also allegedly sold versions of the software to the drug enforcement agencies of Cyprus, Pakistan, Syria, Kuwait, and Turkey, according to a former DEA agent, Lester Coleman.[22]

Juval Aviv, whom we encountered earlier in connection to his testimony to the House Judiciary Committee's Inslaw investigation, also maintained that the software was eventually in use by the CIA, NSA, NASA, the National Security Council—a point whose relevance to 9/11 will become apparent shortly—as well as by Interpol, the Israeli Air Force, and Egypt.[23] Most importantly, Aviv even "stated that INSLAW's Enhanced PROMIS software *was converted for use by both the United States and British Navy nuclear submarine intelligence data base.*"[24]

Pause and consider now the list of nations, U.S. corporations, and U.S. Federal government agencies, that were using some version of PROMIS:

    1)   *The Nations:*
        Canada
        Cyprus
        Egypt
        Germany
        Great Britain
        (Interpol)
        Iran
        Iraq
        Ireland
        Israel
        Jordan
        Kuwait
        Libya
        Pakistan

---

[21] Michael C. Ruppert, "Promis Software—Bin Laden's Magic Carpet," www.rense.com/general17/maf.htm, emphasis added.

[22] History Commons, *Inslaw and PROMIS: Use of Enhanced PROMIS by US Gov't Agencies Other than DoJ and Countries Other than US,*
    www.historycommons.org/timeline.jsp?inslawpromis.

[23] Ibid. See also House Committee on the Judiciary, *The Inslaw Affair*, p. 60.

[24] Ibid., p. 60, emphasis added.

    Singapore
    South Korea
'   Syria
    The Soviet Union
    With indicators of use by:
    The Russian Mafia
    Osama Bin Laden (which in turn implicates the Bin Laden Group, and the Kingdom of Saudi Arabia)

2) *The U.S. Defense Contractors:*
    Boeing
    DynCorp
    Martin Marietta/Lockheed-Martin
    Raytheon,
    SAIC (Science Applications International Corporation)

3) *The U.S. Federal Agencies:*
    CIA (Central Intelligence Agency)
    DEA (Drug Enforcement Agency)
    FBI (Federal Bureau of Investigation)
    FINCEN (implicating the SEC)
    NASA (National Aeronautics and Space Administration)
    NSA (National Security Agency)
    The National Security Council
    U.S. Navy nuclear submarines

Now let us recall the observation of Thierry Meyssan from the Preface, that sometime during the morning of 9/11, after the departure of President G.W. Bush from the Booker Elementary school, that the behavior of the President, and the messages he was sending, were indicative of a coup attempt, necessitating his personal presence at Barksdale and Offut Air Force bases to reassert personal presidential command authority over the nation's strategic nuclear arsenal:

> And more astonishing still, *World Net Daily*, citing intelligence officers as its sources, said the attackers also had the codes of the Drug Enforcement Agency (DEA), the National Reconnaissance Office (NRO), Air Force Intelligence (AFI), Army Intelligence (AI), Naval Intelligence (NI), the Marine Corps Intelligence (MCI) and the intelligence services of the State Department and the Department of Energy. Each of these codes is known by only a very small group of officials. No one is authorized to possess several of them. Also, to accept that the attackers were in possession of them supposes

either that there exists a method of cracking the codes, or that moles have infiltrated each of these intelligence bodies. Technically, *it appears to be possible to reconstitute the codes of the American agencies by means of the software, Promis, that served to create them.*[25]

In other words, *the pattern of PROMIS dissemination throughout the American military-industrial-intelligence complex closely parallels the revelation on 9/11 by level three of the codes it possessed.* This means something equally profound: *the US command structure may have been penetrated by the very software it disseminated globally during the Reagan era.* This implies the use of the "back doors" built into the program *in reverse*, i.e., by an external entity, to gain access to sensitive American databases, including its code names. We shall return to this possibility in a moment.

d. PROMIS and Continuity of Government Operations

There is, however, another connection of the PROMIS software to the sensitive secrets of the American deep state, and this is that the software may also have been used to compile the lists of individuals to be arrested during any implementation of Continuity of Government operations.[26] Indeed, the name Al-Qaeda itself was never a name that the members of that organization used to refer to itself. Rather, as Nafeez Mosaddeq Ahmed pointed out,

> The late Robin Cook (2005), former British Foreign Secretary, 1997-2001, and Leader of the House of Commons, 2001-2003), revealed... that the term "al-Qaeda" referred to a database contained in a computer file, listing "the thousands of Mujahideen who were recruited and trained with help from the CIA to defeat the Russians."[27]

The links between Osama Bin Laden and the CIA are well-known, so it should come as no surprise that he may have acquired a copy of

---

[25] Ibid., p. 44, emphasis added.

[26] History Commons, *Inslaw and PROMIS: Use of Enhanced PROMIS by US Gov't Agencies Other than DoJ and Countries Other than US*, www.historycommons.org/timeline.jsp?inslawpromis.

[27] Nafeez Ahmed Mosaddeq, "Terrorism and Statecraft," in Paul Zarembka, ed. *The Hidden History of 9-11*, 143-181, p. 145.

PROMIS, nor should it come as a surprise that an entire data base of "terrorist operatives" should exist.

The problem implied, however, is that if the "back door" modifications made on PROMIS prior to its dissemination globally *was* ever turned against it, and used as a gate not of American intelligence penetration into the foreign networks using the software, but rather, as a gate of *external entities' penetration* of the American networks using it, then even the Continuity of Government operations—including its lists of "unfriendlies"—could be modified. In this respect, also recall that PROMIS could be modified to track markets and financial flows, and that Deutsche Bank's computers were suddenly penetrated on the morning of 9/11 and their data downloaded to "somewhere," and one has a security nightmare that could, indeed, have induced panic into the Bush Administration on the morning of 9/11, after it became clear that the carefully planned 9/11 operation was now penetrated by something else.

But is there any evidence that such a scenario is even possible? Indeed there is:

In 2006, there were further allegations of the misuse of Promis. Writing in the *Canada Free Press*, the former Polish CIA operative and now international journalist, David Dastych alleged that "Chinese Military Intelligence (PLA-2) organized their own hackers department, which (exploited) Promis (database systems) (in the) Los Alamos and Sandia national laboratories to steal U.S. nuclear secrets."[28]

However, this is not the *only* evidence that such a penetration was made. The other evidence comes from a consideration of 9/11 itself.

5. The PROMIS Connection to 9/11:
Oliver North's White House Operations Room, and Dick Cheney's Behavior on 9/11

As the PROMIS software was making its way around the world and through the U.S. military-industrial-intelligence complex, a command center was constructed inside the U.S. Department of Justice utilizing the enhanced software, and a smaller command post was additionally

---

[28] "Inslaw," *Wikipedia*, en.wikipedia.org/wiki/Inslaw, citing David Dastych, "Promisgate: World's longest spy scandal still glossed over," *Canada Free Press*, Jan 31, 2006. Q.v. also

constructed in *the White House Operations room* by none other than Marine Colonel Oliver North.[29]

It was *this* operations room to which Vice President Cheney retreated on 9/11, and from which he attempted to coordinate the federal government's response. Why is this significant? For one thing, it was Cheney himself who was put in charge of coordinating the planning of Continuity of Government Operations under President Ronald Reagan. Thus, *in all likelihood, he would have been made aware of the powers and properties of PROMIS, and most likely would have been informed of Col. North's subsequent utilization of the program in the White House Operations room.*

Consequently, not only was *President Bush's* behavior on 9/11 indicative of a coup, but *Cheney's behavior as well* may reflect the need to reassert personal executive branch authority over the command structure:

> Such a penetration using Promis might also explain why Vice President Dick Cheney was hurriedly whished out of sight and reportedly taken to a secure underground facility, where he reportedly works to this day. *Cheney's prolonged (post-9/11) absences from the public eye would also be explained by such a breach of security.*[30]

Cheney was indeed mostly out of public view in the immediate weeks and months after the 9/11 attacks, and given his familiarity with the Continuity of Government Operations that he had helped plan during the Reagan era, he would have been the likely person to spearhead any clean-up of America's databases and networks. In this respect, it is important to recall once again that the United Kingdom and Germany suspended use of the program. And in the aftermath of 9/11, the FBI did as well,[31] implying its suspension by other agencies.

With the PROMIS story, in other words, one is chin-to-chin with the direct possibility that someone might have penetrated the entire U.S.

---

[29] "The INSLAW Octopus: Software piracy, conspiracy, cover-up, stonewalling, covert action: Just another decade at the Department of Justice," *Wired Magazine*, www.wired.com/1993/01/inslaw. History Commons, *Inslaw and PROMIS: Use of Enhanced PROMIS by US Gov't Agencies Other than DoJ and Countries Other than US*, www.historycommons. org/timeline.jsp?inslawpromis.

[30] Michael C. Ruppert, "Promis Software—Bin Laden's Magic Carpet." www.rense.com/general17/maf.htm, emphasis added. I have added the words "post-9/11" to Ruppert's commentary, which was first written in December of 2001.

[31] Michael C. Ruppert, *Crossing the Rubicon*, p. 171.

command structure, gaining access to top secret codes, databases, and, as its utilization by several major U.S. Defense contractors implies, may also have gained access to a variety of hidden technologies and their platforms. This is an implication that reinforces what was stated in the previous chapter, for such access would in turn imply the ability to gain access to technologies such as micro-nukes, or any directed or exotic energy weapons as those corporations might have developed.[32] In this respect, it is also worth noting that PROMIS also inspired "four new computer languages" and that it had "made possible the positioning of satellites so far out in space that they were untouchable. At the same time the progeny had improved video quality to the point where the same satellite could focus on a single human hair. The ultimate big picture."[33] In other words, there is a space-based connection in PROMIS, one that, if penetrated, as the evidence gathered thus far seems to suggest, might have panicked the level two planners and plotters of 9/11 beyond anything we can imagine.

But what if this "multilingual" ability to read several databases was used to do more than compile lists of terrorists, suspects to be rounded up for Continuity of Government operations, satellite positioning and imaging, tracking financial flows, invading Deutsche Bank computers, or placing puts and shorts on the markets prior to 9/11, or gaining access to exotic weapons technologies? What it if was used in the ultimate alchemical wedding of high technology and deep black magic? What if it was used to coordinate and plan the details of a MegaRitual?

---

[32] In this respect, recall that Boeing and SAIC corporations, companies reputedly working on anti-gravity (and presumably, its weaponization), were mentioned as some of the corporations using PROMIS.

[33] Michael C. Ruppert, *Crossing the Rubicon*, p. 166.

Masonic Pillars Jachin and Boaz

9

THE ESOTERIC ENIGMA

"By choosing to see 9/11 as a ritual on a massive scale, we paradoxically may better be able to understand it, to accommodate its message on a psychological—even spiritual—level..."
Peter Levenda[1]

WHEN I HAD FIRST FINISHED READING S.K. Bain's *The Most Dangerous Book in the World: 9/11 as Mass Ritual*, I had to sit, quietly, for several minutes. It was as if I had been shocked back into reality, or perhaps into a different reality altogether, the reality that we think humanity left long ago, but which in point of fact it did not. For those with an eye to magic and ritual like myself, it was clear that on 9/11 itself that what we were witnessing was a gigantic working of ritual magic. The three biggest symbols that this was so were staring us in the face from our television sets: the Pentagon, and the Twin Towers of the World Trade Center, the twin masonic pillars of Jachin and Boaz. Bain's book confirms the worst suspicions of those who saw the symbols being manipulated on that day, and then some.

It may indeed well be "the most dangerous book in the world", for it confirmed yet another suspicion: there *was* a third level to 9/11, though it was not even what I had thought it to be, for behind the first level — with its patsies flying airplanes into buildings and their alleged links to radical Islam, behind even the second level, with its careful planning by a rogue network inside the American national security state, meticulously coordinating drills and making arrangements to "flip" some of them live—there was a third level, that had carefully planned the entire event as a massive magical ritual of human sacrifice.

It was, if the argument of preceding chapters has been followed, the ultimate alchemical wedding of magic and technology, technology in the form of exotic means of destruction of the Twin Towers, and perhaps also in the form of a software program that allowed and helped coordinate and plan the ritual aspects of the event. It was the alchemical wedding of magic and technology to process "the subconscious Group Mind of the masses,"[2] a fantastic manipulation to create "meaningful coincidences," a "common practice among occultists."[3] And perhaps this

---

[1] Peter Levenda, "Knock, Knock," in S.K. Bain, *The Most Dangerous Book in the World: 9/11 as Mass Ritual* (Walterville, Oregon: Trine Day, 2012), v-ix, p. viii.
[2] S.K. Bain, *The Most Dangerous Book in the World*, p. 51.
[3] S.K. Bain, *The Most Dangerous Book in the World,* p. 54.

deepest level, too, was what dawned on the level two operators that morning, making the President himself declare the post-9/11 world as a cosmological struggle between good and evil.

Bain's book is so important for an understanding of that third level, that to ignore it would be futile, and yet, one can only hope to briefly review its salient points, in order to exhibit their place in the larger scenario outlined in this book. Bain's book is crucial, for as Peter Levenda put the case in his preface to it, to argue that 9/11 was a ritual working requires:

> ...someone who is as versed in Kabbalah as in conspiracy, in gematria as in government. It requires a new science, a new art, a new approach to the old material. Furthermore, it requires a sense that conspiracy may be transcendental, may have its origins in the unconscious mind of the state. The numerology alone is significant: someone, somewhere is pulling these particular quantum strings. The numbers are consistent, insistent. They are either the result of a conscious and deliberate series of acts by agents so powerful and so unknown that a belief in an ultimate Secret Society is our only option, or they are evidence of the workings of an even Darker Force... and no one is in charge.[4]

Levenda's reaction is my own: no one can read Bain's book, and come away from the experience with anything less than a perception that cosmological forces and very deep conspiracy, far transcending rogue networks within American intelligence, was involved.

As such, any "mere review" such as is offered here cannot do Bain's work justice; it must be read in the full experience of its voluminous details. But summarize we must, if the lineaments of that third, deepest, level are ever to be adequately probed.

A. 9/11 as a Textbook, or Grimoire, of High Magical Ritual:
1. Bain's Thesis

Bain notes that for one to fully understand 9/11's "occult script," one must first "learn the basic language and grammar of occult communications and operations,"[5] for the various symbols evident in the event "constitute a grand Magickal Operation" to such an extent that 9/11 itself could be viewed as kind of "contemporary grimoire, or

---

[4] Peter Levenda, "Knock, Knock," in S.K. Bain's *The Most Dangerous Book in the World*, v-ix, pp. vii-viii.

[5] Bain, op. cit., p. 17.

textbook of magic."[6] Thus the central thesis of Bain's book ignores what we have been calling level one and level two, and goes directly to level three and the heart of the matter:

> 9/11 wasn't simply a black op; it was that, and more. Highly compelling evidence shows beyond a reasonable doubt that the perpetrators of this massive criminal act not only employed a broad range of sophisticated psychological warfare tactics, but, even more disturbingly, incorporated a wide variety of occult symbols and other esoteric elements into multiple levels of the event.
>
> This implies the ability to manipulate, to control, on such an enormous scale that it is beyond what most people are prepared to accept. It so strongly conflicts with our perceptions of reality that we dare not even contemplate it.
>
> Unfortunately the evidence points to a worst-case scenario.... (The) picture that emerges is that of 9/11 as an ultra-powerful mind-control and propaganda weapon—a psychological warfare tool of enormous proportions—infused with techno-sorcery and deep-level occult programming. 9/11 was a global MegaRitual, and the painstakingly reconstructed occult script for the event contained herein convincingly shows this.[7]

With this in hand, Bain points out that which was alluded to earlier in the present book: the lack of clarity concerning virtually all aspects of 9/11 is not evidence of the "fog of war," but of deliberate obfuscation of the data and of the deep techniques of psychological warfare.[8] Like most acts of ceremonial magic, 9/11 was also designed as a "globally-televised hideous act of ceremonial magic"[9] *to invoke spirits.*

2. The Symbolism of the Numerology

One key component of Bain's analysis is the numerology of 9/11 itself. Why the numbers 9? 11? Why flight 77, which is a multiple of 11 (11 x 7)? Why an attack on the Pentagon, a 5-sided building with 5 rings, a building which, moreover, had its ground-breaking ceremony on—you guessed it—September 11, 1941, sixty years to the day before it was attacked by flight 77? Is it mere coincidence that the Pentagon sits on

---

[6] S.K. Bain, *The Most Dangerous Book in the World*, p. 17.
[7] Ibid., p. 7.
[8] Ibid., p. 4.
[9] Ibid., p. 18.

the 77th meridian, is 77 feet tall, and was attacked on the sixtieth anniversary of its dedication, by flight 77?[10]

Within esoteric and occult practice, the Pentagon itself is a symbol of protection,[11] and hence an appropriate symbol for a military headquarters building; damaging such a symbol of protection "is also attractive to practitioners of the dark arts,"[12] and hence, a pentagram or five-pointed star, another symbol of protection, must always be drawn carefully so as to leave no open space, "through which the enemy can enter and *disturb the harmony existing in the Pentagon*."[13] And appropriately, five is the number of man, of his five senses, and of death.[14]

As if to drive the non-coincidental, synchronous nature of 9/11 home even more, the pentagram or five-pointed star, and the pentagon associated with it, is also the symbol of Venus; the call sign for American Airlines flight 77 which, according to the official narrative, struck the Pentagon, was "Venus 77."[15]

The number 9 itself has a deep symbolism, from symbolizing the council of the nine supreme Egyptian gods, to the entire council of gods. In other systems, 9 is of course 3 x 3, and 3 is the supreme number of deity. Because of this, some systems view 9 as the "number of earth under evil influences"[16] and thus, 9/11 is, numerologically, a number of supremely evil magic, one accomplished in a twisted fashion by invoking the council of the gods!

The number eleven, Bain notes, citing the occultist William Wynn Wescott, is the symbol in esotericism of "all that is sinful, harmful, and imperfect,"[17] and few would hesitate to describe the events of that day in those terms. But the 11 itself can symbolize the Twin Towers themselves, the pillars of Hermes, who was (another coincidence?) the god of Commerce and Trade.[18] For Solon the Greek, the Pillars of Hermes were also to be associated with Atlantis,[19] an arresting fact since some believe that Sir Francis Bacon, in his essay, *The New Atlantis*, was describing a long social engineering experiment being run by secret

---

[10] S.K. Bain, *The Most Dangerous Book in the World*, p. 40.
[11] Ibid., p. 42.
[12] Ibid.
[13] Ibid., citing Franz Hartman, *Magic: White and Black*, the emphasis has been added by Bain.
[14] Ibid., p. 46.
[15] Ibid., p. 45.
[16] Ibid., p. 80.
[17] Ibid., p. 21.
[18] Ibid.
[19] Ibid.

societies in the New World, in America, the "new Atlantis." With the Twin Towers symbolizing the Pillars of Hercules and thus, Commerce, Trade, and Atlantis, they are also associated with the Great Flood that destroyed it; they are symbols of its destruction. But the Pillars of Hermes also symbolize the Gateway between "this world" or age, and the next. Consequently, their destruction is an invocation of Hermes, and a destruction of the doorway and partition separating the worlds, a "symbolic tearing of the Veil of Isis."[20] Hermes is also the equivalent of the Egyptian god Thoth, the god of Wisdom, Magic, and Judgment.[21]

3. The Symbolism of the Twin Towers: The Trident and Human Sacrifice

Noting the various buildings around the World Trade Center, topped with domes, pyramids, and stepped pyramids, symbols of the monumental architecture by which the ancients gave homage to their gods, Bain wonders if "the entire area around Ground Zero is a massive ritual occult ceremonial center?"[22] He answers his own question immediately:

> The World Financial Center lies directly adjacent to the World Trade Center on the west side, and atop its four tallest buildings are four incredibly powerful occult symbols: 1.) an unfinished pyramid; 2.) a stepped pyramid; 3.) a square pyramid; and, 4.) a dome.
> There is no way to know for certain what these symbols represented to the planners of the 9/11 MegaRitual, or whether they served an active role in the ritual or simply were a part of the ceremonial setting. What is for certain is that they are all of significance to occultists, and their presence at this location cannot be a coincidence.[23]

Bain comments that the completed pyramid, with a capstone, can represent the final perfection of an initiate, but that there are also darker interpretations of the pyramid, which is often used to symbolize the mass of humanity, which is quarried from rough stone, finished, dressed, and placed into a structure as part of a "collective hive awaiting

---

[20] S.K. Bain. *The Most Dangerous Book in the World*, p. 22.

[21] Ibid., p. 63. Bain also notes that the first of the month of Thoth on the Coptic Christian calendar is also the beginning of the new year. (q.v. p. 97)

[22] Ibid., p. 107.

[23] Ibid., p. 108.

the bidding of its masters."[24] An unfinished pyramid, i.e., a pyramid without its capstone, thus symbolizes imperfection, and a work constantly under such bidding. Stepped pyramids represent stairways or ladders to the heavens, and square pyramids are mountains,[25] with its four corners being "the four corners of the world and the four cardinal directions," and as such, symbolize Earth. With its capstone in the heavens, they were also seen as gateways to the gods, as its four sides represented triangles, and three was the number of divinity.[26]

The World Finance Center. The Arrows on the left point to the finished pyramid with capstone, and to a stepped pyramid; in the center is a dome-topped building, and on the right a building with an "unfinished" pyramid on top.

---

[24] S.K. Bain, *The Most Dangerous Book in the World*, pp. 110-111.

[25] For further discussion of the symbolism of Pyramids, see my *The Cosmic War: Interplanetary Warfare, Modern Physics, and Ancient Texts*, p. 74, where pyramids enter a complex symbolic relationship, symbolizing mountains, planets, and specific gods.

[26] Ibid., p. 111.

The World Trade Center Twin Towers themselves, Bain notes, were cladded in steel columns which, toward the ground, came together in the distinctive pattern of a trident, the symbol of Shiva, Poseidon(and therefore, of Atlantis once again), of Satan, and of tongues of fire.[27]

The Trident Classing of the World Trade Center Twin Towers

The symbolism is a familiar one for such events, for the trident is also the predominant symbol in evidence at Dealey Plaza in Dallas, Texas, site of the murder of President John F. Kennedy in 1963:

---

[27] S.K. Bain, *The Most Dangerous Book In the World*, p. 104, citing Dr. Cathy Burns, *Masonic and Occult Symbols Illustrated*.

The Trident of Dealey Plaza, Dallas, Texas. The Texas School Book Depository building is visible in the upper center.

Bain's commentary on the meaning of the Twin Towers and the symbolism in which they were cladded, is chilling, given all the other numerous "non-coincidences" that he marshals in his book:

As you attempt to process the implications of this revelation, consider this: combined with the other evidence, it now becomes extremely difficult to escape the conclusion that these buildings were designed and constructed with their ultimate purpose in mind. It seems that these structures were pre-ordained to become twin towering infernos, the gates of Hell, Hell on earth—filled with tormented victims, innocents, heroes, whole sacrifices, human sacrifices, sacrificed by fire. They were, unmistakably, Satanic MegaAltars.[28]

And if it was here that dark and exotic luciferian technologies of destruction were alchemically wedded to ritual magic and sacrifice, then this points unmistakably to a third level, announcing its malign presence not only in the ritual sacrifice but in the technologies used to plan and accomplish it,[29] for such planning could be accomplished by access to a programming system that had global extent, could manage disparate databases (like databases of occult knowledge), and could access those technologies.

4. The Hanged Man, The Tower, and The Tarot

One of the most disturbing "non-coincidences" and images from Bain's book is the eerie parallel between one of the many "jumpers" on 9/11, to the 12th card of the Tarot deck's "greater trumps," the card known as "The Hanged Man." The Hanged Man is always portrayed hanging upside down, suspended by one leg, forming an inverted "4", from a bar which is sometimes suspended between two trees or pillars, the pillars of the "gateway". It represents the suspension of normal patterns of thinking and behavior, and a hovering between two worlds, seeing things in a very different way than one has ever saw them, which

---

[28] S.K. Bain, *The Most Dangerous Book in the World*, p. 105.

[29] Bain cites Hans Habe, *Agent of the Devil*: "The secret services of all nations are directed or influence by personalities which are marked by a criminal, a perverted, a criminal-pathological, or in any case, an exceedingly vulgar imagination. ... But the worst perversion of the secret services—and how could there be a worse one—is that of human sacrifice."(S.K. Bain, *The Most Dangerous Book in the World*, p. 103. See also the epigraphs cited by Bain on p. 127.) The relevance of this point to our hidden third level, to Tony Blair's "global network," may not be immediately evident until one recalls the indications in recent years' news of global networks of pedophilia, child and human abduction and sex slavery, and sacrifice, as exemplified in the Franklin Scandal, or the ongoing scandals in the U.K. and the Vatican.

seems appropriate to 9/11. And the Hanged Man was definitely present on 9/11, in the form of one of the "jumpers" from the Twin Towers:

The "Hanged Man" Jumper from the Twin Towers

The 12th Greater Trump of the Tarot: the Hanged Man

5. While People Burn, Bush Reads about Pet Goats

The most disturbing bow to ritual and esoteric practice was, perhaps, most in evidence by President G.W. Bush's weirdly nonchalant behavior at Booker Elementary school, where, having already been informed that America was under attack, he continued to read the children's story, "My Pet Goat." Here, too, there is an occult symbolism in action, for the goat symbolizes Baphomet, the sacred androgyne, the god Pan, half-human, half goat, and used in the western esoteric tradition since the Middle Ages to symbolize the devil.[30]

Baphomet: Half-Man, Half Goat, symbol of Pan, Dionysius, the Sacred Angrogyne, and the Devil.

---

[30] S.K. Bain, *The Most Dangerous Book in the World*, p. 31.

So what was going on? Bain's answer must be cited in full to gain the full impact of this aspect of the 9/11 ritual:

> A satirical ceremony, a Commander-in-Chief that wouldn't leave his seat until the reading of a story about a pet goat was completed... during which time hundreds of his fellow Americans were in harm's way, many of them meeting horrific ends as they burned alive or plunged to their deaths from the towers—conjuring the image of The Tower tarot card (variously referred to as "the Devil's House," "the house of the damned" and "Inferno," or "hell")—all taking place in— ... "Paradise," the city of Sarasota's unofficial yet widely-used and acknowledged nickname. Well, how about that?[31]

The story itself, as summarized by Bain, also has its themes and memes:

> Ostensibly a children's story about a girl and her goat, *The Pet Goat* was in reality a strategically employed device used to introduce this key occult element into the 9/11 MegaRitual; yet it is more than this. A deeper reading of the text reveals that this children's story is an allegory of the Luciferian Doctrine: the Father is an overbearing hyper-authoritarian, and the goat—whose initial poor behavior is, in broader context, relatively benign—saves the day. Praise the Goat.[32]

On this interpretation, it was necessary to the *ritual* that Bush finish the story, in order to complete the "invocation" of the "god" to whom all of it was dedicated.[33]

Perhaps Andrew Card was instructed to tell the President to sit still, and finish the story, and neither of them knew the purpose. But in any case, the vast amount of detail of occult symbol in play on 9/11—and we have scratched only a very *small* part of the surface presented by Bain—is yet another indicator that Mr. Bush, if aware of any degree of the level two planning, could hardly have mastered the details of level three.[34]

---

[31] S.K. Bain, *The Most Dangerous Book in the World*, p. 30. See also page 33.

[32] Ibid., p. 32.

[33] Bain also noted that rituals are often timed by the use of "electional astrology," i.e., selecting dates on which planetary alignments are condign to the working that is being undertaken. In the case of 9/11, there was an opposition of Saturn and Pluto. Saturn is the planet of time and death, and Pluto the ruler of the underworld. (Q.v. Bain, op. cit., pp. 83-84)

[34] S.K. Bain, *The Most Dangerous Book in the World*, p. 132: Bain does not believe that members of the Bush administration were involved at the deepest level: "The

B. The Other Twin Towers Involved on 9/11:
Deutsche Bank Symbolism

One cannot leave the occult aspects of the events of 9/11 without considering one final, very curious "non-coincidence" of that day, one not considered even by Bain: the involvement of Deutsche Bank. As is now commonly known in the 9/11 research community, many of the puts and shorts placed prior to 9/11, were placed by Deutsche Bank subsidiary Alex Brown, and as was also noted previously, the computers of Deutsche Bank, as the attacks were taking place, were suddenly invaded, and information downloaded in a matter of seconds.

It should come as no surprise that the giant German bank—with its ties to the Bin Ladens, to Mohamed Atta via its associations to Atta's bizarre links to I.G. Farben—also is a structure of the Masonic pillars Jachin and Boaz, of Twin Towers, placed on a base building that many think is a deliberate symbolization of the placement of the feet of a candidate standing for Masonic initiation.

The Twin Towers of Deutsche Bank in Frankfurt

---

involvement of the administration seems a foregone conclusion, but the weight of the evidence doesn't support the idea that they were the masterminds... not by a long shot."

In an operation that left little to chance in its ritual aspects, perhaps its presence in the ritual working of that day is meant to symbolize a break—a divorce—within a system that was once an alliance, as symbolized by the two Twin Towers of finance on both sides of the Atlantic. That financial alliance came about as a result of bargains struck with the former Axis elite after World War Two, to gain access to a vast supply of loot, loot which could be kept off the books, and fund and fuel an enormous postwar expansion of secret infrastructure, the development of black, exotic technologies, and covert operations. But the bargain was struck with those who, like their conquerors, knew the practices of the occult, and sacrifice, very well.

The Sixteenth Greater Trump of the Tarot:
The Tower

10
CONCLUSIONS AND OVERVIEW

"'9/11', then, was a weapon used to inflict further trauma on an unsuspecting public. By pre-programming the public consciousness for decades with the formulation that 911= help, a form of subconscious injury was inflicted through the abrupt reversal of 911=terror."
S.K. Bain[1]

I F THERE WAS A "THIRD LEVEL" TO THE 9/11 OPERATION, above and beyond that of rogue networks inside the American military-industrial-intelligence complex that revealed its hand on that day, and panicked the Bush administration into patterns of behavior that resembled those of a regime under threat of a coup d'etat, then how, precisely did that third level reveal its presence? If it is there, what are its principal features? In saying that there are two deeper levels to 9/11, and that they may be in conflict, then what are the goals and motivations of each?

As I indicated in the Preface, the argument of this book has not been that even of a "rationalized" or "reasoned speculation," but more resembles the less robust case of "an elaborated suspicion."

That there was a second, deeper level to the 9/11 operation is all but undisputed within the 9/11 research community. And the questions which dogged the early stages of 9/11 research after the event of whether the event was *allowed* to happen, or *planned* to happen, have, at the locus of level two, been resolved in favor of the latter hypothesis. The global foreknowledge of the events that are in evidence, plus the American intelligence community's own domestic forewarnings, might at one time have argued favorably for the LIHOP (Let It Happen On Purpose) scenario..

But when one adds foreknowledge of the specificity of a Vreeland, or the intricacy of planning of the operation to have several concurrent drills running on the same day, many of which mirrored and duplicated exact features of the real event, the MIHOP becomes the most reasonable scenario for level two's involvement. Additionally, the fact that the Pentagon and World Trade Center Towers were so *specifically* targeted to obliterate damning and incriminating evidence of financial fraud, is again an indicator of level two MIHOP planning, for the perpetrators of that financial fraud involved many of the same players

---

[1] S.K. Bain, *The Most Dangerous Book in the World*, pp. 79-80.

as planned the operation, and the same family political dynasty was in power in both instances.

Like all such operations, many objectives were combined, and it has been the consistent argument of the 9/11 truth community that the strikes were planned with a view to create a false flag event that would allow the projection of American military power into the Middle East, to secure the region's oilfields. In this respect, it should be recalled that at this deep level, warnings came from Egypt, Jordan, and Israel, while Saudi Arabia was suspiciously absent from the nations warning the USA of impending attacks. At least, we are not aware of any official warnings, though the close association of the Bush dynasty and of its close business associates with the Saudi regime certainly allow for the possibility of warnings through more informal channels.

In any case, as was noted in the main text, it would have been sufficient for all of the objectives of level two merely to have created great damage to the Pentagon and Twin Towers, and to create great loss of life, to destroy the evidence of crimes, and to project American power into the Middle East. In this respect, the objective of Level Two may not have even been to destroy the Towers. And, as was seen in the main text, if one follows the evidence of prior preparation of the Towers for demolitions, or the evidence of explosives at the Pentagon, then if the objective *was* to destroy the Towers, then the use of micronukes or exotic energy weapons seems like overkill.

So what, then, are the indications of an even deeper player, of a third level? And what are its motivations?

When one casts the net widely as I have attempted to do in this and previous books, then the presence of this third level is revealed in a variety of ways, and one of these is precisely the arresting presence of exotic technologies of destruction New York City, for regardless to which theory—micronukes or exotic energy weapons—that one might subscribe, their presence is overkill; they are unnecessary to the objectives of level two.

But they are quite necessary to level three, if it wishes to announce its presence on the world stage that day, and to demonstrate its capabilities.

These capabilities, it will be recalled, were also in evidence in yet other ways, chiefly in the revelation by level three to level two, as the events of 9/11 were under way, that it possessed sensitive codenames of virtually the entire US military-industrial-intelligence "deep state." This, as argued in the main text, might have been yet another legacy of the Inslaw-PROMIS scandals of the Reagan administration, for with the enhanced and corrupted software spreading around the world with tis "back door," it may have come into the possession of Mr. Blair's "global network," which then used it to ride into the American computer networks. Such capabilities would have revealed the entire extent of the 9/11 planning of level two, and allowed them to choose the point and manner of their penetration of that operation. If this scenario be true, then this was, in essence, the blackest of the black magic of that day, for now the level two plotters were pinned to their agenda, knowing that another player was now in evidence. In this respect, it is quite interesting to note that in the wake of 9/11, Germany and Britain suspended use of the program, and quietly, the FBI indicated that would do so as well.

This scenario, as unreal as it sounds on its own, does fit a wider context of evidence, some of it uncovered in this book, and some of it in the news of recent years. If there was such a global network—a third level—that revealed its presence and hand on 9/11, then the clues to the nature of that network are very clear: it is not afraid to slaughter human life on an enormous scale, but it possesses the means, and very possibly the exotic technologies, to do so, *and the more exotic the technology it possesses, the more unlikely it is to be identified with the level two aspects of the operation.* In other words, micro-nukes might indeed come from a rogue network within the American military, but exotic energy weapons would be known to a much narrower circle, one out of reach even of the rarefied reaches of command such as NORAD and STRATCOM.

As the Russian economist Dr. Tatyana Koryagina also stated in the previous pages, the fact that this network had access to assets in excess of $300 trillion places it beyond the reaches of any merely American, level two, rogue network, and also means that it would have the financial resources to develop such technologies.

Finally, there are the bizarre connections of Mohamed Atta to the Carl Duisberg Society, and its connection to I.G. Farben, infamous wartime Nazi advanced technology, weapons, and chemicals cartel. We have encountered the strange connection of the Bin Ladens to the postwar banker François Genoud, postwar finance manager of the Nazi International, and his connections as a financial backer to international terrorism and as a sponsor to the 1970s Barcelona terrorists "conference."

Since 9/11, America hardly resembles itself any more, for it has taken on an increasingly brutal, fascist culture, a kind of jingoistic plastic patriotism. Perhaps Webster Tarpley was correct when he noted that rather than "Bush knew allowed it, or made it happen" that he "surrendered." But if that be so, then to whom did he surrender?

Perhaps Russian economics minister Sergei Glazyev informed us, when in response to the American meddling in the Ukraine, he stated that the problem wasn't with the Nazis in Kiev, it was with the Nazis in Washington. And those connections, when the string is pulled, fan out into postwar terrorist networks—to Intifada, Hezbollah, the Muslim Brotherhood—to the Saudis and Iraqis and Iranians, even to the Israelis, and certainly those connections also fan out into the postwar association and alliance with the American fascists of Sullivan and Cromwell.

Thus, while the role of those states might indeed exist at a very deep level within the architecture of 9/11, ultimately they could not have pulled it off on their own, even given their vast financial resources, their intelligence and covert operations prowess, and even given their possession of the software that flowed like acid through the veins of the body of American national security. A global network of finance, of terrorism, of the possession of technological sophistication from cyber warfare to exotic weapons of destruction, and a thorough knowledge of occult practice and a willingness to sacrifice countless innocent lives to invoke evil for ultimate power, is indicated.

Money, power, occult knowledge, exotic technology, and financing in the trillions of dollars do not signify any merely *American* "rogue network," even a network possibly involving Saudis and/or Israelis in a false flag operation to project American power into the Middle East.

These characteristics indicate a much deeper player, a player with no recognizable center of power, a player everywhere and nowhere.

And, perhaps, a player with old scores to settle...

BIBLIOGRAPHY

No Author. "Angel is Next." http://www.911myths.com/htm/angel_is_next .html.

No Author. "EM Weapons: Theories that Directed Electromagnetic Energy weapons Destroyed the Twin Towers." 9-11 Research. 911research.wtc7.net/wtc/analysis/theories/energybeam.html.

No Author. "François Genoud." *Wikipedia.* En.wikipedia.org/wiki /Fran%C3%A7ois_Genoud.

No Author. "Inslaw." *Wikipedia.* en.wikipedia.org/wiki/Inslaw.

No Author. "Inslaw and PROMIS: Use of Enhanced PROMIS by US Gov't Agencies." www.hitsorycommons.org/timeline.jsp?inslawpromis.

No Author. "The INSLAW Octopus: Software Piracy, Conspiracy, cover-up, Stonewalling, Covert Action: Just Another Decade at the Department of Justice." *Wired.* www.wired.com/1993/01/inslaw/

No Author. "Repudiations." (Statements from Jim Hoffman). 9-11 Research. 911research.wtc7.net/about/repudiations.html.

No Author. "Russian Economist Predicted Strikes on America: Says Shadow Power Planning More," apfn.org/thewinds/2001/11/ prediction.

Ahmed, Nafeez Mosaddeq. *The War on Freedom: How and Why America Was Attacked, September 11, 2001.* Joshua Tree, California. Tree of Life Publications. 2002. ISBN 978-0-930852-40-0.

Ananda, Rady. "April Gallup versus Dick Cheney: Court Dismisses 9/11 Suit against Bush Officials." *Global Research.* April 29, 2011. www.globalresearch.com.

Arkin, William M. *Code Names; Deciphering U.S. Military Plans, Programs, and Operations in the 9/11 World.* Hanover, New Hampshire. Streerforth Press. 2005. ISBN 978-1-58642-083-6.

Bearden, T.E. (Lt. Col., Ret) *Gravitobiology.* Chula Vista, California. Tesla Book Cmpany. 1991. No ISBN.

Bibliography

Bearden, T.E. *Star Wars Now! The Bohm-Aharonov Effect, Scalar Interferometry, and Soviet Weaponization.* No Place. Energetic Productions, Inc. 1986. Second Edition. No ISBN.

Bearden, Tom, Ph.D. (Lt. Col., US Army, Ret.) *Fer De Lance: Briefing on Soviet Scalar Electromagnetic Weapons.* Santa Barbara, California. Cheniere Press. Second Edition. 2002. ISBN 0-9725146-1-9.

Bellzer, Richard; Noory George; and Wayne, David. *Someone is Hiding Something: What Happened to Malaysia Airlines Flight 370?* New York. Skyhorse Publishing. 2015. ISBN 978-1-63220-728-9.

Bollyn, Christopher. *Solving 9-11: The Deception that Changed the World.* Christopher Bollyn. 2012. ISBN 978-0-9853225-8-8.

Bull, Chris, and Erman, Sam, eds. *At Ground Zero: 25 Stories from Young Reporters Who Were There.* New York. Thunder's Mouth Press. 2002. ISBN 978-1-56025-427-0.

Childress, David Hatcher, ed. *The Fantastic Inventions of Nikola Tesla.* Kempton, Illinois. Adventures Unlimited Press. Adventures Unlimited Press. 1993. ISBN 978-0-932813-19-4.

Chossudovsky, Michel. *War and Globalisation: The Truth Behind September 11.* Shanty Bay, Ontario, Canada. Global Outlook. 2002. ISBN 978-0-9731109-0-2.

Cook, Nick. "Anti-Gravity Propulsion comes 'out of the closet.'" *Jane's Defence Weekly.* July 29, 2002.

Farrell, Joseph P. "Boeing Admits Antigravity Work." www.gizadeathstar. com, January 29, 2014.

Farrell, Joseph P. "The Baghdad Museum Looting: Some More Thoughts. August 20, 2008. www. Gizadeathstar.com/2008/08/the-baghdad-museum-looting-some-more-thoughts/

Farrell, Joseph P. *Covert Wars and Breakaway Civilizations: The Secret Space Program, Celestial Psyops, and Hidden Conflicts.* Kempton, Illinois. Adventures Unlimited Press. 2012. ISBN 978-1-935487-83-8.

Bibliography

Farrell, Joseph P. *Covert Wars and Breakaway Civilizations: The Secret Space Program, Celestial Psyops and Hidden Conflicts.* Kempton, Illinois. Adventures Unlimited Press. 2012. ISBN 978-1-935487-83-8.

Farrell, Joseph P. *Covert Wars and the Clash of Civilizations: UFOs, Oligarchs, and Space Secrecy.* Kempton, Illinois. Adventures Unlimited Press. 2013. ISBN 978-1-939149-04-6.

Farrell, Joseph P. *The Nazi International: The Nazis' Postwar Plan to Control Finance, Conflict, Physics, and Space.* Kempton, Illinois; Adventures Unlimited Press. 2008, ISBN 978-1-931882-93-4.

Farrell, Joseph P. *The Philosophers' Stone: Alchemy and the Secret Research for Exotic Matter.* Port Townsend, Washington. Feral House. 2009. ISBN 978-1-932595-40-6.

Farrell, Joseph P. *The SS Brotherhood of the Bell: The Nazis' Incredible Secret Technology: NASA's Nazis, JFK, and MAJIC-12.* Kempton, Illinois. Adventures Unlimited Press. 2006. ISBN 1-931882-61-4.

Farrell, Joseph P. *The Third Way: The Nazi International, European Union, and Corporate Fascism.* Kempton, Illinois. Adventures Unlimited Press. 2015. ISBN 978-1-939149-48-0.

Fetzer, James, PhD. *The 9/11 Conspiracy.* Peru, Illinois. Catfeet Press. 2007. 978-0-8126-9612-7.

Gaffney, Mark H. *Black 9/11: Money, Motive, and Technology.* Walterville, Oregon. Trine Day. 2012. ISBN 978-1-936296-46-0.

Goode, Timothy. *Alien Context:*

Griffin, David Ray. *Debunking 9/11 Debunking: An Answer to **Popular Mechanics** and Other Defenders of the Official Conspiracy Theory.* Northampton, Massachusetts. Olive Branch Press. 2007. 97815665668655.

Griffin, David Ray. *The New Pearl Harbor: Disturbing Questions about the Bush Administration and 9/11.* Northampton, Massachusetts. Olive Branch Press. 2004. ISBN 978-1-56656-552-9.

Bibliography

Griffin, David Ray. *The New Pearl Harbor Revisited.* Northampton, Massachusetts. Olive Branch. 2008. ISBN 978-1-56656-729-9.

Griffin, David Ray. *The 9/11 Commission Report: Omissions and Distortions.* Northampton, Massachusetts. Olive Branch Press. 2005. ISBN 978-1-56656-584-7.

Guyénot, Laurent. *JFK-9/11: 50 Years of Deep State.* San Diego. Progressive Press. 2014. ISBN 978-1-61577-631-3.

Heidner, E.P. "Collateral Damage: U.S. Covert Operations and the Terrorist Attacks on September 11, 2001." www.futurefastforward.com/feature-articles/3988-collateral-damage-us-covert-operations-and-the-terrorist-attacks-on-september-11-2001-by-ep-heidner-6810.html.

Hoffman, Jim, and Faulkner, Bonnie. "Your Eyes Don't Lie: Common Sense, Physics, and the World Trade Center Collapses, An Interview of Jim Hoffman by Bonnie Faulkner. *Guns and Butter.* (Radio show.) Transcript. www.911researchwtc7.net/interviews/radio/youreyesdontlie/index.html.

Hopsicker, Daniel. *Welcome to Terrorland: Mohammed Atta and the 9-11 Cover-up in Florida.* Venice, Florida. The MadCow Press. 2007. ISBN 2007.

House Committee of the Judiciary. *The Inslaw Affair: Investigative Report by the Committee on the Judiciary together with Dissenting and Separate Views.* Washington, D.C. U.S. Government Printing Office. 1991. https://w2.eff.org/legal/cases/INSLAW/inslaw_hr.report.

Hufschmid, Eric. *Painful Questions: An Analysis of the September 11th Attack.* Goleta, California. No Publication Data. (This work appears to have been self-published by Hufschmid.) 2002. ISBN 1-931947-05-8.

Johnson, Andrew. *9/11: Finding the Truth.* Andrew Johnso. 2009. ISBN 5-800031-292536.

Johnson, Ian. *A Mosque in Much: Nazis, the CIA, and the Rise of the Muslim Brotherhood in the West.* Boston. Houghton Mifflin Harcourt. 2010. ISBN 978-0-15-101418-7.

Bibliography

Kanter, Katharine. "François Genoud: 60 Years as an Anglo-Swiss Spook. *Executive Intelligence Review,* EIR Books, July 5, 1996.

Kieth, Jim, ed. *Secret and Suppressed: Banned Ideas and Hidden History.* Venice, California. Feral House. 1993. ISBN 0-922915-14-8.

Kostin, Sergei, and Raynaud, Eric. *Farewell: The Greatest Spy Story of the Twentieth Century.* Trans. from the French by Catherine Cauvin-Higgins. Las Vegas, NV. Amazon Crossing. 2011. ISBN 978-1611090260.

Mann, James. *Rise of the Vulcans: the History of Bush's War Cabinet.* New York. Penguin Books. 2004. ISBN 0-14-303-489-8.

Marrs, Jim. *Inside Job: Unmasking the 9/11 Conspiracies.* San Rafael, California. Origin Press. 2004. ISBN 978-1-57983-013-7.

Marrs, Jim. *The Terror Conspiracy: Deception, 9/11, and the Loss of Liberty.* The Disinformation Company, Ltd. 2006. ISBN 978-1-932857-43-6.

Martinez, Brandon. *Grand Deceptions: Zionist Intrigue in the 20th and 21st Centuries.* San Diego. Progressive Press. 2014. ISBN 978-1-61577-841-6.

Meyssan, Thierry. *9/11: The Big Lie.* London. Carnot Publishing Ltd. 2002. ISBN 978-1-59209-026-5.

Meyssan, Thierry. *Pentagate.* London. Carnot Publishing. 2002.

Mizuno, Tadahiko. *Nuclear Transmutation: The Reality of Cold Fusion.* Trans. from the Japanese by Jed Rothwell. Concord, New Hamprshire. Infinite Energy Press. 1998. ISBN 1-892925-00-1.

National Commission on Terrorist Attacks upon the United States. *The 9/11 Commission Report: Final Report of the National Commission on Terrorist Attacks upon the United States.* New York, London. W.W. Norton. First Edition. No Date. 978-0-393-32671-3.

Bibliography

Paul, Don, and Hoffman, Jim. *Waking Up from Our Nightmare: The 9/11/01 Crimes in New York City.* No Location. IR. 2004. ISBN 0-94309605-12.

Pond, Dale, and Baumgartner, Walter. *Nikola Tesla's Earthquake Machine with Tesla's Original Patents.* Santa Fe, New Mexico. The Message Company. 1997. ISBN 1-57282-008-x.

Rea, Paul W., PhD. *Mounting Evidence: Why We Need a New Investigation into 9/11.* Bloomington, Indiana. iUniverse. 2011. ISBN 978-1-4620-0066-1.

Reed, Terry, and Cummings, John. *Compromised: Clinton, Bush, and the CIA: How the Presidency was Co-opted by the CIA.* S.P.I. Books. 1994. ISBN 978-1-56171-249-3.

Ruppert, Michael C., with Hecht, Jamey, ed. *Crossing the Rubicon: The Decline of the American Empire at the End of the Age of Oil.* Foreword by Catherine Austin Fitts. Gabriola Island, British Columbia, Canada. New Society Publishers. 2004. ISBN 978-0-86571-540-0.

Ruppert, Michael C. "Promis Software—Bin laden's Magic Carpet." www. rense. com/general17/maf/htm.

Ryan, Kevin Robert. *Another Nineteen: Investigating Legitimate 9/11 Suspects.* Microbloom. 2013. ISBN 978-1489507839.

Seymour, Cheri. *The Last Circle: Danny Casolaro's Investigation into The Octopus and the PROMIS Software Scandal.* Walterville, Oregon. Trine Day. 2010. ISBN 978-1936296002.

Smith, Dennis. *Report from Ground Zero.* New York. Plume (Penguin Putnam). 2003. ISBN 0-452-28395-7.

Stich, Rodney. *Defrauding America: A Pattern of Related Scandals: Dirty Secrets of the CIA and Other Government Operations.* Expanded Second Edition. Alamo, California. Diablo Press. 1994. ISBN 09-932438-08-3.

Sweet, Christopher, ed., and Photographers of the New York City Police Department. *Above Hallowed Ground: A Photographic Record of*

Bibliography

September 11, 2001. New York. Viking Studio (Penguin Group). 2002. ISBN 0-670-03171-2.

Tarpley, Webster Griffin. *9/11 Synthetic Terror: Made in USA.* 4th Edition. Joshua Tree, California. Progressive Press. 2008. ISBN 978-0930852370.

Tarpley, Webster Griffin. *9/11 Synthetic Terror: Made in USA.* 5th Edition. Joshua Tree, California. Progressive Press. 2011. ISBN 97801615771110.

Thompson, Paul. "Angel is next": The Terrifying message pilot of Air Force One got as he flew President Bush on 9/11." *The Daily Mail.* 7 September 2011. http://www.dailymail.co.uk/news/article-2034423/9-11-message -Air-Force-One-pilot-Mark-Tillman-got-flew-President-Bush.html.

Tompson, Paul, and The Center for Cooperative Research. *The Terror Timeline: Year by Year, Day by Day, Minute by Minute: A Comprehensive Chronicle of the Road to 9/11 and America's Response.* New York. Harper. 2004. ISBN 978-0-06-078338-9.

Tiradera, Peter. *9-11 Coup Against America!: The Pentagon Analysis.* North Charleston, South Carolina. Book Surge LLC. 2006. ISBN 978-1-4196-3822-X.

Unger, Craig. *House of Bush, House of Saud: The Secret Relationship between the World's Two Most Powerful Dynasties.* New York. Scribner. 2004. ISBN 978-0-7432-5339-0.

Vassilatos, Gerry. *Declassified Patents of the Cold War and SDI: Companion Study Guide for "Secrets of Cold War Technology."* Bayside, California. Borderland Sciences. No date. No ISBN.

Vysotskii, Vladimir I., and Kornilova, Alla A. *Nuclear Transmutation of Stable and Radioactive Isotopes in Biological Systems.* New Delhi. Pentagon press. 2010. ISBN 978-81-8274-430-1.

Zarembka, Paul, ed. *The Hidden History of 9-11.* Second Edition. New York. Seven Stories Press. 20080. ISBN 978-1583228258.

ROSWELL AND THE REICH
The Nazi Connection
By Joseph P. Farrell

Farrell has meticulously reviewed the best-known Roswell research from UFO-ET advocates and skeptics alike, as well as some little-known source material, and comes to a radically different scenario of what happened in Roswell, New Mexico in July 1947, and why the US military has continued to cover it up to this day. Farrell presents a fascinating case sure to disturb both ET believers and disbelievers, namely, that what crashed may have been representative of an independent postwar Nazi power—an extraterritorial Reich monitoring its old enemy, America, and the continuing development of the very technologies confiscated from Germany at the end of the War.
540 pages. 6x9 Paperback. Illustrated. $19.95. Code: RWR

SECRETS OF THE UNIFIED FIELD
The Philadelphia Experiment, the Nazi Bell, and the Discarded Theory
by Joseph P. Farrell

Farrell examines the now discarded Unified Field Theory. American and German wartime scientists and engineers determined that, while the theory was incomplete, it could nevertheless be engineered. Chapters include: The Meanings of "Torsion"; Wringing an Aluminum Can; The Mistake in Unified Field Theories and Their Discarding by Contemporary Physics; Three Routes to the Doomsday Weapon: Quantum Potential, Torsion, and Vortices; Tesla's Meeting with FDR; Arnold Sommerfeld and Electromagnetic Radar Stealth; Electromagnetic Phase Conjugations, Phase Conjugate Mirrors, and Templates; The Unified Field Theory, the Torsion Tensor, and Igor Witkowski's Idea of the Plasma Focus; tons more.
340 pages. 6x9 Paperback. Illustrated. $18.95. Code: SOUF

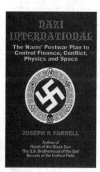

NAZI INTERNATIONAL
The Nazi's Postwar Plan to Control Finance, Conflict, Physics and Space
by Joseph P. Farrell

Beginning with prewar corporate partnerships in the USA, including some with the Bush family, he moves on to the surrender of Nazi Germany, and evacuation plans of the Germans. He then covers the vast, and still-little-known recreation of Nazi Germany in South America with help of Juan Peron, I.G. Farben and Martin Bormann. Farrell then covers Nazi Germany's penetration of the Muslim world including Wilhelm Voss and Otto Skorzeny in Gamel Abdul Nasser's Egypt before moving on to the development and control of new energy technologies including the Bariloche Fusion Project, Dr. Philo Farnsworth's Plasmator, and the work of Dr. Nikolai Kozyrev. Finally, Farrell discusses the Nazi desire to control space, and examines their connection with NASA, the esoteric meaning of NASA Mission Patches.
412 pages. 6x9 Paperback. Illustrated. $19.95. Code: NZIN

ARKTOS
The Polar Myth in Science, Symbolism & Nazi Survival
by Joscelyn Godwin

Explored are the many tales of an ancient race said to have lived in the Arctic regions, such as Thule and Hyperborea. Progressing onward, he looks at modern polar legends: including the survival of Hitler, German bases in Antarctica, UFOs, the hollow earth, and the hidden kingdoms of Agartha and Shambala. Chapters include: Prologue in Hyperborea; The Golden Age; The Northern Lights; The Arctic Homeland; The Aryan Myth; The Thule Society; The Black Order; The Hidden Lands; Agartha and the Polaires; Shambhala; The Hole at the Pole; Antarctica; more.
220 Pages. 6x9 Paperback. Illustrated. Bib. Index. $16.95. Code: ARK

REICH OF THE BLACK SUN
Nazi Secret Weapons & the Cold War Allied Legend
by Joseph P. Farrell

Why were the Allies worried about an atom bomb attack by the Germans in 1944? Why did the Soviets threaten to use poison gas against the Germans? Why did Hitler in 1945 insist that holding Prague could win the war for the Third Reich? Why did US General George Patton's Third Army race for the Skoda works at Pilsen in Czechoslovakia instead of Berlin? Why did the US Army not test the uranium atom bomb it dropped on Hiroshima? Why did the Luftwaffe fly a non-stop round trip mission to within twenty miles of New York City in 1944? *Reich of the Black Sun* takes the reader on a scientific-historical journey in order to answer these questions. Arguing that Nazi Germany actually won the race for the atom bomb in late 1944,

352 PAGES. 6x9 PAPERBACK. ILLUSTRATED. BIBLIOGRAPHY. $16.95.
CODE: ROBS

THE GIZA DEATH STAR
The Paleophysics of the Great Pyramid & the Military Complex at Giza
by Joseph P. Farrell

Was the Giza complex part of a military installation over 10,000 years ago? Chapters include: An Archaeology of Mass Destruction, Thoth and Theories; The Machine Hypothesis; Pythagoras, Plato, Planck, and the Pyramid; The Weapon Hypothesis; Encoded Harmonics of the Planck Units in the Great Pyramid; High Freqquency Direct Current "Impulse" Technology; The Grand Gallery and its Crystals: Gravito-acoustic Resonators; The Other Two Large Pyramids; the "Causeways," and the "Temples"; A Phase Conjugate Howitzer; Evidence of the Use of Weapons of Mass Destruction in Ancient Times; more.

290 PAGES. 6x9 PAPERBACK. ILLUSTRATED. $16.95. CODE: GDS

THE GIZA DEATH STAR DEPLOYED
The Physics & Engineering of the Great Pyramid
by Joseph P. Farrell

Farrell expands on his thesis that the Great Pyramid was a maser, designed as a weapon and eventually deployed—with disastrous results to the solar system. Includes: Exploding Planets: A Brief History of the Exoteric and Esoteric Investigations of the Great Pyramid; No Machines, Please!; The Stargate Conspiracy; The Scalar Weapons; Message or Machine?; A Tesla Analysis of the Putative Physics and Engineering of the Giza Death Star; Cohering the Zero Point, Vacuum Energy, Flux: Feedback Loops and Tetrahedral Physics; and more.

290 PAGES. 6x9 PAPERBACK. ILLUSTRATED. $16.95. CODE: GDSD

THE GIZA DEATH STAR DESTROYED
The Ancient War For Future Science
by Joseph P. Farrell

Farrell moves on to events of the final days of the Giza Death Star and its awesome power. These final events, eventually leading up to the destruction of this giant machine, are dissected one by one, leading us to the eventual abandonment of the Giza Military Complex—an event that hurled civilization back into the Stone Age. Chapters include: The Mars-Earth Connection; The Lost "Root Races" and the Moral Reasons for the Flood; The Destruction of Krypton: The Electrodynamic Solar System, Exploding Planets and Ancient Wars; Turning the Stream of the Flood: the Origin of Secret Societies and Esoteric Traditions; The Quest to Recover Ancient Mega-Technology; Non-Equilibrium Paleophysics; Monatomic Paleophysics; Frequencies, Vortices and Mass Particles; "Acoustic" Intensity of Fields; The Pyramid of Crystals; tons more.

292 pages. 6x9 paperback. Illustrated. $16.95. Code: GDES

ANCIENT ALIENS ON THE MOON
By Mike Bara
What did NASA find in their explorations of the solar system that they may have kept from the general public? How ancient really are these ruins on the Moon? Using official NASA and Russian photos of the Moon, Bara looks at vast cityscapes and domes in the Sinus Medii region as well as glass domes in the Crisium region. Bara also takes a detailed look at the mission of Apollo 17 and the case that this was a salvage mission, primarily concerned with investigating an opening into a massive hexagonal ruin near the landing site. Chapters include: The History of Lunar Anomalies; The Early 20th Century; Sinus Medii; To the Moon Alice!; Mare Crisium; Yes, Virginia, We Really Went to the Moon; Apollo 17; more. Tons of photos of the Moon examined for possible structures and other anomalies.
348 Pages. 6x9 Paperback. Illustrated.. $19.95. Code: AAOM

ANCIENT TECHNOLOGY IN PERU & BOLIVIA
By David Hatcher Childress
Childress speculates on the existence of a sunken city in Lake Titicaca and reveals new evidence that the Sumerians may have arrived in South America 4,000 years ago. He demonstrates that the use of "keystone cuts" with metal clamps poured into them to secure megalithic construction was an advanced technology used all over the world, from the Andes to Egypt, Greece and Southeast Asia. He maintains that only power tools could have made the intricate articulation and drill holes found in extremely hard granite and basalt blocks in Bolivia and Peru, and that the megalith builders had to have had advanced methods for moving and stacking gigantic blocks of stone, some weighing over 100 tons.
340 Pages. 6x9 Paperback. Illustrated.. $19.95 Code: ATP

THE ILLUSTRATED DOOM SURVIVAL GUIDE
Don't Panic!
By Matt "DoomGuy" Victor
With over 500 very detailed and easy-to-understand illustrations, this book literally shows you how to do things like build a fire with whatever is at hand, perform field surgeries, identify and test foodstuffs, and form twine, snares and fishhooks. In any doomsday scenario, being able to provide things of real value—such as clothing, tools, medical supplies, labor, food and water—will be of the utmost importance. This book gives you the particulars to help you survive in any environment with little to no equipment, and make it through the first critical junctures after a disaster. Beyond any disaster you will have the knowledge to rebuild shelter, farm from seed to seed, raise animals, treat medical problems, predict the weather and protect your loved ones.
356 Pages. 6x9 Paperback. Illustrated. $20.00. Code: IDSG

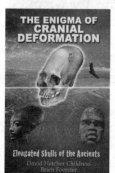

THE ENIGMA OF CRANIAL DEFORMATION
Elongated Skulls of the Ancients
By David Hatcher Childress and Brien Foerster
In a book filled with over a hundred astonishing photos and a color photo section, Childress and Foerster take us to Peru, Bolivia, Egypt, Malta, China, Mexico and other places in search of strange elongated skulls and other cranial deformation. The puzzle of why diverse ancient people—even on remote Pacific Islands—would use head-binding to create elongated heads is mystifying. Where did they even get this idea? Did some people naturally look this way—with long narrow heads? Were they some alien race? Were they an elite race that roamed the entire planet? Why do anthropologists rarely talk about cranial deformation and know so little about it?
250 Pages. 6x9 Paperback. Illustrated. $19.95. Code: ECD

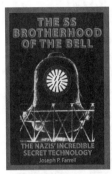

THE SS BROTHERHOOD OF THE BELL
The Nazis' Incredible Secret Technology
by Joseph P. Farrell
In 1945, a mysterious Nazi secret weapons project code-named "The Bell" left its underground bunker in lower Silesia, along with all its project documentation, and a four-star SS general named Hans Kammler. Taken aboard a massive six engine Junkers 390 ultra-long range aircraft, "The Bell," Kammler, and all project records disappeared completely, along with the gigantic aircraft. It is thought to have flown to America or Argentina. What was "The Bell"? What new physics might the Nazis have discovered with it? How far did the Nazis go after the war to protect the advanced energy technology that it represented?

456 pages. 6x9 Paperback. Illustrated.References. $16.95.
Code: SSBB

SECRETS OF THE HOLY LANCE
The Spear of Destiny in History & Legend
by Jerry E. Smith
Secrets of the Holy Lance traces the Spear from its possession by Constantine, Rome's first Christian Caesar, to Charlemagne's claim that with it he ruled the Holy Roman Empire by Divine Right, and on through two thousand years of kings and emperors, until it came within Hitler's grasp—and beyond! Did it rest for a while in Antarctic ice? Is it now hidden in Europe, awaiting the next person to claim its awesome power? Neither debunking nor worshiping, *Secrets of the Holy Lance* seeks to pierce the veil of myth and mystery around the Spear. Mere belief that it was infused with magic by virtue of its shedding the Savior's blood has made men kings. But what if it's more? What are "the powers it serves"?

312 PAGES. 6x9 PAPERBACK. ILLUSTRATED. BIBLIOGRAPHY. $16.95.
CODE: SOHL

MAPS OF THE ANCIENT SEA KINGS
Evidence of Advanced Civilization in the Ice Age
by Charles H. Hapgood
Charles Hapgood has found the evidence in the Piri Reis Map that shows Antarctica, the Hadji Ahmed map, the Oronteus Finaeus and other amazing maps. Hapgood concluded that these maps were made from more ancient maps from the various ancient archives around the world, now lost. Not only were these unknown people more advanced in mapmaking than any people prior to the 18th century, it appears they mapped all the continents. The Americas were mapped thousands of years before Columbus. Antarctica was mapped when its coasts were free of ice!

316 PAGES. 7x10 PAPERBACK. ILLUSTRATED. BIBLIOGRAPHY & INDEX. $19.95. CODE: MASK

PATH OF THE POLE
Cataclysmic Pole Shift Geology
by Charles H. Hapgood
Maps of the Ancient Sea Kings author Hapgood's classic book *Path of the Pole* is back in print! Hapgood researched Antarctica, ancient maps and the geological record to conclude that the Earth's crust has slipped on the inner core many times in the past, changing the position of the pole. *Path of the Pole* discusses the various "pole shifts" in Earth's past, giving evidence for each one, and moves on to possible future pole shifts.

356 PAGES. 6x9 PAPERBACK. ILLUSTRATED. $16.95. CODE: POP

THE COSMIC WAR
Interplanetary Warfare, Modern Physics, and Ancient Texts
By Joseph P. Farrell

There is ample evidence across our solar system of catastrophic events. The asteroid belt may be the remains of an exploded planet! The known planets are scarred from incredible impacts, and teeter in their orbits due to causes heretofore inadequately explained. Included: The history of the Exploded Planet hypothesis, and what mechanism can actually explode a planet. The role of plasma cosmology, plasma physics and scalar physics. The ancient texts telling of such destructions: from Sumeria (Tiamat's destruction by Marduk), Egypt (Edfu and the Mars connections), Greece (Saturn's role in the War of the Titans) and the ancient Americas.

436 Pages. 6x9 Paperback. Illustrated. $18.95. Code: COSW

TECHNOLOGY OF THE GODS
The Incredible Sciences of the Ancients
by David Hatcher Childress

Childress looks at the technology that was allegedly used in Atlantis and the theory that the Great Pyramid of Egypt was originally a gigantic power station. He examines tales of ancient flight and the technology that it involved; how the ancients used electricity; megalithic building techniques; the use of crystal lenses and the fire from the gods; evidence of various high tech weapons in the past, including atomic weapons; ancient metallurgy and heavy machinery; the role of modern inventors such as Nikola Tesla in bringing ancient technology back into modern use; impossible artifacts; and more.

356 PAGES. 6x9 PAPERBACK. $16.95. CODE: TGOD

ANCIENT ALIENS ON MARS
By Mike Bara

Bara brings us this lavishly illustrated volume on alien structures on Mars. Was there once a vast, technologically advanced civilization on Mars, and did it leave evidence of its existence behind for humans to find eons later? Did these advanced extraterrestrial visitors vanish in a solar system wide cataclysm of their own making, only to make their way to Earth and start anew? Was Mars once as lush and green as the Earth, and teeming with life? Chapters include: War of the Worlds; The Mars Tidal Model; The Death of Mars; Cydonia and the Face on Mars; The Monuments of Mars; The Search for Life on Mars; The True Colors of Mars and The Pathfinder Sphinx; more. Color section.

252 Pages. 6x9 Paperback. Illustrated. $19.95. Code: AMAR

LBJ AND THE CONSPIRACY TO KILL KENNEDY
By Joseph P. Farrell

Farrell says that a coalescence of interests in the military industrial complex, the CIA, and Lyndon Baines Johnson's powerful and corrupt political machine in Texas led to the events culminating in the assassination of JFK. Farrell analyzes the data as only he can, and comes to some astonishing conclusions. Chapters include: Oswald, the FBI, and the CIA: Hoover's Concern of a Second Oswald; The Mafia; Hoover, Johnson, and the Mob; The FBI, the Secret Service, Hoover, and Johnson; The CIA and "Murder Incorporated"; Ruby's Bizarre Behavior; The French Connection and Permindex; Big Oil; The Dead Witnesses: Jack Zangretti, Maurice Gatlin, Guy Bannister, Jr., Mary Pinchot Meyer, Dorothy Killgallen, Congressman Hale Boggs; LBJ and the Planning of the Texas Trip; LBJ: A Study in Character, Connections, and Cabals; The Requirements of Coups D'État; more.

342 Pages. 6x9 Paperback. $19.95 Code: LCKK

ORDER FORM

**10% Discount
When You Order
3 or More Items!**

One Adventure Place
P.O. Box 74
Kempton, Illinois 60946
United States of America
Tel.: 815-253-6390 • Fax: 815-253-6300
Email: auphq@frontiernet.net
http://www.adventuresunlimitedpress.com

ORDERING INSTRUCTIONS

✓ Remit by USD$ Check, Money Order or Credit Card

✓ Visa, Master Card, Discover & AmEx Accepted

✓ Paypal Payments Can Be Made To:

    info@wexclub.com

✓ Prices May Change Without Notice

✓ 10% Discount for 3 or More Items

SHIPPING CHARGES

United States

✓ Postal Book Rate { $4.50 First Item / 50¢ Each Additional Item

✓ POSTAL BOOK RATE Cannot Be Tracked!
Not responsible for non-delivery.

✓ Priority Mail { $6.00 First Item / $2.00 Each Additional Item

✓ UPS { $7.00 First Item / $1.50 Each Additional Item

NOTE: UPS Delivery Available to Mainland USA Only

Canada

✓ Postal Air Mail { $15.00 First Item / $2.50 Each Additional Item

✓ Personal Checks or Bank Drafts MUST BE

US$ and Drawn on a US Bank

✓ Canadian Postal Money Orders OK

✓ Payment MUST BE US$

All Other Countries

✓ Sorry, No Surface Delivery!

✓ Postal Air Mail { $19.00 First Item / $6.00 Each Additional Item

✓ Checks and Money Orders MUST BE US$
and Drawn on a US Bank or branch.

✓ Paypal Payments Can Be Made in US$ To:
info@wexclub.com

SPECIAL NOTES

✓ RETAILERS: Standard Discounts Available

✓ BACKORDERS: We Backorder all Out-of-
Stock Items Unless Otherwise Requested

✓ PRO FORMA INVOICES: Available on Request

✓ DVD Return Policy: Replace defective DVDs only

ORDER ONLINE AT: www.adventuresunlimitedpress.com

**10% Discount When You Order
3 or More Items!**

Please check: ✓

This is my first order ☐	I have ordered before ☐

Name

Address

City

State/Province	Postal Code

Country

Phone: Day   Evening

Fax   Email

Item Code	Item Description	Qty	Total

Please check: ✓

	Subtotal ▶	
	Less Discount-10% for 3 or more items ▶	
☐ Postal-Surface	Balance ▶	
☐ Postal-Air Mail (Priority in USA)	Illinois Residents 6.25% Sales Tax ▶	
	Previous Credit ▶	
☐ UPS	Shipping ▶	
(Mainland USA only)	Total (check/MO in USD$ only) ▶	

☐ Visa/MasterCard/Discover/American Express

Card Number:

Expiration Date: —   Security Code:

✓ SEND A CATALOG TO A FRIEND: